THE HISTORY OF HIGHER EDUCATION IN LOUISIANA

THE HISTORY OF HIGHER EDUCATION IN LOUISIANA

Curtis A. Manning

To order additional copies of this book, contact:
Xlibris Corporation
1-888-795-4274
www.Xlibris.com
Orders@Xlibris.com
32536

CONTENTS

PART II
Formative Period of Higher Education in Louisiana:
1928-1972

PART III
Contemporary Higher Education in Louisiana:
1972-2004

DEDICATION

This book is dedicated to Lani and Chloe Manning, with love. Thanks to Don and Karen Manning, for your advice and support; to Malcolm McLeod, for your editorial sensibilities; and to Donna Clark, Stanley Raymond, Brian Keating, Jim Killacky, Amy Wells, Barbara Johnson, and Jimmy Sawtelle, for your suggestions.

FOREWORD

The book has two major goals: to serve as a history of higher education for a general audience and to offer a perspective on how to improve conditions in Louisiana-based on the lessons of history. I approach this challenge from the unique perspective of being both a theorist looking at the big picture as well as teacher on the front lines of the struggle. I have fairly extensive graduate-level studies in both History and Education. I teach history at a community college. Also, I am not originally from Louisiana and I have had no involvement in politics, so I do not know what is not possible. Though I did not attend one, I have an admitted community college perspective, which is fundamentally different from most commentators who attended a four-year college or university. There is a certain elitism inherent in university graduates about two-year colleges (I had it as well before working at one) that is not suited to objectively considering the importance of two-year colleges.

Education is a retail activity—in the end accomplished through the interaction of two individuals. It does not lend itself well to regulation by high-level governmental officials painting with a broad brush. Nonetheless, given the modern system, most reform in public education is driven by politicians and administrators that are far from the front lines. For any higher educational reform to touch successfully the lives of the Louisianans who need it most, this contradiction must be examined and proper responsibilities meted out to the institutions and individuals that can have the proper impact.

I take a simple, practical approach to the importance of history. History is not interesting to me (or, I have found, my students) when it is a series of dates, individuals and ideas that are seemingly disconnected from contemporary life. History is fascinating when it is a series of facts organized in a compelling story that explains who we are today. When history is relevant in a way that explains the name of a street, the action of a governor, the song of a Mardi Gras ball or the poignant plight of a relative, it comes alive and is useful.

Even more important are the rare times when history can impact the future in a positive way. I do not believe that "history repeats itself" because society continuously becomes more complex. However, I absolutely believe that patterns can be discerned by the successes and failures of those who came before. On an individual level, these patterns can simply be labeled "experience" or "common sense." On a societal level, these patterns can ideally serve as lessons that inform the decisions of the people making the laws and policies.

I hope that this history of higher education will serve as a foundation of knowledge for the decision-makers currently in the midst of higher education reform in Louisiana. My approach has been to look at the current public institutions of higher education and work backwards to the beginning. The story traces the threads of how we got to where we are today. The history ends in 2004, but the story goes further.

INTRODUCTION

In a 2004 national ranking of higher education performance, Louisiana was 49th, a slight improvement over a last place ranking in 2002.[1] Why did Louisiana score so low? Is this a recent phenomenon, or has Louisiana higher education historically lagged the national average? More importantly, what is being done to remedy the situation?

Soon after moving to the state and becoming a community college history professor, the answer to these questions became more than just a theoretical exercise. Having a child in 2004, the answers took on a greater urgency, as I wondered about the choices she would face in 18 years as she considers going to college.

My attempt to find the answer to these questions is contained herein. I hope this will add to the discussion. The issues are complex and it seems results will only come in the long-term. By starting now, I hope that my daughter—whether she chooses a two or four year option—will have strong and vibrant higher education establishment—one that is not ranked at the bottom of the nation.

Improvement in higher education is the key for Louisiana to emerge from the bottom of virtually every national quality-of-life indicator. It will not happen in the short run. Louisiana desperately needs business and industry to relocate to the state and bring jobs. Once the jobs are here, the increased salaries will lead to greater prosperity that in turn should lead to an increase in all manner of quality-of-life indicators. This—in a nutshell—is the theory put forth by state leaders, and it is sound.

The primary currency for luring business and industry is a large pool of educated workers. Most of the other inducements—tax breaks, access to natural resources, cheap unskilled labor—pale in comparison. It is an asset that Louisiana cannot sufficiently offer now. Only by improving the system of higher education can the virtuous cycle of jobs and prosperity be achieved. This book will seek to aid in the process of bringing this future to fruition.

The goal of the book is to impart the story of Louisiana and its people—through the lens of higher education. To attempt a comprehensive history of such a complex institution would be both folly and boring. I endeavor to tell an entertaining and informative, yet historically accurate, story. At times, it might be necessary to forego a full explanation of a complex subject—a decision that might disappoint academic historians. For example, I do not delve into all aspects of each college and university in the state. Instead, I give a taste of what college life was really like.

The book has two intertwined thematic histories. First, obviously, is an examination of higher education in Louisiana over its entire history. While higher education in a technical sense did not begin until the mid-nineteenth century, the foundation was laid much earlier. The second major thread is the strength of governors in Louisiana, especially after 1928. Unlike in many other parts of the country, Louisiana governors have often played a central role in the establishment and reform of colleges and universities.

Within these two strands, three major characteristics of Louisiana emerged. First, Louisiana has had a low emphasis on education throughout its history. Second, LSU and Tulane have emerged as the most important and influential universities in the state. Finally, Louisiana leaders consciously set up a "dual system" of higher education, segregated by race. These characteristics emerged from the most distinctive cultural foundation in America.

Two stylistic decisions merit a fuller discussion. First, I sought to define the "character" of the individual institutions of higher education in Louisiana, to answer the question "What makes a college?" This was not a straightforward process when the people, locations and even buildings were often not static. To determine the character, I looked to important events that indicated some fundamental transformation, e.g. a change in name, mission, or location. The "business as usual" actions of running the school, learning, and graduating, while vital, were not considered historically interesting. The character issues are charted in the Appendix.

Another challenge was finding the proper middle-ground between the story of statewide higher education as a whole versus the histories of individual institutions. To include a full institutional history of each college would make the book unreadable for a non-academic. To include only the actions at the state level would not give a glimpse of the true character of higher education—the interaction with students. I chose to start with the existing public and private colleges and universities, and then to concentrate on the "most important" sixteen institutions—either because of size or history. In turn, I dealt with especially vital "character" issues of the individual colleges while giving overall "illuminating examples" for a feel of the times.

Exploring the history of higher education in Louisiana was a complex but necessary undertaking. I hope the reader will take an interest in the past events of colleges and universities in the state, especially the whimsical glimpses of a very different time. More importantly, however, I hope the lessons of the past will make their way to the shapers of today's higher education, who in turn will use the ideas to construct a better future. If this happens, then history will become practical—and thus worthwhile.

PART I

Early History of Higher Education in Louisiana

Louisiana's cultural upbringing was schizophrenic, a child of three parents that cared little for her. The French, Spanish and Americans all put their indelible stamp on the territory, and the complex interplay contributed to the uniqueness of the state. The famous "French Quarter" has Spanish architecture and an American ethos. Louisianans have parishes instead of counties and "neutral grounds" instead of medians. The examples abound.

Louisiana's youth was first imprinted by the culture of France and Spain. Both countries featured a "strong king" system and Roman Catholicism, radically different from the English roots of the Thirteen Colonies. The state did not merge with the rest of "English" America until its adolescence—with the Louisiana Purchase of 1803. The culture shock initially resulted in a state of virtual civil war and was followed by two centuries of an uneasy merging of French, Spanish and American folkways.

When Louisiana was bought by America, it became part of the American Deep South. It benefited from the antebellum King Cotton economy and suffered the vicissitudes of the Civil War and Reconstruction. Its uniqueness endured—in good and bad ways. Alone in the South, New Orleans had a substantial population of Free People of Color, some of whom owned slaves. Sugar was a major crop only in Louisiana, and conditions on the sugar plantations were so harsh that many slaves on cotton plantations were threatened with being "sold down the river" to Louisiana. By the end of the nineteenth century, Louisiana's elite was among the richest in the South, and her poor were among the most downtrodden.

Among the vast cultural differences of French Louisiana, Spanish Louisiana and the American South, there was at least one commonality: a lack of emphasis on education for the common person. Wealthy families hired tutors or sent their children to Europe or the North to be educated. Educational opportunities were in short supply for almost everyone else. Louisiana consistently ranked near the bottom nationally on measures of literacy. This culture of eschewing education took a toll on the emergence of higher education in the late 19th and early 20th century.

Another defining characteristic of the French/Spanish upbringing shaped Louisiana government and higher education. This was the concept of "executive centralism." On a smaller scale, Louisiana followed the model in France and Spain where a "strong king" held an inordinate amount of power and zealously guarded and exercised that power without much input from other institutions. In the colony of Louisiana, the governor was the executive in charge. While following orders from the home country, he was given great personal power. For example, Alejandro "Bloody" O'Reilly earned his sobriquet by ruthlessly carrying out his dictatorial powers in 1769.[2] This power centralized in the hands of an executive, and the people's acquiescence, set the stage for later governors. Most famously, Huey Long had the nickname "America's Dictator" in the 1930s.

CHAPTER 1

History of Education to 1845: Cultural Foundation

Context of Renaissance Europe & Cultural Development of America

The story of Louisiana higher education really began even before the first Europeans "discovered" the territory. La Salle formally claimed the territory in 1682 for France somewhere in modern-day Plaquemines Parish. He had spent two months traversing the Mississippi River from Canada along with Henri de Tonti who was considered an imposing warrior among the native tribes because of the weapon-like iron hook that had replaced his blown-off right hand. The return trip up the Mississippi to Canada going against the current took much longer. Later, La Salle attempted to return to Louisiana by finding the mouth of the Mississippi from the Gulf of Mexico. He failed, likely because of poor navigational equipment, and landed in Texas. He was murdered by his own men, and the rest of the expedition died of exposure, starvation or at the hands of the Native Americans or Spanish. [3]

Before this discovery, an emerging competition between France and England was played out in the Europe of the 1500s and 1600s. The two countries chose very different paths in government and religion, and these differences have reverberated down through the ages—affecting, among many other things, the story of higher education in Louisiana.

France at the turn of the 18th century featured a "strong king" system of government, exemplified by Louis XIV, for whom Louisiana was named. The king held almost complete power and did not need to negotiate with other groups to raise taxes or perform other functions of government. Louis was called the "Sun King" because both inhabited a position at the top, looking down on a lesser society. Religiously, France was a Roman Catholic country. Catholicism, the sanctioned state religion, played a strong role in society and operated in a hierarchical, top-down mode, much like the style of government. In the French colonies, the Catholic Church generally administered any educational efforts. Though a competitor, Spain was similar to France—with a "strong king" system and Roman Catholicism.

England[4] developed a different governmental and religious model. The English kings would have preferred the absolute power of their French counterparts. They did not have enough power to ensure sufficient revenues for their ambitions, however, and thus went by a "weak king" model. Over a period of time, the kings were forced to cede increasingly more power to a group of nobles, the Parliament, in exchange for increased tax revenue. At first, shared decisions extended to a tiny, elite group, but the rights slowly spread to ever more of the "average" citizens. This "weak king" model evolved to a governmental system marked by broad participation of the citizenry in political affairs. Religiously, England broke from Catholicism. While England also had a state religion, the Anglican Church (the Episcopal Church in America) exerted far less power over society and education in the English colonies.

The "weak king" model naturally shaped the English-owned colonies of America. The governors of the Thirteen Colonies had less power than their Spanish and French colonial counterparts, and the citizens had more chances to participate in government. Most of the continental American states other than Louisiana can trace their cultural beginnings to the original Thirteen Colonies. While many diverse peoples contributed to American development, the basic institutions like participatory democracy, religious pluralism and a common-law based legal system emerged from the original English colonies and spread across the nation. Louisiana did not confront these institutions until 1803, and the result was almost a civil uprising.

The original Colonies were more akin to thirteen separate, feuding, competing countries than to a single nation. By the 1800s, the states had coalesced into two competing regions with cultural differences so extreme that only the horror of a Civil War could truly create a single, unified nation. Beyond language and the most basic institutions, the North and the South in the colonial and antebellum eras shared very little in common, and views of education were among the starkest differences.

Northerners placed a high value on education. The region that became the North was first influenced by the settlement in New England of the Puritans who came seeking religious freedom as well as economic stability. Education was extremely important to the Puritans though not for its own sake. Literacy was needed to read the Bible, and reading the Bible was a necessary step to salvation. The geography of the area, as well as customs brought from England, indicated the settlement of small family farms clustered around villages. The concentration of population allowed the support of schoolhouses within walking distance of much of the population. To this day, the northeastern states display a considerable advantage in educational attainment.

Southerners placed a comparatively low value on education. Reading did not offer a heavenly reward and was seen as time away from work. Geography and customs indicated the development of plantation-style agriculture, especially after the early discovery of the cash crop of tobacco. Unlike the small, independent farms of the

North that featured a large middle class, the success of large plantations tended towards a class-based society. A small, wealthy elite coexisted with a large lower-class of laborers—first English indentured servants and later African slaves. The elite hired tutors for their children or sent them to Europe for an education. Growing tobacco or cotton well did not require much of an education. Even with a desire for an education, the vast distances between plantations, the lack of cities and villages, and the decentralized population in the South made establishing a school uneconomical for the average community. In the antebellum period, education for slaves was generally illegal because illiteracy was an impediment to organizing rebellions. To this day, the southern states score among the bottom of education statistics.

Higher education was to be a province of the elite until well into the twentieth century, and its roots lie in the North in general and in New England specifically. Rising out of such an educational tradition, a majority of the most respected colleges and universities are located in the northeast, exemplified by the prestigious Ivy League schools. The most famous university, Harvard, was also the first; a Puritan institution founded in 1636 and it—not a commercial business—is the oldest corporation still in existence.[5] The South seriously lagged in the development of higher education institutions until well into the twentieth century.

Another prominent feature of higher education in early America is that it developed without a centralizing tendency. Unlike other countries where the national government organized colleges, in America, it was an uncoordinated effort by communities, states, churches, commercial ventures or other entities. In this "capitalist" approach, there was no central planning, and the haphazard development eventually resulted in the most respected higher education establishment in the world.

French/Spanish Louisiana (up to 1803)

The context of the American parents who will adopt Louisiana in 1803 is set—now back to its other parents—France and Spain. The thirteen colonies and their progeny were born of English parents beginning in the early 1600s. Louisiana was founded over a century later. Her birth parents were French. She was adopted out to Spain during adolescence. She spent a brief time in French hands once again. She became part of America with the Louisiana Purchase in 1803.

Growing up French/Spanish as opposed to English

The French and Spanish had a similar approach to government and religion. These philosophies shaped the institutions of Colonial Louisiana and became part of its cultural DNA. The governmental influence was the "strong king" model where the monarch exerted virtually unfettered power. The religious influence was the infusion of Roman Catholicism, the state religion in both countries. Of course, France and

Spain had competitive differences that carried over to Louisiana, but they shared these fundamental similarities that greatly impacted later higher education.

The "strong king" model was exemplified by Louis XIV in France, the namesake of Louisiana. The idea was transferred to a colony without monarchs under the name of "executive centralism" where great power was centralized in the hands of the governor. Executive centralism was the norm in Louisiana under France and Spain where governors generally ruled with an iron fist. Average citizens played a relatively small role in government.

In the rest of America, descending from the English "weak king" model of governance, various legislative bodies had a much greater check on the executive. Since these legislative bodies were generally elective, the average citizen had some say in his government. The system was not equitable by contemporary standards—since the only eligible voters were literate, property-owning, white males over a certain age. Yet it was the most representative government in the world at the time. The average citizen of New Orleans could only hope for such a role.

The Catholic Church played an integral role in administering Spanish colonies, and Louisiana was no exception. There was relatively little official religious tolerance for non-Catholics, though the remoteness of places outside of New Orleans allowed unofficial religious freedom at times. This Catholic upbringing has contributed to Louisiana's uniqueness even today. The use of parishes as the official governmental unit, instead of counties, is a remnant of the early organization of the territory into religious parishes. Louisiana's Catholicism also played a big role in education, because it was the Church that took responsibility for the delivery of education.

French Louisiana (1699-1763)

It took another seventeen years for the French to follow up on La Salle's initial claim to Louisiana. An expedition reached the mouth of the Mississippi River in 1699—fittingly on Mardi Gras day. Though he died seven years later of yellow fever, also a Louisiana staple, Sieur d'Iberville established the first European settlement in a land area that covered about one-third of the present continental United States. New Orleans became the capital of French Louisiana by 1721 and had a population of 1,000 by 1728,[6] though the rest of the vast territory remained sparsely populated by Europeans. As with other colonies, Louisiana was intended to be a profit-making venture. By the time it was turned over to the Spanish in 1763, Louisiana was the foundation of numerous failed financial ventures.

In French Louisiana, most children simply did not receive any type of formal education, though some families provided private tutors or sent their children to private schools.[7] The best way to get an education was to send the children to France, but this was prohibitively expensive for all but the wealthiest families.[8] The French government did not help matters, because it "always minimized the importance of

Louisiana and throughout the period refused to make any appreciable concessions for education." [9] In 1742, Sieur d'Bienville, Iberville's brother who became a leading figure in early New Orleans, made one last appeal to France for a college after many similar ones over his forty years of association with the colony. A French minister reported that Louisiana was "'too unimportant for such an establishment.'" [10] Historian Adam Hebert, Jr. argued that this lack of attention was the main reason the residents of Louisiana did not make significant educational progress, not because the inhabitants were uninterested in education. [11]

As befitting a colony, the educational policies in Louisiana were really an extension of those in France. In eighteenth century France, the absolute monarchy form of government was characterized by a close interaction between church and state. As elsewhere in the world, wherever the Roman Catholic Church dominated an area, it also controlled education. This was definitely the case in French Louisiana.[12] Thus the main educational event was the establishment of the Ursuline Academy in New Orleans in 1727, which was probably the first girls' school in what is now the United States.[13]

Spanish Louisiana (1763-1800)

Spain took over Louisiana—sort of—in 1763 as a provision of the peace treaty following the French and Indian War (known elsewhere as the Seven Years War). Great Britain defeated an alliance of France and Spain in the conflict that started in the hinterlands of the American colonies. The treaty had two major effects on Louisiana. First, a group of individuals in the French Acadiana region of Canada refused to take an oath of allegiance to the victorious British and were expelled. A number of these Acadians, or "Cajuns," made their way to the south-central part of Louisiana and instilled a unique culture. Secondly, Great Britain forced Spain to take the financial liability of Louisiana as a punishment for being France's junior partner in the war. France lost all remnants of its once bountiful colonies in North America, a blow to its pride that the ambitious Napoleon sought to reverse at the end of the century. For the time being, however, it took Spain several years to get around to claiming its new possession.

Spain's lack of enthusiasm set the stage for colonial Louisiana's most notorious example of executive centralism, General Alejandro "Bloody" O'Reilly. Spain finally sent a governor to formally take possession of the territory in January of 1767, but with an inadequate military contingent. The French New Orleanians rebelled, and the governor was expelled. By mid-1769, the Spanish king sent O'Reilly with sufficient reinforcements. After a month-long trial with O'Reilly serving as judge and jury, six people, including leading citizens and government officials, were executed by firing squad and six others received long prison sentences. O'Reilly had asserted his executive power in no uncertain terms.[14]

When Spain received Louisiana in 1763, the influence of the Catholic Church persisted. O'Reilly restructured the colony into twenty-three parishes presaging their use as political units instead of counties. However, the Spanish priests had conflicts with the French priests who remained. For example, a 1780s attempt to introduce the Spanish Inquisition to the colony was successfully blocked by the French priests. [15] This was but one example of friction between the Spanish and French.

The Catholic Church, especially the Jesuit order, also oversaw education in Spanish Louisiana, though the state of education was deplorable. An official report after the takeover noted that more than fifty percent of the colony was unable to read or write. Only eighty of 169 people were able to even sign their names to a document in Pointe Coupee.[16] The Spanish government attempted to establish a public school system in 1771, but the effort was not successful. The elite sent their children to private, French-speaking academies that had a total attendance of about 400 in 1788.[17] The masses remained illiterate, though the Spanish set up an apprenticeship system that offered a rudimentary education.

Neither the Spanish nor French set up any type of higher education. The typical European approach was to set up universities that delivered training for a career as a priest, lawyer or doctor. Based on the precedent of their other colonies, Spain likely would have established a university in Louisiana as well. However, King Charles III realized that French institutions infused the colony, and he decided to wait until the people had become assimilated with Spanish customs.[18] The colony was taken back over by France before that could happen.

French Louisiana II (1800-1803)

In the 1790s, Napoleon Bonaparte rose to power in France and, after military successes in Europe, sought to re-build a French empire in North America, starting with Louisiana. In October of 1800, Napoleon forced Spain to return Louisiana to France with the Treaty of San Ildefonso. Napoleon wanted the treaty to remain secret while he built a military force, but the arrangement became known. He dispatched a French force but it was decimated by rebellion and disease in an intermediate stop in the West Indies. Napoleon's lack of replacement soldiers, and a need for revenues to fund his ongoing battles in Europe, set the stage for what would become the Louisiana Purchase in 1803. No substantive change in education or higher education took place in this brief era.

Education in Early American Louisiana (1803-1845)

With the Louisiana Purchase, Louisiana changed hands once again, this time going over to its adoptive American parents. Under the executive centralism of France and Spain, Louisianans had little control over their political fortune. As an American territory, they were force-fed democracy through a system of representative government by a flood of "immigrants" that seemed culturally deficient, spoke a different language and practiced a different religion. They reacted not with meek submission but with a rebellion that bordered on civil war. Before, the disagreements were just between the French and Spanish. The introduction to the mix of the more powerful Americans created a cauldron of simmering rivalries. The nascent emergence of higher education was one of the casualties of the bickering.

Education in the South to the 1930s

Before discussing higher education in Louisiana during this period, it is important to discuss the cultural context of the America, and specifically the South, to which Louisiana was involuntarily joined. In British America, the New England colonies developed a strong emphasis on education, and this emphasis generally spread to the Midwestern states along with out-migration. The Southern colonies viewed education as less important, and this attitude also spread as the population spread from the coast to the inland areas. By the 1860s, these differences, among many others, coalesced into two regions which had cultural differences so stark that only a Civil War could unite them.

The antebellum South that absorbed Louisiana had three general social groups: the elite, poor whites and slaves. The society was more class-based than the North, but less so than European countries such as France, Spain and Great Britain. The elite, for example the Tidewater Gentry of Virginia, comprised the large plantation-owners and merchants and was a small percentage of the populace. They generally provided tutors and sent their children off to college, so they had no incentive to support broad-based educational efforts. The poor whites, for example the Scots Irish immigrants, generally eked out a subsistence living through small inefficient farms, and did not have the time, inclination or money to devote to education. Slaves had many of the difficulties of the poor whites, and additionally were often denied education by law as literacy was an effective tool in organizing rebellions.

Not surprisingly, the difference in emphasis on education was reflected in educational statistics. In the 1860 census, 94% of the northern population was found to be literate, compared to only 54% of the South. 72% of northern school-age children were enrolled in school versus 35% in the South. The average length of the school year was 135 days in the north and only 80 days in the south.[19]

The Civil War from 1861 to 1865 did not help Southern educational efforts. It was fought on the territory of the South, so virtually all colleges and universities were either closed or occupied. A larger percentage of Southern young men fought and died, so there were very few students and teachers during the war and relatively fewer afterward. The Confederacy lost a "total" war that prescribed the infliction of economic and social devastation on the populace so that a similar war would never be fought again. It was effective but the negative social effects persisted, in education and other parts of life.

The period of Reconstruction in the South (1865 to 1877) was even worse for higher education than in the antebellum era. The newly freed slaves took advantage of the new-found opportunities for education in large numbers, reflecting the pent-up demand that had been denied them under slavery. This education, however, was at a basic elementary level. Despite these advances, the overall literacy rate decreased. Due to the general economic deprivation and a backlash against the institutions that might benefit members of the former Confederacy, colleges and universities struggled to survive. Historian W. J. Cash wrote that "'the state universities ceased in effect to exist for loyal whites in the Thorough[20] period and went for long years thereafter with empty halls and skeleton facilities.'" [21] With the Civil War and Reconstruction, a generation of college graduates was lost.

After Reconstruction, "Bourbon" Democrats dominated most Southern governments. The name, like that of Bourbon Street in the French Quarter of New Orleans, comes not from the alcoholic beverage, but from the family line of French Kings. Louis XVI was beheaded during the French Revolution. The rule of the Bourbon kings thus came to an end for the duration of the French Revolution and the reign of Napoleon. When Napoleon was exiled after the Battle of Waterloo, the Bourbon line of Kings was brought back to rule France. A similar pattern was followed by the ruling elite of South. In power before the Civil War, they were generally forbidden from entering government during the period of Reconstruction. After this interregnum, the group (or their descendants) came back into power, and being part of the Democratic Party, were given the sobriquet "Bourbon Democrats."

The Bourbon Democrats sought to bring back as much as possible the social and political life before the Civil War. While much had irrevocably changed, in education, the Bourbon governments had two significant effects. First, a philosophy of low taxes and low government spending did not provide the wherewithal to ameliorate the poor state of education. The Southern states fell even further behind their Northern neighbors. Second, public education was segregated by race. This separate and unequal system, and its legacy, affected Louisiana and the rest of the South through the twentieth century.

The Bourbon Democratic governments generally prevailed in the South until populist or progressive governments emerged in the 1920s and 1930s. Governors were elected that sought to use the power of government not for the elites but for the average citizen. Huey P. Long of Louisiana, for example, delivered free textbooks to public school students who could not otherwise afford them.

The legacy of the past, as well as the Great Depression, left the South in dire straits. A governmental report concluded that by the 1930s, "the educational base of the South had been decimated." Illiteracy in the South was double the rate in the New England and the Middle Atlantic states. The financial condition was even worse. The total endowment of all of the Southern colleges and universities combined was less than just the endowments of Harvard and Yale.[22] In 1936, the South spent $25.11 per child for secondary education, about ½ the average of the country, and far less than the New York State average of $141.43.[23] On the eve of cataclysmic changes after World War II, the South had a great need for educational improvement.

The last thing on the minds of the French/Spanish, or "creole"[24] residents of Louisiana was the inherited American values. They did not lament that the primary American cultural influences were not the values of the education-rich Northeast, but the education-indifferent culture of the Southern states. Instead, the creoles sought to resist the American influx of "foreign" people, values and practices. Most of the Americans they had known were from Tennessee and Kentucky. These rough pioneers brought their produce down the Mississippi to the markets in New Orleans and many became infamous for "their hard drinking, ardent winching, and murderous brawling when drunk, and sometimes when sober."[25] Also, most of the Americans were Protestants who had religious practices very different from the predominantly Catholic populace. For example, Baptists kept the Sabbath and judged the creoles harshly for dancing and drinking on Sundays. [26]

The social distinction between creoles and "Anglos" existed into the twentieth century—and maybe beyond for some regions. As late as the 1880s, the president of LSU viewed them as distinct ethnic groups. Though his colleagues were not convinced, he held the "belief that the association of Creole and Anglo-American was good for both. The gentle manners of the former served as a check upon the rough, impetuous ways of the latter while the American in turn stimulated the Creole to energy and enterprise. His policy was to mingle the two nationalities in the dormitories as well as in classes and in play." [27]

Another culture shock stemmed from the creoles' lack of experience with representative government and its accompanying institutions. In the French and Spanish periods of executive centralism, citizens had participated relatively little in the governing process. When given the chance to perform civil duties, like voting, they saw them as impositions on their time, not as privileges. [28] In the negotiations for the Constitution of 1812, some lawmakers sought to "'please the people' by producing 'a constitution as little tainted with democracy as a delegated republic can be.'"[29] Trial by jury had to be introduced to Louisiana, but the creoles were dissatisfied at having to perform jury duty. The American government introduced for the first time the offices of sheriff and coroner to local government and renamed the parishes to "counties," though this latter measure was soon reversed due to the resentment of the creoles.

The local officials were appointed by the governor, but the parish judge had to meet with the justices of the peace and twelve citizens of the parish at least once a year to oversee the levees, roads and police. These twelve citizens, or "jurors," formed the basis of the "police jury," a form of government unique to Louisiana and still used in many parishes. Slaves lost many rights under the American system as they could no longer own or inherit property, could no longer practice the Spanish custom of *coartacion* (self-purchase), and lost the right to complain of ill treatment. [30]

The most influential American in all of these changes was William Charles Cole Claiborne, the governor of Louisiana during its territorial period and after statehood. Claiborne strongly supported Thomas Jefferson over Aaron Burr when neither received a majority of electoral college votes in the 1800 presidential election and the decision was made in the House of Representatives. Jefferson rewarded Claiborne with the governorship of Louisiana in August of 1804.

Claiborne had de facto dictatorial powers as governor of Louisiana. The president or Congress could overturn Claiborne's actions, but Washington, D. C., was too far way in a time of difficult travel to have much of an effect. Congress decreed a Legislative Council of thirteen citizens, appointed by the president, to assist Claiborne in governing. President Jefferson had enough confidence, however, that he let Claiborne fill in the names. [31] Claiborne did appoint several prominent creoles to the Council. When Louisiana became a state on April 30, 1812, the governors had extensive power which included the appointment of all state officials though some needed the approval of the legislature. [32]

Claiborne faced a unique and difficult task. Both Napoleon's top official and the former Spanish governor stayed around in the territory in the hopes that the American occupation would not work. There was at least one plot to take over the territory, and if given a vote, a good majority of the citizens would likely prefer French rule to that of the Americans. Also, Claiborne had to somehow assimilate into America a people with different languages, different cultures, a different religion, and a sense of hostility. [33]

This creole versus American dichotomy plagued Claiborne and lasted to the middle of the 1800s, almost reaching a civil war in the 1820s. [34] In New Orleans, the creoles and Americans settled on different sides of Canal Street, the most important downtown street where space for a planned but unbuilt canal resulted in a large, empty median. This swiftly became a demilitarized zone between the feuding parties and was labeled a "neutral ground." Throughout contemporary Louisiana, medians are almost exclusively called "neutral grounds."

At times, the extraordinary diversity of cultures gave a glimpse of the positive future where America parlayed a "melting pot" mentality into the freest and most prosperous country in the world. For example, Andrew Jackson won one of the most stunning underdog victories at the Battle of New Orleans in 1815—and arguably saved the full independence of the country—by raising a motley collection of creoles, Americans, free men of color, Jean Lafitte's Baratarian pirates, and Choctaws. [35] Most times, however, the bitter infighting led to obstruction and an inability to marshal the state's limited resources in a bid to efficiently move the state forward. Education was a primary example of this.

Education remained underdeveloped in the early American period. In 1804, as provisional governor, W. C. C. Claiborne wrote to Secretary of State James Madison with an overview of the education and the culture of the newly acquired territory. He wrote that

> 'by far the greater part of the people are deplorably uninformed. The wretched policy of the late Government having discouraged the education of the youth . . . Frivolous diversions seem to be among their primary pleasures, and the display of wealth and the parade of power constitute their highest objects of admiration.' [36]

Claiborne noted that he was essentially starting from scratch in regard to education. He reported that there were no colleges and only a single Spanish-language, public school—located in New Orleans. He estimated that illiteracy was over 50% and that not more than 200 people could read and write well.[37] Another assessment was that except for the Ursuline school in New Orleans and a few private ones, schools hardly existed.[38]

Despite the low starting point, Claiborne believed that education was vitally important to a prosperous future for the citizens of Louisiana. Thomas Jefferson thought that the primary benefit of education was to train citizens to have the good judgment necessary for a properly functioning republic. European kings were certain that average citizens—uneducated, unenlightened, and often drunken—were not capable of electing proper leaders. The still-young country of America depended on them being wrong. Jefferson argued that a general education was vital to America as a whole and his political protégé, Claiborne, sought to apply the lessons to Louisiana.

Whereas the population did not necessarily place a high value on education, Claiborne had a zeal. He placed education as one of his top priorities and "earnestly believed that universal education, provided by the state, offered the only safeguard to democracy. He conceived the problem of preparing the heterogeneous population of Louisiana for self-government as essentially a problem of education."[39]

Some of his early plans were inhibited by Louisiana's status as a territory, not a state. When Louisiana became a state in 1812, any efforts toward advancing education were put on hold due to the War of 1812 and the attention paid to defending New Orleans, culminating in the Battle of New Orleans in 1815. No mention was made about public education in Louisiana's first state constitution in 1812. [40]

Claiborne's main educational effort, the College of Orleans, was hampered by partisan bickering among the French, Spanish and American inhabitants. The College closed in 1826, and during its existence, it "amounted at best to a second-rate high school."[41] Raphael Cassimere wrote that public secondary education officially began in 1841 over a dispute between the American and Creole divisions. The Americans in uptown New Orleans started their own school system after the Creole state officials would not implement the recently enacted education laws. The Creoles started their own French-speaking schools in order not to fall behind. [42]

College of Orleans (1805-1826)

Claiborne's establishment of the College of Orleans was the first try at higher education in Louisiana. From the beginning of his administration, Claiborne pushed for a system of public schools, and a plan was instituted by an act of the Louisiana legislature on April 19, 1805. Originally, the plan was ambitious and included a series of academies, schools and a college, all encompassed in a "University of Orleans."[43] Only the college came to fruition. It had success and by 1823, the College of Orleans had 44 boarding students and 35 day students. The students were all male, as the Ursuline Academy for girls came later. [44]

Unfortunately, the College could not overcome the disagreements within the diverse elements of the state population. It depended on funds from the state legislature for its continued existence, and the political differences caused the state to transfer disbursements to the newly established College of Louisiana at Jackson. The College of Orleans closed its doors on March 3, 1826, mostly because the "French and Spanish elements of the population of New Orleans, generally distrusted each other. They tended toward being united only in their mutual hostility toward the English-speaking 'Americans' who were aggressive as concerning the affairs of the territory and the state." [45] Historian Rodney Cline added that "[j]ealousies between rural and urban sections of the state, lack of understanding between the 'American' and the French-Spanish elements of the population, together with religious differences all contributed to its early demise." [46]

Centenary College of Louisiana (1825)

Following the failure of the College of Orleans, the legislature established the College of Louisiana at Jackson (later Centenary College of Louisiana) in 1825. It is the oldest currently-existing college in Louisiana and was touted as the "oldest chartered liberal arts college west of the Mississippi River."[47] Apparently tiring of the previous attempt of embracing diversity, the Legislature established the College and deemed it "to be an 'American' college to be dominated by the protestant English-speaking people outside of New Orleans."[48]

The College of Louisiana had a relatively short life. The first classes began in January of 1826. It had some success as seen by the conferring of the bachelor of arts degree in 1837. A rapid decline ensued, however, and by 1843, there were only 46 students and 3 faculty members. In the new constitution in 1845, all appropriations were discontinued and the College Trustees returned the charter to the state and closed the school. Echoing modern Louisiana, the legislature had authorized a lottery in 1827, expecting to produce $40,000 per year for the school. The lottery seems never to have been initiated. Showing a very different era, Robert Perry, a subcontractor who furnished the bricks on an early school building, "gave a mortgage on his slaves in lieu of performance bond."[49]

Meanwhile, in 1839, the Mississippi Conference of the Methodist Church, which included Louisiana in its purview, established a college at Clinton, Mississippi. The college was named "Centenary" in honor of the 100th anniversary of the founding of the first Methodist Society by John Wesley. It moved to Brandon Springs, Mississippi, before opening. Then, the property of the defunct College of Louisiana was purchased on Centenary's behalf on June 5, 1845. The property ended up being without charge in exchange for using it for a college. [50]

Centenary College of Louisiana officially came into being on January 14, 1846. The alumni of the College of Louisiana at Jackson were "adopted" which is the basis for tracing the beginning date back to 1825. The College had some success until the onset of the Civil War. By May of 1861, there were only three students remaining, and on October 7, 1861, an entry in the "Records of the Faculty" read: "'Students have all gone to war. College suspended and God help the right.'"[51] The College reopened in October of 1865, but operated with difficulty during Reconstruction, having only 25 students in 1879. On October 8, 1906, the move to its current location in Shreveport was authorized, and in September 1908, classes were held there for the first time. [52]

Medical College of Louisiana (1835-1847)

Another early institution of higher education was the Medical College of Louisiana, established in 1835, the Deep South's first medical school.[53] This College was merged into the University of Louisiana upon the latter's establishment in 1847. Finally, the University of Louisiana became the foundation of Tulane University in the 1880s, the details of which will be discussed in the next chapter.

New Orleans was a dangerous place to live before medical science found a cure for diseases like yellow fever and cholera. Around the time of the opening of the Medical College, New Orleans had earned the sobriquet "the necropolis of the South." [54] The abundance of cadavers, however, made the city an ideal place for the establishment of an early medical school.

In 1834, seven physicians pooled their resources to start the Medical College of Louisiana as a for-profit venture. On April 2, 1835, the legislature granted a charter of incorporation to the College, soon thereafter, it had 11 students. In March 1836 its first medical degree was awarded. [55]

The short period of time for its first graduate was not surprising because the practice of medicine was brutally primitive by modern standards, and the science of medicine was in its infancy. As of 1800, only four small medical schools existed in America, and one of those, Dartmouth, had only one professor. The use of science and technology was increasing rapidly in society, but the effort did not translate to an increase in medical knowledge. Physicians, for example, had little understanding about the causes or cures of infectious diseases. Historian John Duffy noted the tough situation of doctors when he described them as being unable "to comprehend or cure the major ailments of their patients, almost in despair they intensified the traditional remedies of bleeding, blistering, purging, vomiting, and sweating."[56] The "cures" generally did more harm than good.

In this case, Louisiana benefited from its French upbringing. In France, doctors had taken the lead on testing the efficacy of some of these methods. The first area of the United States to benefit from this research was Louisiana, given the French influence in general which caused most physicians to seek their medical training in France. Also, the French Revolution and Napoleonic Wars caused many French physicians to seek refuge in Louisiana by the early nineteenth century. The medical approach stood in stark contrast with the aggressive techniques of doctors in English-speaking America. At this time, the French manner of moderation in medical matters proved more beneficial to patients. [57] This approach greatly influenced the success of the Medical College of Louisiana.

On February 2, 1847, the legislature decreed that the Medical College of Louisiana would be "engrafted" onto the newly established University of Louisiana as its Department of Medicine.[58] Before this transition is discussed, however, it is important to get a feel for higher education from a participant's perspective.

An illuminating example of the times can be seen in the everyday routine of a medical student at the University of Louisiana Department of Medicine. The study of medicine was not for the squeamish, as the "nature of surgery in pre-anesthetic days required physical strength, speed and dexterity, and a measure of ruthlessness."[59] Medical student Robert Patrick described assisting on the amputation of a man's arm that had been caught in a cotton gin: "'I had to hold the arm, which smelled worse than a dead horse, while [the Doctor] performed the operation.'" The next day, Patrick decided against medicine as a career. [60]

A striking feature of early medical training was the brevity of the instruction. In the early years, the stated minimum term of training was one year, but in reality it might have constituted a few months. The primitive level of medical knowledge did not lend itself to a lengthy course of study. John Duffy noted that "the shortness of the school year, which began November 17 and ended February 26, precluded the acquisition of much knowledge."[61] By the middle of the century, the typical course of study was two years of lectures plus one year's practical experience in a doctor's office, though "only conscientious students spent the full required year." [62] A medical student wrote:

> 'When I think of the short time required of a student to prepare for the profession (two years! How short the enormity of labor!) I am astonished at the cupidity of the medical professors.' He added in his letter that the American Medical Association had urged colleges to extend the school year 'but none will take the step for they know they will lose students, who will always go where they can graduate sooner.' [63]

The American Medical Association was formed in 1847 and reform efforts in medical education bore fruit by the turn of the twentieth century. By 1885, the third year of training was firmly required.[64]

The Medical College ranked among the best in the nation,[65] in part because of the proximity to Charity Hospital in New Orleans. Duffy noted that the "one major school asset upon which all observers agreed was the abundance of clinical and anatomical material in New Orleans" due to the fact that the "large transient population and high incidence of malignant fevers in New Orleans provided far more subjects than were needed." [66] Medical students needed cadavers upon which to practice. Medical students in other cities were forced to rely on grave robbers (called "resurrectionists" or "sack-em-up men") to supply them for anatomy lessons. Charity Hospital had an abundant supply. A student could always get a particular body section from a hospital janitor for a few cents. The cost for an arm and two legs for dissection was 15 cents apiece. [67]

University of Louisiana (1847-1884)

The University of Louisiana was born as a state school out of the Constitution of 1845, and it lasted until absorbed by the newly dedicated Tulane University in 1884. The most successful component was a medical school after the University of Louisiana took over the Medical College of Louisiana. The University also had a moderately successful law department and notably unsuccessful academic department. Along with the Medical College of Louisiana, it is considered a lineal descendant of modern Tulane University.

State support for higher education in Louisiana after the closing of the College of Orleans in 1826 was split by nationality. Three colleges received state assistance. As covered earlier, the College of Louisiana (1825-1845) which was located in Jackson in East Feliciana Parish, an "Anglo-American stronghold," had influences that were Protestant and English, and it later became Centenary College. The College of Jefferson (1831-1846) was located in St. James Parish which was under French influence. It had some success until 1844 when the main building burned. The state then sold the property. Finally, Franklin College (1831-1843) was located near Opelousas and was established to meet a local demand. It was not successful and was abandoned in 1845.[68]

The Constitutional Convention of 1845 marked a fundamental turning point for public education in general. The framers determined that "education was to be democratic—free education was a duty of the state, not a charity to the poor." [69] A free public school system was started. Additionally, emblematic of an emerging New Orleans—rural areas split in the legislature, the capitol was to be removed from New Orleans after 1848.[70]

The resulting Constitution called for two state-supported institutions of higher education. The first was the University of Louisiana in New Orleans. Judah P. Benjamin led the charge for the University which was to consist of four departments—medicine, law, letters and natural science. On May 14, 1845, the convention adopted an enabling article directing the legislature to set up the University. On February 16, 1847, the bill was signed into law by Governor Isaac Johnson.[71] The good news was that the University existed. That existence, however came with two sets of bad news. First, the legislature was not forthcoming with proper revenues. While the medical department was somewhat self-funding, the academic department was not. Historian Walter Fleming argued that because of the lack of appropriations, from 1845 to 1878, the academic department of the University was "hardly more than a paper organization." [72]

The second set of bad news for the University of Louisiana was the Constitution's authorization of a "Seminary of Learning" that eventually came to be the most important university in the state. Historian John Dyer contended that the convention had no intention of creating a strong New Orleans institution. It was generally recognized that this Seminary of Learning was to be the official state university and was to be favored by rural legislators for appropriations. This Seminary, which was the precursor to LSU, did not open until 1860, and the details will be covered in the next chapter. [73]

The various departments of the University of Louisiana met with different levels of success. As detailed in the earlier section, the Medical College of Louisiana became the medical department of the University of Louisiana was quite successful. The law school met with some success but did not flourish. It was the first institution in early southwest to teach civil law, itself a curious legacy of Louisiana's unique heritage. Prior to 1803, Louisiana law was based on the French and Spanish system, which in turn was based on Roman law. The introduction of the very different system of English common law, the system in the rest of America, was—not surprisingly—strongly resisted by the creoles. In 1805, Congress decreed that civil law was acceptable as long as it did not conflict with the Constitution. [74] Around 1860, similar to the medical department, the entrance requirements (for males) to the law department were literacy and the ability to pay the $100 tuition. [75]

The academic department of the University of Louisiana had a checkered history. In the 1850s, it was tough to establish the department due to a lack of interest. A yellow fever epidemic in 1853 nearly closed the department.[76] Damning with faint praise, historian John Dyer noted that the "one bright spot in the entire history of the academic department came on July 25, 1857, when a class actually graduated."[77]

The entire University of Louisiana closed during the Civil War when the buildings sat silent and deserted. The 1864 Constitution provided funding for the medical and law departments to open in November of 1865. The academic department did not reopen.[78] The University was in operation during the Reconstruction years, when, according to historian Joe Gray Taylor, it was "almost the only source in the state of professionally trained men."[79] By the early 1880s, its fortunes had declined, and the state considered closing it.

In 1877, there was a legislative battle concerning the potential merger of the University of Louisiana with LSU to unify the state universities. At the time, only the medical and law departments were viable. Proponents of the merger argued that it "would avoid rivalry between state institutions, which had been the curse of education in Louisiana for nearly half a century."[80] As will be discussed further in the next chapter, the merger was not successful.

With additional funding as a result of the failed merger attempt, the academic department was reborn in the Fall of 1878 with three faculty members. The curriculum was so flexible that there were no degree requirements. Students took the classes agreed to by parents and professors.[81] The University limped along and, in the Spring of 1884, graduated its last class.[82] In that same year, the state government was happy to turn over the poorly performing school to the Tulane Education Fund, the vehicle for Paul Tulane's philanthropic efforts.

Despite an auspicious beginning with W. C. C. Claiborne, higher education in Louisiana was stunted in the middle of the nineteenth century. The University of Louisiana's academic department was virtually non-existent. The Seminary of Learning was not established until 1860, and it did not gain a foothold until the 1870s. Despite the uncertain prospects, the next era in Louisiana higher education history, 1853 to 1884, saw the foundation of the three bedrock elements of modern higher education: LSU, Tulane and a "dual system" of higher education separated by race.

CHAPTER 2

1853 to 1884:
Beginning of Top Three Features

The foundation for contemporary higher education in Louisiana was laid in the period from 1853 to 1884 with the establishment of the three most significant universities. Louisiana State University has become the most important public university. Tulane University has become the most important private university. Southern University represents a dual system of higher education for blacks and whites. All were established in one of the most turbulent generations that Louisiana has ever faced.

In the single decade of the 1860s, the city of New Orleans went from stunning prosperity to military occupation to economic devastation. On the eve of the Civil War, New Orleans rivaled New York City as the most prosperous port city in America. King Cotton had given the south one of the most lucrative crops in history, and much of the attendant wealth transited through the Louisiana port. New Orleans was one of the first major cities to be captured by Northern troops—in 1862—and thus Louisiana was among the earliest to begin the painful process of Reconstruction. Until the Union troops were removed in 1877, economic survival was the main goal, and the development of "non-essential" institutions was either abrogated or deferred.

The period encompassing the Civil War and Reconstruction is considered the point of fundamental change in American history, and especially in the South. 1877 was a symbolic year in which the former Confederacy began to join a modern America. Antebellum ways had receded into nostalgia, and the "New South" attempted to turn away from an agrarian past and embrace a future of capitalism and cities. While illiteracy sufficed for sharecropping and chopping cotton, a modernizing economy needed managers, lawyers and engineers. It is not surprising, then, that LSU, Tulane, and Southern were established or re-established within a few years after the end of Reconstruction.

Louisiana State University (1853)

LSU has played a central role in the state's pantheon of higher education. The influence has transcended the narrow confines of academia and has infused into the populace—the educated and uneducated parts. The most apparent evidence is the popularity of the LSU football team. Not so obvious, but likely more important, is the prevalence of LSU graduates among the state's leadership. This section will discuss the history of LSU from its beginning in 1853 to 1884, though, as befitting its importance, following sections will continue the story of LSU as it intersects with— and often becomes synonymous with—higher education in the state.

Early days

LSU's beginning can be traced to the Constitution of 1845 which provided for the establishment of a "Seminary of Learning" along with the University of Louisiana in New Orleans (discussed in the previous chapter). In turn, the genesis in 1845 was the availability of federal land grants, authorized by Congress, for the support of "a seminary of learning." Early in its statehood, when giving up its western lands, Virginia had set aside every 16th section of land to support schools. The Ordinance of 1787 included the provision and added the set-aside of two large parcels of land for the support of "a literary institution." Congress adopted the policy in 1803 and decreed that newly admitted states were to receive 46,080 acres of public lands to fund "a seminary of learning." [83] The idea was that the lands were to be sold to raise the necessary funds.

Upon admission as a state in 1812, Louisiana was eligible to apply to receive the public lands, but the process was glacial—in part due to the lack of consensus among the wide range of interest groups within the state. In 1827, Congress authorized the lands to be located and reserved, and in 1843 authorized the state to sell the lands. [84] In 1844 the Louisiana legislature authorized the sale of the lands by the governor. By 1855 nearly all lands were sold.

After authorization by the 1845 Constitution and with the sale of lands progressing, the legislature began debating a location. Not until March 17, 1852 was the question settled. The State Seminary was to be located "in Rapides Parish, in the pine woods north of Red River, within four miles of Alexandria." [85] In 1853, the legislature authorized the purchase of a specific tract of land near Pineville. Inaction followed due to a defect in the title, then a yellow fever epidemic, then a hard winter. The first bricks were finally laid on February 11, 1856, and the cornerstone was dedicated on March 12, 1856. [86]

The mostly likely reason for locating the State Seminary in Rapides Parish was the fact that it was also the residence of General G. Mason Graham, one of strongest proponents. Also, the State Seminary arguably continued the legacy of the College of the Rapides (1818-1845) which had gotten some state support.[87] Other attributes were the central location in the state, the ease of access by water in a time when transportation was exceedingly difficult, and the general healthfulness of the area.

The State Seminary was modeled after Virginia Military Institute and was to be "'a literary and scientific institution under a military system of government.'" [88] Graham's leadership was the main reason for the military orientation of the institution, but public sentiment in the South also favored military discipline.[89] The impending secessionist passion of the 1850s was not given as a motivating factor, but some expressed the view that military school graduates might be needed at some time in the future. The essential reason was that "Southerners were a military people."[90] In March of 1860, two months after the opening, a new law added "Military Academy" to the official name.[91]

The first superintendent of the State Seminary, William Tecumseh Sherman, was chosen from among 100 applicants.[92] Though relatively unknown at the time, Sherman was to become one of the most important and successful Union generals in the Civil War. Historian J. Fair Harden and others noted that in the application process, Sherman listed as references Col. Braxton Bragg and Maj. P. G. T. Beauregard—two military officers that famously became generals opposed to him in the Civil War.[93] Walter Fleming countered that this tradition was not correct. He contended that Bragg and Beauregard did not know Sherman and were supporting a different West Point graduate.[94]

The first class session started on January 2, 1860, with five professors and nineteen students. The students straggled in over the next several days and Sherman "remarked upon this lack of punctuality as being 'according to Southern fashion.'" Many mothers accompanied their sons and thought attendance to be a "dangerous business." Also, P. G. T. Beauregard requested that his son be assigned a roommate "'who has not seen much of city life.'"[95] The school was extremely isolated and Sherman wrote: "'It does seem to me that our lot is cast in the remotest part of the present civilized world.'" Books had to be purchased from New York, sent by steamer to New Orleans, then up the Mississippi River, to the Red River to Alexandria, before being loaded onto wagons for the final trek.[96]

1861-1877—Civil War & Reconstruction

The nascent college symbolized the poignant upheaval of the Civil War. As the possibility of secession loomed, Sherman was forced to choose sides in a conflict that pitted brothers, friends and countrymen against one another. When the election of Abraham Lincoln as president in 1860 brought matters to a boil, Sherman made clear that he did not believe in abolition or secession. If Louisiana seceded, he would not follow. If it remained in the Union, he would fight for the state.[97] In a secessionist move, Louisiana Governor Thomas O. Moore seized the Baton Rouge Arsenal and the captured arms were sent to Sherman who was Superintendent of the State Central Arsenal. Sherman was placed in an awkward position and "used strong language" but accepted the weapons. After the war, Sherman made a personal appeal for a full pardon for Moore.[98] He also remained friends with many at the State Seminary and retained a fondness for the institution itself.

Sherman's formal resignation was accepted on February 28, three days after he had left the state. In his letter of resignation, he wrote that "[r]ecent events foreshadow a great change, and it becomes all men to choose.'" Sherman chose to fight for the North, and he later successfully carried out the "march to the sea" that demoralized the military and civilian population of the South.[99] An overview of Sherman's military success was that "his hand was heavy on the South."[100]

The State Seminary essentially closed during the War. It is likely that a larger percentage of its students and faculty fought in the war than any other American institution. A single cadet joined the Union army, whereas the rest joined the Confederacy.[101] Before the horrors of the War became obvious, many young men on both sides rushed to enlist before their chance of glory was gone in a quick victory. The State Seminary students who first gained parental approval to enlist were the "envy of those who remained behind." The Seminary closed for the year on June 30, 1861, without the final examination or other events.[102] The college officially released its student body on April 23, 1863, as Union General Nathaniel Banks came up the Red River Valley to subdue remaining pockets of Confederate resistance.[103]

The college also symbolized the paralyzing and divisive effect of the Reconstruction era in Louisiana. Reconstruction refers to the period in the South after the Civil War where the presence of Union soldiers ensured that the policies of Abraham Lincoln and, later, the Radical Republicans in Congress would not be thwarted by opposition from the pre-War elites. It was a time of newly found liberty for the Freedmen, or newly freed slaves, who pursued in vast numbers the opportunity of gaining an elementary education for the first time. It was a time of repression for the whites who had sided with the Confederates as their rights to participate in government were curtailed. Higher education almost ground to a halt. Louisiana was the first Southern state to enter Reconstruction with the capitulation of New Orleans in 1862. In April 1877, it became the last southern state to leave Reconstruction.[104]

From 1865 to 1877, the State Seminary knew only hard times. It reopened in 1865 with four students.[105] For most of the next decade, most activity all but ceased due to lack of funds. At a low point in 1875, only five students remained.[106] The faculty went down to three men,[107] and the few professors who stuck around often had to do without basic necessities. Thomas Boyd, a member of the faculty who later became president, was frequently without proper shoes and clothing. Also, the food was exceptionally bad and "mutiny was threatened on several occasions."[108]

The key individual that helped the State Seminary weather the storm was president David French Boyd. David F. Boyd was the older brother of Thomas "Colonel" Boyd, a man who played a formative role in a later chapter of LSU history. D. Boyd was a member of the very first faculty and felt a calling to keep the doors of the State Seminary open until better times came along. In the especially tough times of the mid-1870s, he was urged by friends and colleagues to leave, especially since he had no salary and sometimes did not get expenses reimbursed. He resisted because he "considered it his duty to the University and to its creditors to keep the institution alive until better days."[109] One of the few positive notes was the continued interest in the State Seminary of William T. Sherman. Sherman lobbied federal officials and visited D. Boyd, who he still considered a good friend. Sherman was received fairly warmly on the campus—at least by D. Boyd. Given his cruel effectiveness as an opposing military leader, at least one professor, a former Confederate officer, refused to shake his hand.[110]

Move from Pineville to Baton Rouge

The facility in Pineville burned in October 15, 1869, and the college was relocated to Baton Rouge.[111] The fire to the Seminary Building had no definitive cause. One theory was that it was accidentally started when a cadet snuck into the cellar underneath the kitchen to partake of the recently unloaded provisions and carelessly threw aside a match.[112] Another theory was that it was intentionally set in retaliation for the death of a black peace officer by "a drunken cadet who was resisting arrest."[113] The boarding cadets were sent home, pending a decision on how to proceed. Since the Louisiana government was essentially bankrupt, D. Boyd did not hold out hope of replacing the building. Instead, he sought out other possibilities.[114]

After consulting with the governor, Boyd settled on part of the building of the Institute for the Deaf and Dumb and Blind, usually called the "Deaf and Dumb Asylum."[115] He arranged for the cadets to use the north half of the building while the deaf students remained in the other part.[116] The State Seminary students were forbidden to communicate with the deaf students, but they often strayed from the rule.[117] The most serious incident came in November 1871. The deaf students rang a large cracked bell, and the State Seminary cadets, "much annoyed by the frequent tolling of the bell, were unable to ascribe any good reason for such a noise in an institution for the deaf."[118] They stole the bell and hid it. The bell was later returned without incident.

The State Seminary reopened in Baton Rouge in 1869 with 170 students. It was understood that the site was temporary and rebuilding at the old site in Pineville was imminent.[119] The College never returned to Pineville and remained at the "temporary" site for 18 years. The official domicile of the College remained in Alexandria/Pineville until 1877 and this is where the Board of Supervisors carried on its business. Having the physical location so far away from its governing board often caused confusion and delay, especially when the Red River was low or at flood stage.[120]

President D. Boyd also took the opportunity of the move to request a name change. He argued that the "unwieldy name of the school caused the faculty much pain" and also that the word "Seminary" in the title caused a misperception that it was a girls' boarding school.[121] In 1870, the name was officially changed from the "Louisiana State Seminary of Learning and Military Academy" to "Louisiana State University."[122]

The main reason the university continued to struggle during Reconstruction was because from 1872 to 1877, it received no state support due to a refusal to admit black students.[123] The chaotic and uncertain Reconstruction era politics was typified by the situation in 1873 where two rival governors were sworn in and two rival legislatures met, though unfortunately LSU "was noticed by neither and hence appropriations ceased." [124] With federal help, William P. Kellogg, the candidate favored by Radical Republicans and blacks, became the recognized governor with a platform that included opening state colleges up to both races. LSU lost the governor's support upon the decision not to comply. [125]

The political contest between Kellogg's Radical Republic government and a majority of white citizens soon devolved into actual warfare. In 1874, the White League opposed the Kellogg government, and the governor's effective control was soon limited to New Orleans and the river towns. [126] After an initial victory on September 14, 1874, where the White League "drove out Kellogg and his officials," the federal troops caused the surrender the League troops and brought back Kellogg. [127]

The sympathies of LSU were clearly with the White League in the contest. Even before the move to Baton Rouge, the loyalties were clear, as a New Orleans newspaper summarized: "'The State Seminary as at present constituted is *not* an aid to reconstruction; on the contrary, it is an obstacle, for it is a Confederate institution for Confederate purposes in Rapides parish, which is itself an *enclave* of the Confederacy.'" [128] Even worse for the University, amidst all of the White League actions, the "energies of the people were so absorbed in the political struggle that there was little hope of arousing interest in educational matters." [129] D. Boyd tried to find some type of compromise between the two positions by advocating free schools for black and white students in each district in return for keeping the Seminary segregated. As noted earlier, his entreaties did not meet with success, and D. Boyd just resolved to try and keep the doors opened until something changed.

Louisiana Agricultural & Mechanical College

While LSU fought the integrationist policies of the Radical Republican state government during Reconstruction, a rival college emerged. The Louisiana Agricultural & Mechanical College (A & M College) emerged due to federal assistance and sought to replace LSU as the most prominent institution of higher education in the state. The political uncertainty of the 1870s prevented the stability of either school. Soon after the end of Reconstruction in 1877, the two colleges merged, and the combined entity became the "Louisiana State University and Agricultural and Mechanical College." [130] The name, no matter how unwieldy, remains the official one of Louisiana's flagship university.

The motivating principle of the A & M College emerged from the ashes of the Civil War South. Amidst the devastation in body and spirit, the South was forced to rebuild. Prominent leaders put the first educational priority as contributing to the South's physical rehabilitation. [131] Medical schools were needed to train doctors how to combat the widespread malaria, typhoid, yellow fever and hookworm. Schools of agriculture were needed to train farmers in new techniques of producing food and commodities. Practical training was need for the engineers and technicians who might do the literal rebuilding. The other side of the consideration was that most leaders saw little need for "lawyers or liberally educated young men who could read Greek and Latin poetry in the original." [132] As the country—and economy—became more modern as the twentieth century approached, the move away from narrowly academic disciplines was coupled with a move toward practical higher education.

The A & M College was the culmination of a series of events beginning with the Morrill Act passed by the U. S. Congress. Sponsored by Senator Justin S. Morrill of Vermont and signed by Abraham Lincoln on July 2, 1862, the Morrill Act fundamentally changed higher education in the nation by providing revenues for most of the leading public, flagship universities of today. Each state was allotted a grant of land equal to 30,000 acres for each member of Congress so long as it was accepted by 1869 and a college was established by 1874. [133] Historian Walter Fleming contended that the land grants were made by the government "in response to a popular demand for 'practical' education" and in "a reaction against the formal cultural education given by the colleges of the time." [134]

According to the federal law, the colleges must teach three subjects: agriculture, mechanic arts, and military tactics. [135] At the passage of the Act during the height of the Civil War, military schools were not as popular in the North, as the South, and this was seen as a problem. Since the Act was instituted by a northern, Union government, the military component was thought to be a type of insurance for future uncertainties. Also, the name "Agricultural and Mechanical College" which was adopted by colleges in many of the states, was not consciously chosen by the drafters of the legislation. Apparently a clerk in Washington simply "hit upon the phrase as a suitable one."[136]

To avoid losing the Morrill Act funds, Louisiana had to establish a college by 1874. After accepting the land grant in 1869, the committee set up by the Legislature to sell the land took until 1873. The Legislature then had to establish the college, and if not done so before July 1, 1874, the grant was to revert to the federal government. [137] It was decided that the A & M College was to be in New Orleans and to be open to both races.

The site for the A & M College was temporarily established at Common and Baronne streets in New Orleans. [138] Walter Fleming noted that this building belonged to the "suspended" University of Louisiana but at the time was being rented out for office space.[139] John Dyer wrote that the administrators were directed to find room in the East Wing of the building and the medical professors situated there found the A & M College to be "an unwelcome intruder." [140] A summer session was held in 1874 with 3 professors and two tutors, so as not to risk losing the Morrill Act funds by missing the opening deadline. [141] One of the main admissions requirements was that students be at least twelve years of age. [142]

The location was considered temporary, and a Board of Control was formed to determine a permanent location "in one of the country parishes."[143] The site settled upon was in St. Bernard Parish on the Chalmette battleground famous for the Battle of New Orleans. The state owned 200 acres of land, and Governor Kellogg transferred the title to the Board of Control in October of 1874. A smaller tract, the "Powderhouse property," was also purchased. Finally, a "questionable" purchase was made of the land lying between the two other tracts. This 400-acre farm "of little value" was owned by government insider "Honest" John Lynch (or his wife) and the price was $20,555, a large sum at the time.[144]

Two criticisms plagued the attempt to establish the A & M College in St. Bernard Parish. First, corruption was alleged with the charge that the whole enterprise was an attempt to reward "Honest" John Lynch. Second, selecting St. Bernard as a "country parish" was unusual since it was adjacent to urban New Orleans.[145] In the end, a demonstration farm was set up at the Chalmette site.[146] Practical and political difficulties, however, forestalled a permanent move from the New Orleans location.[147]

In New Orleans, the first regular session began November 15, 1874, with fifty students of both races. Admission standards were low and the students were generally unprepared. The Legislature did not appropriate needed funds for a building, so the College remained in the "temporary" New Orleans building. Making things more crowded, some of the former occupants refused to move out.[148] It took the end of Reconstruction in the South for the uncertainties surrounding the College to be resolved.

End of Reconstruction / Bourbon Democrats in General

A disputed national presidential election in 1876 ultimately led to the end of Reconstruction. Both candidates received just less than the needed 50% plus one of the Electoral College votes, and in three states, rival legislatures had certified that their own candidate had received the most votes. The dispute was finally resolved when a deal was cut. The Republican candidate, Rutherford B. Hayes, became president in exchange for withdrawing the soldiers from the South, and thus ending Reconstruction. This deal has come to be known as the Compromise of 1877.

In Louisiana, the 1876 gubernatorial election was even more curious. The Democratic Party ran "all that was left of Francis T. Nicholls," a former Confederate general who had lost an arm at the Battle of Winchester and a foot at Fredericksburg.[149] He was opposed by a Radical Republican candidate. After the ballots were counted, both sides claimed victory, both candidates took the oath of office, and both had a distinct legislature that recognized their right to office. After the troops were withdrawn due to the Compromise of 1877, the Republican administration faded away.[150]

Nicholls represented a party and ideology that became grouped under the sobriquet "Bourbon Democrats."[151] The name "Bourbon," as with the famed French Quarter street in New Orleans, comes not from the alcoholic beverage, but from the royal line of French monarchs. The Bourbon kings ruled France through the 1789 beheading of Louis XVI. They were out of power through the French Revolution and the reign of Napoleon. After Napoleon's final exile in 1815, the Bourbons were brought back to rule again. The Bourbon Democrats had a similar pattern in the Southern states. Ascendant in the antebellum period, they were out of power in the interregnum of Reconstruction, and they again dominated Southern life after 1877. A Louisiana history textbook defined the Bourbon Democrats as "the white oligarchs who regained power across the South." [152]

In Louisiana and across the South, the Bourbon Democrats advocated a policy of low taxes and low governmental spending, including on education and higher education. Since the small, wealthy elite was responsible for paying the bulk of the taxes, and since others were the beneficiary of the bulk of the spending, the Bourbon governments— dominated by the elite—chose to minimize both taxes and spending.

The Bourbon Democrats also controlled politics in Louisiana after Reconstruction. They increased the power of the governor's office with the Constitution of 1879, in a measure that "reaffirmed Louisiana's Latin heritage of 'executive centralism,' from which the Radical Republicans who drafted the Constitution of 1868 had briefly and partially strayed." [153] Murphy J. Foster, governor from 1892 to 1900, typified the era and was called the "most powerful and decisive of Louisiana's Gilded Age politicians." [154] Though he contributed relatively little to Louisiana higher education, his grandson, M. J. "Mike" Foster, had a significant impact starting in 1996.

The dominance of the Democratic Party in Louisiana starting with the end of Reconstruction in 1877 also contributed to the legacy of executive centralism. Louisiana did not elect a Republican governor for over a century, and it took until 2004 for the next U. S. Senator from the Republican Party. Louisiana effectively became a one-party state for most of the twentieth century. The lack of a viable opposition concentrated power in the hands of the Democratic Party. Since the governor usually was the most dominant figure in the Party, his office benefited most from this concentration.

Educational policies of the Bourbon Democrats

The damage of the low-spending philosophy on education was especially profound on a state that desperately needed to catch up with the rest of the nation. Historian William Hair wrote that the fiscal conservatism exceeded even other Southern states. Louisiana was the only state to show an increase in illiteracy among whites—from 18.4% in 1884 to 20.1% in 1894. [155] Black illiteracy was above 70%. Louisiana's public school system was the worst in the nation, and as of 1890, Louisiana had the highest illiteracy rate. [156]

The basic elitist policies of the Bourbon Democrats continued past the turn of the century and were sustained until Huey Long's election in 1928. Upon taking office, Newton Crain Blanchard, governor from 1904 to 1908, was appalled by the "deplorable condition of public education in Louisiana, the result of almost three decades of official neglect and even, at times, hostility by the state's conservative Democrats." [157] Despite the outrage, he and other governors did not successfully ameliorate the situation. Though governmental policies did not reflect it, interest in education for the populace increased markedly after 1900. For example, between 1904 and 1908, accredited high schools doubled from 26 to 53 in Louisiana. [158] The increasing dichotomy between the desires of the people and a government for the benefit of the elite led to a fundamental change in the governing philosophy with the ascent of the dynamo that was Huey P. Long. Long was the first to use the centralized power of the governor on behalf of the non-elite. As will be seen in the next chapter, higher education and Louisiana itself would never be the same.

Merger of LSU and the Louisiana A & M College

Amidst the chaos of Reconstruction, LSU and the Louisiana A & M College were both struggling institutions with uncertain futures in temporary locations. A merger in 1877, giving LSU the upper hand, strengthened the institution and eliminated much of the uncertainty over governance. The resumption of state appropriations increased the financial stability. Finally, a move to a more permanent location a decade later provided a geographical foundation. The reconstituted LSU and A & M College emerged from this era as the most important state university, ready to meet the fundamental changes of the twentieth century.

The actual merger, as can be imagined during the times, was both accidental and chaotic. While the colleges were separate and in competition, the supporters of LSU insisted that the two institutions should be merged. The Board of Control, the responsible group for the A & M College, considered this position "absurd and illegal." [159] In January of 1876, David F. Boyd, the head of LSU, made a request of the Legislature to unite the state universities. For a number of years, he had requested a consolidation of one or the other competing colleges, and the action was essentially perfunctory. To his surprise, the legislature passed the bill.[160]

Governor Kellogg indicated he would sign the bill, if it passed, but he had not actively supported it. [161] If Kellogg did not veto it on the first day of the next Legislature session, it would become law—even without his signature. Whether or not he would veto is not known because before the January 1, 1877 deadline, the state was thrown into uncertainty with the dual governors. The government of Stephen B. Packard controlled the archives and the state house. The government of Nicholls "had the support of the people and the assurance that the Federal government would not now interfere as it had done heretofore." [162]

Since Kellogg did not send in the veto, the bill became law—promulgated on January 23, 1877, by the Packard government. [163] Since the Packard government did not survive; however, the Act "was of no validity and passed unnoticed." [164] After more machinations, the merger was approved by the Nicholls government. Since the state archives were under the control of the Packard government, it took until May 19, 1877, for the official copy of the act of union to make it to the Secretary of State for certification. It was again formally promulgated on June 1, 1877. [165] Officially, Act 145 of 1876 united the Louisiana State University and the Louisiana State Agricultural and Mechanical College, at the time located in St. Bernard Parish, into the "Louisiana State University and Agricultural and Mechanical College," [166] still the official name of the university. Walter Fleming, thinking back to the original "Louisiana Seminary of Learning and Military Academy" noted that the new name was "a monstrosity equal to the original name." [167]

The union of the colleges did not dispel the uncertainty over a proper site. The Act left the question of a permanent site unsettled but indicated the initial plan of locating in Baton Rouge. The University had been in "temporary" quarters in the Deaf and Dumb Institute since the Seminary building in Rapides Parish burned in 1869, but the University did not own the land. The University did still own the land in Rapides, but there were still no suitable buildings on it. [168] While still "temporary," the deaf and dumb residents were transferred to other locations in 1878. [169] The University had a location, but D. Boyd sought a more permanent and suitable one.

The merged institution opened on October 5, 1877. Because of the uncertainty of the dual governor situation, the new Board of Supervisors did not appoint a President or a faculty until twelve days after the University had opened. [170] David Boyd was named President and Professor of Engineering though he felt that his resignation was imminent due to the controversies during the merger. Reflecting a situation that few presidents might face today, Boyd's report to the Board on February 22, 1878 noted that the "'Board of Supervisors, the public, and the Legislature, should please bear in mind that we opened the school *first* and *organized* it afterwards; that students were actually here and recitations going on before President or Professors were appointed.'" [171]

With the A & M College merger complete and classes resumed, D. Boyd returned his energies to a merger between LSU and the other state institution, the University of Louisiana. For several years, he had set out to unite LSU with at least the moribund Academic Department, if not the Medical and Law departments as well. Walter Fleming argued that the merger "would avoid rivalry between state institutions, which had been the curse of education in Louisiana for nearly half a century." [172] Of course, D. Boyd thought the merger should be on LSU's terms and that the institutions should be located in Baton Rouge, not the New Orleans home of the University of Louisiana. After several years of negotiations, the Board of Trustees of the University of Louisiana accepted Boyd's plan and sponsored a constitutional amendment favoring "partial amalgamation."[173] The resulting protests caused the Board of Trustees to renege on their support. In turn this embittered D. Boyd and split the supporters of the respective institution so that perhaps "no educational issue in the history of the state, up to that time, had engendered more heat." [174] The constitutional amendment resolution on unification was defeated in November 1878.

1886 Move to the Barracks

The crowning achievement of David F. Boyd's tenure was the acquisition for LSU of the old United States Barracks in Baton Rouge on July 12, 1886. [175] He had worked toward securing a donation of the property of the United States military post at Baton Rouge as early as 1870. [176] The possibility gained new life during the Compromise of 1877 that ended Reconstruction since part of the deal was removal of Northern troops which likely meant the vacating of the Barracks in Baton Rouge.[177] Finally, through the influence of General Sherman, Congress approved a bill in the Spring of 1886 that granted temporary use of the buildings and 211.56 acres of ground.[178] LSU had to insure and keep the property in repair, and the United States government could resume possession if the property was no longer used for educational purposes or if needed by the War Department.[179]

The Barracks, before begin turned over to LSU, had a remarkable history— changing hands among France, England, Spain, West Florida, the United States, "Independent" Louisiana, the Confederate States, and finally the United States again.[180] The first Europeans to own the land were French when the tract was granted by John Law's Mississippi Company to an individual who was later massacred in Mississippi by Indians.[181] From 1718 to 1763, the French maintained a military post. They turned the post over to the English as a result of the Treaty of Paris after the French & Indian War. The British built a garrison and called the area "New Richmond" though this name did not catch on. By 1768, it was the main British post on the Mississippi River. Some Royalists on the losing side of the American Revolution took refuge there. In 1779, Governor Bernardo de Galvez of Louisiana drove out the British and planted a Spanish flag.[182]

Baton Rouge (including the Barracks) was not included in the Louisiana Purchase in 1803—instead it was considered part of the Spanish colony of West Florida. In 1810, restless backwoods Americans under Fulwer Skipwith and Philemon Thomas captured the fort and established the Republic of West Florida with its capital at Baton Rouge. Within a few months, the United States government took possession of the post and the so-called "Florida Parishes." On the eve of the Civil War, the "Independent State of Louisiana" seized the fort. (At this time, Governor Moore transferred munitions to William Sherman at the Louisiana State Seminary.) It was soon transferred to the Confederate States of America which held it for one year. Finally, the Federal military recaptured the Barracks on behalf of the United States in 1862. It remained under American military ownership until the turnover was directed by Special Orders, No. 86, Department of the South on May 31, 1879. One June 6, the garrison was withdrawn.[183]

The transfer of the Barracks property did not go as smoothly as Boyd wanted. It did put off plans that had been in the works for the University to go to Alexandria and the A&M College to stay in Baton Rouge. [184] However, Governor McEnery opposed the acceptance of the property from the federal government because it was only a temporary situation. He did not advocate that the state build permanent buildings on a tract of land not owned by the state. [185] Despite McEnery's opposition, in July of 1886, the LSU Board of Supervisors accepted the donation. The Board later secured full title to the property. [186] At the time of the turnover, the structures were very dilapidated.

The subsequent removal of the University to the new Barracks location was the last hurrah of President D. Boyd. The numerous political battles over the years had taken a toll, and he felt an "undercurrent of opposition" in his final administration.[187] D. Boyd resigned in December 1886 but stayed until July 1888.

Executive centralism before Huey Long

A theme of higher education in Louisiana after 1928 is the intense involvement by governors, especially with LSU. Executive centralism had been alive and well in Louisiana, but Huey P. Long took this involvement to another level. He was emulated by most of the succeeding governors in the twentieth century. However, the special relationship with LSU was in place well before 1928.

The political interference likely began soon after the 1877 merger of LSU with the A & M College. Though relatively small and insignificant before the union, the merged institution gained prestige and "[s]tate politicians now began to meddle in the affairs of the University." [188] During the years 1877-79, President D. Boyd had eschewed granting minor university positions as patronage rewards to the governor.[189] A bill was successfully put forth in the 1880 legislature with the purpose of giving control of the LSU Board of Supervisors to the incoming governor, Louis Wiltz. Wiltz was opposed to the Boyd administration, and at a July 1880 meeting, the Board dismissed all members of the faculty including Boyd. All but Boyd and another were re-hired. [190] On October 4, 1880, the Board hired William Preston Johnston who "soon became involved in political entanglements and it became only a question of time when he would be forced to resign." [191] He resigned in 1883 to become president of Tulane University of Louisiana.

Tulane University (1884)

Tulane University has been the most important private institution of higher education in Louisiana's history. Second only to LSU, but more than any of the other colleges and universities, Tulane University has influenced the affairs of Louisiana and its leaders. Though beyond the scope of this work to attempt to quantify the "influence" of universities, one anecdotal example is offered. In a biographical interview after his 2004 election to the U. S. Senate, David Vitter said that he had been accepted into Harvard and Yale law schools but instead chose Tulane Law School because "he knew the importance of state loyalty if he was going to run for office." [192] Thomas Langston, a political science professor, explained that if a person wants "to get somewhere in Louisiana politics, a Tulane or LSU law degree gets you a lot farther than a Harvard or Yale law degree."[193]

The modern Tulane University had its roots in the University of Louisiana established in 1847, as well as the Medical College of Louisiana, established in 1835, which became the medical department of the University of Louisiana. In the early 1880s, the University of Louisiana was foundering. At the same time, Paul Tulane, an industrialist with roots in New Orleans, sought to give back something to the city that made him wealthy. His career had coincided with the prosperous era of the steamboat, [194] and he contrasted the hard times after the Civil War and Reconstruction. He planned to give enough money to establish a new college with a technical curriculum. Instead, in 1884, Tulane University of Louisiana was started on the foundation of the University of Louisiana, and it went on to become a premier academic university.

A glimpse of a very different time in 1883 comes from a *New York Times* article about Paul Tulane's plans for the university he wanted to establish in New Orleans. The reporter noted that Tulane's "form is bent, and the long, thick, black eyebrows are gray; but the eye is clear, the voice round and full; the gesture quick, the brain active, shrewd, and penetrating, the heart generous as ever." Tulane made his fortune in Louisiana and his "most intimate" friends were from there. These friends had been "well to do" before the Civil War and had been able to send their sons to the North or to Europe to get an education "as was the custom of the day." The War impoverished his old friends and their sons and grandsons could not go to "Harvard or Yale or London or Paris for the education they sought and ought to have." Tulane thus determined that he should enable the young men (intentionally excluding girls) to be able to get an education at home. Tulane said that their "grandfathers had made his fortune; it was his duty as well as his pleasure to help the grandsons." Tulane spoke of the conditions in Louisiana that "we have the boys there to become such men, only they lack the educational resources. The common school system of the State is defective."[195]

As the American economy industrialized at an unprecedented rate in the latter part of the nineteenth century, Tulane realized a need for an applied or technical education that could immediately be put to use by accountants, factory superintendents and middle managers. Most colleges and universities offered a liberal arts education better suited for priests and lawyers. For example, the study of Latin and Greek was at the heart of the curriculum. Tulane thought a more practical education was more appropriate for the less educated South, especially for Louisiana.[196]

Tulane set up the Tulane Educational Fund[197][198] (Fund) which in turn was charged with determining the best way to spend his money. The Fund's Board of Administrators held its first meeting on April 17, 1882. The Act of Incorporation occurred on May 23, and Tulane's Act of Donation was on June 10. [199] The Fund had two major decisions to consider. First, should the struggling University of Louisiana be taken over or should a completely new institution be established? Second, should the primary curriculum be practical or academic in nature? The outcomes on both, ironically, seemed to contradict the expressed wishes of Tulane himself. Also, despite Tulane's desire for an all-male university, the early leaders pioneered "a new pattern of education for women" [200] which will be discussed later in the chapter.

In 1881, a Committee of Education met to determine how Tulane's money would be used, and submitted two reports: opinions of the majority and the minority. The majority recommended taking over the University of Louisiana, including the academic department, and creating a manual training school—for vocational and engineering education—as a branch of the university. [201] The minority group argued that Tulane himself wanted an independent institution. They also pointed out the "'pressing demand for an institution which shall afford practical instruction in the application of theoretical studies to the industrial pursuits of life.'" They also noted that an institution of practical training was what Tulane had in mind when he gave the money. [202] The majority plan was adopted by 9 to 7 vote, and by this slim margin, Tulane University avoided being a technical school. [203]

When the plan was presented to Paul Tulane, he "virtually vetoed the plan" by noting his objection to his money being spent on the academic department. He commented that "'I mean to foster such a course of intellectual development as shall be useful and of solid worth, and not be merely ornamental or superficial.'" [204] He also expressed a strong preference for a new institution with a technological curriculum.[205] He also felt strongly about two other issues. He was adamant that any university was not to be subject to politics or political control of the state. [206] This insistence was especially prescient. The other was that the school be tax exempt.

Two individuals were credited with changing Paul Tulane's mind and laying the foundation for the modern Tulane University. First, U. S. Senator Randall Lee Gibson carried on much of the personal contact with Tulane. Historian Mary G. McBride wrote that Gibson "contributed most to the initial formation of Tulane" and was notable for "the cosmopolitan and even scholarly vision that he brought to the design of Tulane."[207] Gibson also played a key role in securing the Barracks as a campus for LSU.[208]

The other key individual was William Preston Johnston, the first president of Tulane. Johnston[209] had been on the staff of Jefferson Davis and spent three months in solitary confinement upon their capture. [210] In January of 1883, he was selected as president of the then-non-existent university despite the fact he happened to be the president of LSU at the time. He accepted the position. In changing Tulane's mind on the key issues, he felt the board should take over the University of Louisiana because it "had buildings, a student body, a faculty, and a history." [211]

Tulane University of Louisiana was authorized by Act 43 of the 1884 Legislative Session, which was signed into law on June 5, 1884, by Gov. S. D. McEnery.[212] The name was officially changed from "The University of Louisiana." The first session opened on October 4, 1884, and included 73 students in Tulane College (as the academic department was known), 136 in the high school department, 223 in the medical department, and 17 in the law department.[213] The union was voted on and approved by the people of Louisiana in 1887.[214]

Two major themes characterized Tulane University from its beginnings into the twenty-first century. The first was a commitment to higher education for elite students as opposed to higher education for the masses. While this philosophy was not fully formed until after the turn of the twentieth century, the roots were apparent even in the beginning. Essentially, Tulane sought to educate the individuals who were to become leaders of society. In contrast, the other universities in Louisiana were to remain open-admission well into the twentieth century and were charged with educating all students that might benefit from college—not just the most capable. Also, Tulane was a privately endowed university free from political or religious control.[215] Though this was a disadvantage at first, it later gave Tulane great flexibility for growth and stability. In addition, there was not a similar institution within 500 miles of New Orleans, so Tulane had the potential of becoming a regional university.[216] Tulane soon became an important Southern academic institution, and it had the Deep South's first schools of architecture, business and social work.

The second theme was that, after an incident in 1906, Tulane was clearly a private university but—due to its beginning—it also retained elements of a public university. These public attributes, most notably tax advantages normally reserved only for public colleges, engendered controversy at many times over Tulane's later history.

The most notable dispute came in the 1990s and involved tuition vouchers for Tulane to be awarded by state legislators. Under the 1884 law, all Louisiana legislators were entitled to nominate one student annually for a one-year tuition waiver at Tulane. This benefit was worth $19,550 as of 1996. In return, the university received exemption from state sales and local property taxes. The benefit became controversial in 1996, as a study discovered that legislators often assigned them to other legislators, relatives and campaign supporters.[217] The relevant part of Act 43 was as follows:

> The said Board further agree and bind themselves to waive all legal claim upon the State of Louisiana for any appropriation, as provided in the Constitution of this State, in favor of the University of Louisiana. Besides the waiver of the claim, as aforesaid, as an additional consideration between the parties of this act, the said Board agrees to give continuously, in the academic department, free tuition to one student from each Senatorial and from each Representative district or parish, to be nominated by its member in the General Assembly from among the bona fide

citizens and residents of his district or parish, who shall comply with the requirements
for admission established by said Board. [218]

The property tax breaks, the quid pro quo for the scholarships, became another part
of the controversy as Tulane University took on elements of a commercial property
business in the 1990s and after. In the midst of the controversy in 1996, one tax study
showed that Tulane received $23.5 million in property tax breaks, though Tulane
disagreed and contended it was $5 million.[219] Into the twenty-first century, the unique
public-private arrangement has engendered some controversy.[220]

"Dual system" of segregated higher education

In addition to the final establishment of LSU and of Tulane, the third major
feature of higher education in Louisiana, a segregated approach, was established
during this period. With the establishment of Southern University in 1880, Louisiana
embarked on a system of rigid segregation in higher education. Over the next century,
a consistent feature of this system was the establishment of two colleges or universities
in very close proximity for students of different races. For example, primarily white
LSU and primarily black Southern University are separated by about ten miles in
Baton Rouge. A similar pattern can be seen in New Orleans, Shreveport, and north-
central Louisiana. This dual system led to a desegregation lawsuit that began in the
early 1970s and spanned two decades, ending with a Settlement Agreement in 1994.
By 2004, both LSU and Southern University were both slightly *more* segregated than
before the $120 million dollar remedy. With some notable exceptions, it can be
argued that a dual system of education still exists.

Louisiana before Reconstruction was noted for the absence of educational
opportunities for African-Americans. Free People of Color had some opportunities
to gain an education, but these were gradually lessened by the change in laws and
attitudes after the American takeover of Louisiana in 1803. In 1830, the Louisiana
legislature passed a law that prohibited the teaching of even basic literacy to slaves. [221]
On the eve of the Civil War, a significant majority of African-Americans had received
no formal education.

The Reconstruction period from 1865 to 1877 saw an explosion of educational
demand among the Freedmen, or newly freed slaves. The Freedman's Bureau and
northern philanthropies set up schools that generally provided an elementary education.
This period also saw the establishment of four institutions of higher education for
African-Americans, including Southern University and the precursors to Dillard
University.

The emergence of the Bourbon Democrats at the end of Reconstruction brought
a segregated system of education—both secondary and higher—that hardened by the
1890s. Historian Joe Gray Taylor argued that "in Louisiana, the master class when
restored to power almost destroyed the public school system. This was not primarily

because of race prejudice . . . [but because of the] mandate for low taxes and economy; and this program hit the schools especially hard."[222] Whether because of prejudice or governmental philosophy, the result was a poor system of education for whites but a deplorable one for blacks. An 1898/1899 report of public school Superintendent J. V. Calhoun noted the presence of 35 public high schools for whites and none for blacks.

An interesting coincidence in this period was that two of the most influential U. S. Supreme Court cases establishing the constitutionality of segregation originated in Louisiana. The most famous, *Plessy v. Ferguson*, handed down in 1896, created the standard of "separate but equal" that governed the practice of segregating public accommodations, such as schools, until overturned by *Brown v. Board of Education* in 1954. The second instance was the so-called *Slaughterhouse* cases of 1879 where the Supreme Court ruled that individual states could continue to make laws allowing segregation without interference from the federal government.

During the era of segregation that emerged with the end of Reconstruction and "hardened" after the 1896 *Plessy* decision, historically black colleges and universities (HBCUs) were usually the only viable way for African-Americans in the South to get a college education, so the mission was clear. However, during the period of Reconstruction (and in the immediately succeeding years), it was possible for blacks to attend white colleges. An important debate during this period was how best to achieve the long-term goal of a greater number of college-educated African-Americans. One side argued this was best achieved by advocating for more resources to be given to the segregated HBCUs. The other side argued for a greater integration of higher education. The debate was cut short before the turn of the century by the policy of strict segregation in Louisiana. However, the debate was reopened with the landmark case of *Brown v. Board of Education* in 1954, and it became a central feature of higher education in Louisiana in the fifty years afterward.

The national *fin de seicle*[223] debate over the best methods of black higher education was symbolized by two leading figures, Booker T. Washington and W. E. B. Dubois. Washington, a Southerner and son of a slave, became the "apostle of industrial education" and argued the best course was proficiency in manual tasks—not "academic" pursuits. Once blacks reached a level of economic self-sufficiency, the next generation would be prepared for the rigors of universities. DuBois, a Northerner and Harvard graduate, feared a reliance on such basic instruction—of a largely agricultural nature— would result in the exclusion of blacks from general American higher education.[224] Implicit in the debate on higher education was a disagreement over the proper course for blacks to obtain civil rights in society. Washington was noted for an "accommodationist" approach of gaining economic self-sufficiency first and demanding equal social and political rights afterward. Dubois was famous for the advocacy of the "talented tenth" of black leaders who would push for equal rights immediately.

Booker T. Washington, who had a great impact on higher education in Louisiana, touted the benefits of occupational preparation over abstract reasoning. Often recognized as one of the principal founders of vocational education, he was one of the first people to espouse a philosophy of education that emphasizes the practical nature of learning. Born a slave in 1856, he received some informal education as a youth. He was later admitted to the newly opened Hampton Institute established to teach newly freed slaves. He followed a curriculum that included traditional academic subjects and some industrial trades, and upon graduation, he joined the faculty.

In 1881, he founded the Tuskegee Institute in Alabama. Based on the pragmatic philosophy of Hampton Institute, Washington instituted a curriculum of academic subjects as well as vocational programs such as painting, plumbing, carpentry skills, blacksmithing, basket making, harness making, brick laying, brick making, wheelwrighting, and tinsmithing. By the time of Washington's death in 1915, Tuskegee had grown from a $2,000 initial endowment to 2,300 acres of land, 123 buildings, and more than $1,000,000 worth of equipment.

Washington believed that the ultimate goal of education is to be able to solve everyday problems. This practical knowledge could elevate individuals and the surrounding community. Making a distinction between practical understanding and the abstract book-learning common in the elite colleges of the day, he instilled an emphasis on learning by doing. He was one of the few to recognize that learning encompasses more than just memorization. An educated person was defined as having self-discipline, high moral standards and a sense of service. He summed up his philosophy and distance from the traditional liberal arts education when he wrote that

> (h)appily the world has at last reached the point where it no longer feels that in order for a person to be a great scholar he has got to read a number of textbooks and that he has got to master a certain number of foreign languages; but the world has come to the conclusion that the person who has learned to use his mind. that the person who has mastered something, who understands what he is doing, who is master of himself in the classroom, out in the world, master of himself everywhere, that person is a scholar.[225]

Washington put forth many of the same arguments made by proponents of vocational education in the twenty-first century.

Washington's famous "Atlanta Compromise" speech in 1895 was the first shot in what would become his heralded debates with Dubois over the best approach to education for African-Americans. The two scholars came from very different backgrounds and primarily dealt with groups of African-Americans from different regional and socio-economic conditions. The differing approaches would frame the debates over education as well as the best path to civil rights throughout the 20th century.

Dr. W.E.B. DuBois was born to a well-to-do free black family in the primarily middle-class town of Great Barrington, Massachusetts, in 1868. After a receiving a formal education through high school, he enrolled in Fisk University in Nashville, Tennessee, at the age of 17. His traditional liberal arts training prepared him for attendance at Harvard, and he graduated in 1890 with a Ph.D. After further study at the University of Berlin for two years, DuBois became a professor at Wilberforce University in Ohio, the University of Pennsylvania, and Atlanta University.

Dubois believed that the best road to prosperity for American-Americans was to provide a liberal arts education for an elite few who could then oppose the leaders of Southern society that upheld segregation. He favored a more typical theoretical curriculum for the "Talented Tenth" who would then become leaders of the African-American community and would be prepared to push for economic, social and political equality. He opposed the Tuskegee model of practical education and challenged black youth to "hitch their wagons to a star rather than to a mule."[226] This view seemed a better choice for the relatively more prepared African-Americans in the North.

The motivation behind Washington's more practical educational orientation was the desire to see a different ascent for African-Americans in society. In opposition to Dubois, he felt that African-Americans first had to establish themselves as economically self-sufficient before it would be advantageous to seek political and social equality. Since slavery had put African-Americans so far behind the rest of society, he argued that it was necessary to start with some of the less well-respected occupations. The necessary preparation had yet to be done for the elite, leadership roles in society. He outlined this philosophy in his "Atlanta Compromise" speech:

> Our greatest danger is that in the leap from slavery to freedom we may over—look the fact that the masses of us are to live by the production of our hands, and fail to keep in mind that we shall prosper in proportion as we learn to dignify and glorify common labor, and put brains and skill into common Occupations of life; shall prosper in proportion as we learn to draw the line between the superficial and the substantial, the ornamental gewgaws of life and the useful.[227]

Washington believed that the best road to prosperity was in pursuing manual occupations, especially in the agricultural and mechanical fields. This view was a more popular choice for the relatively less-prepared African-Americans in the South.

In addition to vocational education, Washington is credited with other pioneering educational programs. First, at Tuskegee, Washington developed an emphasis on adult education. At the turn of the century, higher education was synonymous with traditional-age students. Washington saw the great need of farmers for practical knowledge of how to increase food production. He developed an educational program that was geared to the adult farmers. Also, to reach a wider audience that needed knowledge of better agricultural techniques, he instituted an early form of extension education. He bought a wagon that was then loaded with tools and information and dispatched to farmers' homes.

Southern University (1877)

Washington's influence was seen in the establishment of Southern University in 1877. Southern is the oldest surviving HBCU and historian Joe Gray Taylor wrote that Southern University was "probably the most important institution of higher education for Louisiana blacks."[228] Southern historian Charles Vincent wrote that the University was considered "the largest predominantly black institution . . . in the world."[229] Southern University became the most important HBCU in the dual system of higher education in Louisiana.

During the Civil War and Reconstruction, education for blacks emerged in a nascent form after the days of slavery. During the Union occupation, General N. P. Banks proposed a program of elementary education.[230] The Freedmen's Bureau, the federal government agency set up to assist the newly freed slaves, at first did not include promoting education, but this was soon added as a service.[231] Prior to the establishment of Southern University, three institutions of higher education were established. Leland University was established by Baptists in 1870. Straight University was established by Congregationalists in 1870. Finally, New Orleans University emerged in 1873 and grew out of Union Normal School which had been founded earlier. The former no longer exists and the latter two were later merged into Dillard University.

The founding of Southern University had its genesis in a political compromise proffered by P. B. S. Pinchback in the tumultuous political year of 1877. Just as the election results for the governor and legislature were unclear, so were other elections. Pinckney Benton Stewart Pinchback, a black Republican, thought he had won the U. S. Senate seat, but the outcome was disputed. He did not get general Republican support and decided to use his position to make a political compromise with Francis T. Nicholls, one of the competing governors. Pinchback gave his support in exchange for "securing a promise from Nicholls to promote the political, educational, and material interest of black people as he would those of white people."[232] After becoming the recognized governor, Nicholls came through with the establishment of Southern.

Pinchback was a colorful and important figure in the tumultuous times of the 1860s and 1870s. He was the son of a white Mississippi planter and slave mother. Prior to and during the Civil War, he worked on steamboats. In 1862, after Union occupation, he abandoned his ship and ran a Confederate blockade to reach New Orleans. He enlisted in the Union Army and served as a recruiter and captain. After the war, Pinchback was a delegate to the Constitutional Convention of 1867, a state senator, lieutenant governor, and governor for approximately thirty-five days.[233]

Southern University was officially established in New Orleans with Article 231 of the Constitution. The "Act of Incorporation or Charter" of the Board of Trustees was established on March 3, 1881. Southern opened for classes on March 7, 1881, with 12 undergraduates.[234] It remained in New Orleans until 1914 before moving to its permanent location in Baton Rouge.

In the first decade, Southern provided a practical education in the model of Booker T. Washington. Dubois described it as a "manual training school."[235] Among the graduates were seamstresses, joiners, carpenters, brickmasons, and mattress-makers.[236] Like LSU and the other colleges and universities established up to this time, Southern did not yet have what would become the "typical" university curricular offering of four-years of college-level work that resulted in a Bachelor's degree. In a chart of the educational institutions in the state, Southern was listed under "Four-Year Colleges", "Two-Year Colleges or Normals" and "State-Approved High Schools."[237] Completion of grade school was the main admission requirement at Southern.[238]

The early years in New Orleans were fraught with uncertainty, exemplified by three presidents in the first four years.[239] Internal administrative controversy almost closed the school. Also, the act establishing the University made no provisions for a building. The University obtained a facility located a 158 Calliope Street in a building that formerly housed the Hebrew Girls School.[240] The property was obtained August 15, 1881.

Southern faced some early opposition from the black community. The first point was that another university was not needed, and instead the resources should be put towards more secondary schools. A second concern reflected a trade-off concerning the unique mission of historically black colleges and universities. Joe Gray Taylor noted that "some black Radicals were opposed to the new school because they thought it an extension of Jim Crow policies already in effect in the public schools."[241] A petition by black Delegate Henry Demas of St. John the Baptist Parish reportedly had 1300 signers protesting the University on the grounds "'that it made a distinction between citizens in organic law.'"[242] This latter debate was destined to flare anew after the *Brown v. Board* decision in 1954 that outlawed segregation in schools.

Dillard University's Predecessors (1868-1930)

Dillard University, a private historically-black institution, was formed in 1930 from two predecessors that were established during Reconstruction: Straight University and New Orleans University. Straight University[243] was established by the American Missionary Association of the Congregational Church[244] and chartered by the State of Louisiana in 1869. It was a named for Seymour Straight, "a prominent white, Baptist, New Orleans businessman and philanthropist, concerned with ameliorating the conditions of blacks during Reconstruction."[245] Straight also donated the land for the school.[246] The Freedman's Bureau gave assistance in the establishment. Its normal (teacher-training) school opened in October of 1869. Straight became arguably the first integrated college in Louisiana history, with eight white law graduates (of ten total) in 1878.[247]

Straight had early success for two main reasons. First, it received a great deal of support from the black community, in part because blacks had a large voice in the operations, serving on the faculty and board of trustees.[248] Second, the segregationist policies of the Louisiana State Seminary (named LSU after 1870) caused an increase in appropriations. When LSU refused to admit black students in 1873, black legislators and Radical Republican allies cut off state appropriations and instead channeled the previous LSU funds to Straight. [249] Much of the momentum dissipated when a fire in 1877 destroyed most of the main building, and many students transferred to Southern University.[250]

The other predecessor college, New Orleans University, was itself the result of a merger. Union Normal School for Blacks which was established in 1868 joined with Thompson Biblical Institute (or Thompson University) which was established in Franklin by Northern Methodists.[251] The merged institutions were chartered in 1873 by the Freedmen's Aid Society of the Methodist Episcopal Church. New Orleans University also operated Flint-Goodridge Hospital for blacks, and its campus was located on St. Charles Avenue.[252]

Both schools maintained an independent existence until the 1930 merger to form Dillard University. Historian Joe Richardson summarized that although "both schools were probably mediocre, had serious financial and housing problems and taught more elementary and secondary than college students, they offered post secondary work and were equal to the average black college. Unfortunately, both schools were under funded and competed for the same students."[253] The existence of these universities in New Orleans was one of the reasons cited for the removal of Southern University to just outside Baton Rouge in 1912. The merged school was named for James Hardy Dillard and will be discussed in Chapter Four.

Though the prospects might have seemed fleeting at the end of this era in the mid-1880s, Louisiana was on the verge of a proliferation of new colleges and a modernization of higher education. The decades on either side of the turn of the twentieth century became a golden age of higher education for Louisiana and the nation.

CHAPTER 3

1884 to 1928: Proliferation

At the turn of the twentieth century, the city of New Orleans was far simpler than at the turn of the twenty-first. The wealthy still fled during the summer yellow fever season while everyone else contended with "the omnipresent stench of animal carcasses, full privy vaults, stagnant ditches, and . . . tons of manure dropped daily on city streets by hundreds of horses and mules." [254] As in the early days of the Medical College of Louisiana, New Orleans still had one of the highest death rates among American cities. [255] There were no bridges that connected New Orleans to another land mass. And after the move of Southern University to Baton Rouge in 1912, there were no public colleges or universities in the largest city in the state.

The national economic and educational milieu at the turn of the twentieth century was also much simpler. The nature of occupations did not require a high level of education. Consequently, a small percentage of Americans went to high school and fewer went to college. The college-going populace consisted of mostly a small elite training in liberal-arts type settings for occupations such as being a lawyer or priest. As seen with Paul Tulane's philosophy, an emphasis on more technical subjects, such as business, was growing, but this would not begin to change the nature of higher education until well after 1900.

Executive centralism was alive and well in the state of Louisiana. A textbook on Louisiana history described the state as "a place that had never really accepted the American principle of representative government. Of all the states, Louisiana was the least democratic, the least responsive to majority opinion." [256] The Bourbon Democratic governors had enough power that they did not even feel the need to hide political manipulation. Governor Murphy J. Foster won reelection in 1896, outpolling his opponent 9,499 to 1 in four plantation parishes where black voters would have voted for Foster's opponent if allowed. [257] In response to the obviously rigged vote total and similar measures, the Bourbon Democrats "seldom bothered to deny fraud. 'Rob them! You bet! What are we here for?' exclaimed Shreveport's most vociferous Bourbon newspaper, the *Evening Judge*." [258]

This 1896 election was the high point for a wave of Populism that swept Louisiana and the country. Arising from the grass-roots appeal of small farmers in the South and West, this third-party political movement sought to get the government to provide what is today considered basic needs to the struggling farmers and poor people in general. Examples included protection from the monopolistic practices of large corporations, decent roads and free textbooks in public schools. In Louisiana, the Bourbon Democrats were able to suppress the Populist uprising for a generation, but Huey Long revived Populist rhetoric in his 1928 gubernatorial victory when he successfully overturned the elitist, Bourbon Democratic hierarchy.

Though powerful, Louisiana governors did not yet play a central role in higher education reform, mainly because colleges and universities were just beginning a move from elitist institutions to a staple of general society. In the 44-year era under consideration, only John Parker, governor from 1920 to 1924, attempted to deal with public higher education as a statewide system. In the adoption of the 1921 Constitution, two governing boards for higher education in the state were established, the State Board of Education and the Louisiana State University Board of Supervisors. This was a nascent attempt to organize the proliferating colleges and universities across the state.

The lack of governor involvement reflected a trend that had characterized early Louisiana colleges as well as national higher education development from its beginnings with Harvard in 1636. The primary actors in the establishment and nurturing of individual colleges and universities had been college presidents, philanthropists or other non-governmental leaders. Historian John Thelin stated that the "national history of American Higher Education favors college and university presidents and the 'captains of erudition,' or industrialists turned philanthropists, as the pioneers who built institutions and stoked the fires of university greatness between 1880 and 1910."[259] In Louisiana, Paul Tulane, an industrialist, was the driving force behind the 1884 forming of Tulane University. This characterization—the absence of the governor as a driving force in higher education—is an important one that binds early Louisiana and national higher education because it will stand in stark contrast to the situation in Huey Long's Louisiana after 1928.

The era from 1884 to 1928 saw an explosion of higher education institutions— with the establishment of twelve currently-existing colleges and universities. Unlike many other countries where higher education was centrally planned and administered by the federal government, American higher education was noted for a "capitalist" approach. At the turn of the nineteenth century, the early American government considered and then rejected the notion of coordinating the expansion of higher education. Instead, colleges and universities developed on their own in response to the need or whim of a local community, religious organization or other groups or individuals. The institutions that filled a need and could recruit enough students prospered. The others closed or merged with more successful colleges. This era in Louisiana reflected the burgeoning need for higher education in the rapidly expanding economy and saw the establishment of a large number of public, private, religious, four-year, two-year, academic, and technical colleges. As befitting the general American pattern, a majority of these colleges no longer exist, but the ones that prospered are detailed in the chapter.

Continued development of LSU and Tulane

Before the newly established institutions are discussed, it is important to detail the continued development of LSU and Tulane—both of which solidified much of their character as universities during this era. From shaky beginnings, both emerged with their lofty positions in the state's higher education hierarchy intact. LSU became the recognized public flagship university of the state, charged with providing a quality education to the citizens of Louisiana. Tulane became the premier private university, with the mission of providing elite education to prepare the future leaders of the state, and increasingly the Gulf South region. Both outcomes, however, were far from certain looking forward in 1884, and even the survival of the schools was by no means assured.

LSU barely survived the political opposition and lack of revenue during the 1870s but had emerged as the unquestioned state university with the elimination of its two competitors. LSU had merged with the Louisiana Agricultural and Mechanical College, and Tulane had absorbed the University of Louisiana. LSU needed to solidify its position. To oversee the changes, it turned to former president David F. Boyd's brother.

Thomas Duckett "Colonel" Boyd became president in 1896 and arguably did more to determine LSU's character than any other individual. His presidency capped a long association with the institution. His father was a good friend of Thomas Jefferson, having been born in sight of Monticello. Thomas Boyd grew up with Confederate generals Joseph E. Johnston, Albert Sidney Johnston, and J. E. B. Stuart.[260] He came to attend the Seminary in 1868, living with his older brother, D. Boyd, and enrolled at the age of 14.[261] He was briefly named president in 1875 when D. Boyd resigned to head up the Royal Military School in Cairo, Egypt. When revenues were not forthcoming for that venture, D. Boyd returned to LSU presidency.[262] Thomas Boyd was also appointed acting president in 1887, in a political battle, after his brother offered his resignation. When D. Boyd rescinded his resignation, Thomas Boyd turned down the presidency out of deference, though he was "crushed" to take the action.[263] He left LSU to be the president of Louisiana State Normal School and served with distinction, before leaving to become president of LSU.

Under T. Boyd's direction, LSU developed from a small military school to an established state university. In March of 1876 there had been 22 students,[264] but by 1919-20, the school passed the 1000 mark in attendance, ending with 1028.[265] In 1881, two courses of study led to the bachelor's degree. In 1906, a Law School was established, followed by a Graduate Department in 1908.[266] T. Boyd also seemed to "modernize" the social life of the students, as he was criticized for allowing "sinful" amusements—fiddle music and dancing.[267]

T. Boyd did not face political interference until Luther E. Hall became Governor in 1912. Dr. Charles McVea, the university surgeon, had opposed Hall in a high-profile way. The Governor asked T. Boyd to request Dr. McVea's resignation. In a tough position, T. Boyd agreed to pass along the message. [268] The matter went before the LSU Board. Hall did not control the Board and the move was defeated. When Hall subsequently filled four vacancies, McVea resigned when faced with the impending decision. When Ruffin G. Pleasant was elected governor, McVea was named to his former position. T. Boyd did not face any other instances of negative political interference. [269]

When T. Boyd accepted the LSU presidency in 1896, he was arguably downgrading his position from the presidency of Louisiana State Normal College. [270] Normal was bigger and more stable, and the salary was the same. At LSU, he found a "dissatisfied student body and a jealous and discordant faculty." [271] In the Spring of 1896, about two-thirds of the students mutinied over alleged favoritism shown in the promotion of two student officers. [272] Some of the students were dismissed, and the resulting legislative investigation led to the resignation of the sitting president. T. Boyd hesitated for four weeks before accepting the position on July 6. He had been successful at Normal but preferred university work, saying that "I still feel somewhat like a fish out of water [at Normal] and sometimes would fain return to my old love." [273]

T. Boyd instituted two major changes that fundamentally contributed to the character of LSU. The first was a revision of the strict military discipline that had characterized LSU from almost the beginning. In 1896, T. Boyd realized that the university had outgrown its rigid military bearing. The strict discipline and constricting military regulations caused frequent disturbances. Appealing to a broader range of students was necessary for growth.[274] By 1926, the growth had occurred, and a select committee reported "that the disciplinary plan then in operation was deficient in that it failed to differentiate clearly between the requirements of academic discipline, which should apply to all students alike—male and female, military and non-military— and military discipline, which concerned only members of the cadet corps." [275] A separate approach to the different types of students was adopted.

The second change, far more influential, was the acquisition of the final site of the University with the ample assistance of Governor John Parker. The University had inhabited a succession of locales—the old Seminary building in Rapides Parish starting in 1859, the School for the Deaf and Dumb in 1869 in Baton Rouge, and finally the former U. S. Barracks in 1885.[276] T. Boyd and Parker relocated the campus to larger grounds south of Baton Rouge, beginning in 1922. Historian Matthew Schott argued that this laid "the foundation for L.S.U.'s growth into an important southern university." [277]

In 1919, John Parker ran for governor on the issue of establishing a "Greater Agricultural College" in place of the current LSU.[278] At first he wanted to expand just the College of Agriculture, but his vision soon expanded. [279] He wanted to use the Gartness Plantation for the site and get funds for building with a severance tax of two per cent on the natural resources of the State. After he won the election in 1920, he asked members of the "Greater Agricultural College" commission to tour the best sites and bring back recommendations. They reported the agricultural college should not be separate from the University, and Parker's goal then became a "Greater University." [280] The first dirt was turned on March 29, 1922. The goal was to offer "to all young men of the State, rich and poor alike, unlimited educational opportunities." [281] Parker's devotion to LSU was matched by the succeeding governor, Henry L. Fuqua, who might have been one of the youngest students ever to enroll at LSU. [282]

T. Boyd was also notable for fending off a final challenge to LSU's supremacy—this time from Tulane University—in 1906. The opening gambit in the competition between LSU and Tulane was initiated by T. Boyd. He wanted to organize a medical school in New Orleans though he maintained it was not "an act of aggression or hostility toward Tulane University." [283] In 1906, a group of doctors in New Orleans had organized the "Louisiana College of Medicine" and sought to have it taken over by LSU. The attempt was defeated and another medical school at LSU was not considered until the present one was established in 1930. [284]

The more serious challenge was the attempt by Tulane to gain state support. Marcus Wilkerson called this legislative fight "[o]ne of the bitterest struggles in the career of Colonel Boyd." [285] The key issue came down to whether or not Tulane was a state institution and, thus, whether or not it was eligible for state aid. The legislative debate was spearheaded by the respective presidents—T. Boyd and Dr. E. B. Craighead of Tulane—and their supporters throughout the state.[286] The publicity battle was fierce, and the New Orleans Times-Democrat reported that "'[t]ension between the warring camps was so strong that violence was talked of if not actually contemplated for practice'" and that "'the war of the colleges was begun anew.'"[287]

For T. Boyd, the issue was quite simple—any funding and support given to Tulane must be taken from LSU. Boyd felt that there "was no need for two state universities; one or the other would die, for there were not enough white students for the support of two." [288] T. Boyd and LSU had made enemies in recent political contests, including the A & M College merger, and many prominent citizens were supporting Tulane.

Craighead, on the contrary, sought to obtain state aid so that Tulane could prosper. Tulane's financial prospects had been dealt a blow when on March 27, 1887, Paul Tulane died intestate. With no will, Tulane University was cut off from anticipated future revenues. The lack of a will was somewhat mysterious, though in the last few months of his life, Paul Tulane had "an obsession that the administrators were spending his money recklessly and for purposes which he did not approve." [289] Regardless, the lack of the expected endowment caused Tulane University to struggle financially past the turn of the century.

William Preston Johnson, the long-serving president, died in July of 1899 in the bed where he was born.[290] His successor, Craighead, became president and saw a solution to the financial difficulties. He argued that "'Tulane is a public institution, entitled to state aid.'" [291]

Two things contributed to Tulane's eventual loss in the state legislature. The first, as described by historian John Dyer, was Craighead's "qualities of truculence and impatience [which] came out most obviously when he was drinking." [292] The second was that Act 43 of 1884, Tulane's founding legislation, clearly stated that Tulane was not a state institution. Craighead's position was that Tulane was a continuation of the University of Louisiana. [293]

Tulane had some prominent proponents arguing its case, including Senator Randall Lee Gibson, Governor Newton C. Blanchard, and Judge Charles E. Fenner who served 14 years as a justice of the State Supreme Court. All of these men studied law at the University of Louisiana. [294] Governor Blanchard was in favor of providing state funds to Tulane. He argued that Tulane was a "quasi-state institution" because Act 43 simply lent the property of the University of Louisiana to Tulane University, it did not transfer the title from the state. [295]

During the legislative proceedings of June 1906, the final bill was completed in executive session. In a bit of skullduggery, when the printed measure of the bill reached the legislators' desks, changes had been made in pencil concerning the Tulane item. The change read that in exchange for $25,000 state appropriations, Tulane must offer free tuition to all Louisiana students. Historian Marcus Wilkerson wrote that "[j]ust who made the changes and by whose authority was not disclosed." [296] The bill was sent back to the Appropriations Committee and the Tulane part was deleted. The political maneuvering continued. [297]

T. Boyd and the LSU supporters then decided to use their main weapon. They produced a telegram from Edward Douglas White, Associate Justice of the United States Supreme Court (and later Chief Justice). He had been a member of the Board of Administrators first selected by Paul Tulane to figure out his bequest. The Tulane side had publicly stated that White would side with them. White sent the telegram in reply to the question of whether Tulane was a state college and entitled to state aid. He wrote: "'My opinion is very decided that it is not, and should not ask or receive (aid) on the footing that it is a state institution.'" [298] He also wrote that he did not want to influence the debate. The telegram was read on the floor of the House, and the measure was defeated by a 2 to 1 margin.

For LSU, the victory was the final hurdle in becoming the unquestioned premier state university. After surviving challenges by the Louisiana A & M College, the University of Louisiana and Tulane University, its position was safe. It is difficult to imagine the appearance of state higher education in the twenty-first century had LSU not fended off the challenges.

For Tulane, the defeat had two implications. First, it was another chapter in the continuing theme where Tulane occupies an ambiguous middle ground between public and private universities. The Tulane administration and supporters unquestionably considered the University to be more public than private. It was only after a hard-fought defeat that they reluctantly resigned themselves to lean heavily towards the private side.

The second implication was that, ironically, the fight to become a state university defined Tulane as a private university. More out of desperation than forward-thinking enthusiasm, Tulane trod a path towards becoming an elite, regional, liberal arts university. Tulane's emphasis changed to a more defined role of educating top students. The university was forced to reject an emphasis on the "mass education for Everyman" and instead to concentrate on "developing potential leaders with general enlightenment for the professions and for citizenship." [299] The University did not de-emphasize its more vocational programs of law, medicine and engineering, of course, but a liberal arts education increasingly became the main focus.[300]

The path turned out to be a successful one, but after the legislative loss in 1906, the mood was pessimistic among the Tulane community. At the turn of the century, a more practical curriculum was more valued, especially in the South. Also, given the low state of educational preparation in the New Orleans region, having rigorous admissions requirements was a move fraught with danger. In 1890, New Orleans was the only place in Louisiana that had a public high school. [301] Also, the lack of an accreditation system for high schools made it difficult to even use high school graduation as an admissions requirement.[302] Finally, though the Tulane administrators did not conceive of Tulane being a regional university at this time, the entire Gulf South region had a similar level of academic preparation as Louisiana. From the vantage point of 1906, Tulane's subsequent success is especially impressive.

Two other highlights of the early years included Tulane's move to its present location and the medical school's association with leprosy. Tulane moved to its present location on St. Charles Avenue in 1894. Much of the land was bought on April 27, 1891, and was described as "a monotonous stretch of barren crawfishy land broken intermittently by live oak trees, a vegetable patch grown up in winter dead weeds, or occasional pools of stagnant water defying one and all to drain them." [303] Also, doctors from the medical school were influential in the establishment of the United States Public Health Service Hospital for lepers at Carville, Louisiana, called "the world's hope for the eradication of leprosy." [304] With the combination of such debilitating symptoms and ignorance of the cause, the public often showed "unbelievably callous treatment" to the sufferers. The location of a leper hospital was so routinely fought by the public, that the site for the Carville hospital had to be secured under the guise of establishing an ostrich farm. [305]

New Colleges Established

While LSU and Tulane were establishing important elements of their characters, a fantastic proliferation of colleges and universities reflected the increasing demand for higher education around the turn of the century. Twelve currently-existing institutions were established during this era, as were many more that are now defunct. The enrollments were extremely small by modern standards, but the foundations were set to handle the influx of students after World War II.

Northwestern State University (1884)

The first college founded during the era, Louisiana State Normal School (later Northwestern State University) was established in 1884. "Normal" was the name generally given to institutions of higher education specifically assigned the task of preparing teachers for elementary and secondary schools. These schools were vital to a nation where universal education and literacy was increasingly expected and needed for the modern economy. At first, the level of instruction was generally more akin to a high school. Thus normal schools were sometimes considered a "college" and sometimes not.

Normal schools were first developed in France. The tenets of the French Revolution called for a push for broad-based, basic education. The French government created a set of institutions—called *ecoles normale*—dedicated to the training of the large number of elementary and secondary school teachers needed to educate the masses. The term *normale* referred to the norms or standards to be applied in teaching. The first American normal school was based on the French model and was founded in Massachusetts in 1839. By 1860, there were twelve normal schools in the nation. By 1910, there were 264 normal schools with 132,000 students. [306] Normal schools provided the vast majority of teachers in America for the following century. [307]

After the mid-twentieth century, stand-alone normal schools declined in popularity for two main reasons. First, they were increasingly forced to give up their monopoly on education degrees, and other colleges provided competition. Second, most normal schools had been located in rural settings "away from large cities and the temptations which might corrupt young, innocent students." [308] This became a significant disadvantage after the 1940s, when a large population base became crucial to growth.

Louisiana State Normal School (Normal) was founded on the site of a school whose history showed the ravages of life in rural Louisiana. In 1847, the Sisters of the Religious of the Sacred Heart established the first Catholic school in north Louisiana with six pupils. [309] Yellow fever hit Natchitoches in both 1853 and 1854, so by November of 1855, the sisters decided to close the school. They were convinced to open a new and expanded convent in 1857, on the edge of town. [310] In the Red River campaign of the Civil War, in 1864, federal troops occupied Natchitoches. Suspecting that ammunition or Confederate fugitives were in the convent, a Union colonel trained artillery guns on the convent and sent a note demanded the right to search the premises.[311] Nothing was found. The school stayed open ten years after the war, but it could not overcome Reconstruction. The nuns closed the school in September of 1875. For another ten years, the vacant property deteriorated. [312]

Normal was officially established by Act 51, signed by Governor Samuel D. McEnery on July 7, 1884, which called for the "the establishment of a State Normal

School 'for the benefit of such white persons of either sex, of suitable age and mental qualifications, as may desire and intend to teach in the public schools of Louisiana.'" [313] There was a competition among towns for the school, and Natchitoches won—locating the school on the vacant grounds of the former convent. Dr. Edward Sheib, the first president of Normal, wrote that the school opened in a "'half-ruined building surrounded by a wilderness of thorns and trees . . . without desks, without benches, without books and black boards, with the rain pouring through the broken roof, and the wind sweeping through halls that could not be closed.'" [314]

The first classes were held November 3, 1885, with 60 students. [315] The lack of preparation among potential students provided the greatest obstacle. There was no public grammar school or high school within a hundred miles. [316] Also, the original legislation had prohibited a preparatory department. Sheib was unprepared for such difficulties which stemmed from his "naivete in underestimating the obstacles and resistance he would encounter from people unconvinced of the value of public education and from students inadequately prepared for normal school." [317] He resigned within two years.

In 1888, Thomas Duckett Boyd left LSU to become president of Normal. T. Boyd had turned down the LSU presidency in deference to his brother, David French Boyd, in 1887. When T. Boyd accepted the Normal presidency at age 34, he admitted that he knew nothing about normal schools, and the offer came as a surprise. Later looking back at his first days at Normal, he recalled that "'the outlook for the school was gloomy in the extreme.'" [318] He went on to write in an open letter that "'[w]eighed down by an oppressive debt, her people not yet recovered from the ravages of war and the horror of reconstruction, Louisiana is poorly prepared to give the masses of her people the education which modern progress demands.'" [319]

Normal under T. Boyd started with nine instructors and 64 students, about half in preparatory classes. The "advanced" curriculum consisted of a two-year course in teacher-training that was roughly equivalent to the junior and senior years in high school. [320] The degree was extended to three years in 1886, and to four years by the legislature in 1892. [321]

Given the precarious beginnings, T. Boyd had a successful tenure at Normal, but he returned to be president of LSU in 1896. In June, he was elected president of LSU, but he hesitated before accepting. Normal was running smoothly, it had a larger enrollment than LSU, the salaries were the same, and LSU was experiencing student and faculty unrest. [322] He at first declined the position but later accepted on July 6, 1896. In the end, he just preferred university work.

Beverly C. Caldwell followed T. Boyd as president of Normal. Reflecting the norms of a different era, Caldwell recalled that one of the great joys of his first teaching assignment in 1886 was his marriage to Ida Underwood, his fifteen-year-old student. He was 31 or 32 years old at the time. [323]

Caldwell faced many difficulties at the rural college. Just getting to Normal was tough. There was no direct rail service to other parts of the state. The most convenient connection was at Cypress, "eleven long, muddy, difficult miles" from Natchitoches. [324] There was relatively poor heating from fireplaces, no running water, and no electricity. [325] Caldwell commented that with the combination of wooden buildings and heating provided by 145 stoves and 27 open fireplaces, "'the fire risk is little less than appalling.'" [326]

Disease was also a constant worry. There were outbreaks of measles and smallpox in 1896. [327] After a 1912 outbreak of paratyphoid fever, the department of health found an "infestation of the school by bedbugs, 'filthy disease-bearing insupportable vermin of the night.'" To combat the pests, 452 of 544 mattresses were burned. [328] The school was closed in 1918 due to the Spanish influenza epidemic that claimed about 500,000 lives in the United States. At Normal, there were 132 cases but no fatalities.[329]

Caldwell had Normal running smoothly until politics intervened in 1908. He was asked to resign in June by the newly elected governor, Jared Y. Sanders. [330] Caldwell recounted: "'I had voted against him in the race for governor and I accepted my dismissal without demur.'" [331] Criticism of the dismissal mounted and was publicly fought in the press. In a curious situation, the Normal Board of Administrators, with Sanders presiding, even adopted resolutions noting Caldwell's "excellent leadership" of Normal. [332] Sanders had not commented publicly but broke his silence in November because of the continuing criticism. He cited financial improprieties and dispatched an auditor who "reported that the books of . . . the entire institution . . . were so poorly kept that it was impossible to determine accurately the financial condition of the school." [333] Caldwell avoided indictment on the financial improprieties, but he was out as president. James Benjamin Aswell became president in 1908, but he resigned in 1911 to campaign for governor. [334]

Victor Roy became president in 1911 amidst political opposition on two fronts. The first criticism was that Roy had been an instructor at Southern University in New Orleans,[335] a black university. He was vociferously opposed by much of the community who argued that merely teaching black students was sufficient to disqualify Roy. Also, Roy had contributed to the opponent of the governor in the election of 1912, and educational leaders surmised the governor wanted him dismissed for this reason. [336] Roy briefly lost his job but, due to public support, was quickly renamed to the presidency and remained in the position for 18 years.

The most notable occurrence of Roy's tenure was Normal's promotion to four-year college status. In July of 1918, the Legislature authorized state institutions to confer bachelor's degrees, and in May of 1919, the Normal Board of Administrators established a four-year course. [337] The Constitution of 1921 resulted in a name change to "Louisiana State Normal College," and the college was placed under the governance of the State Board of Education (along with seven other state institutions). [338] This new State Board of Education officially took office in January of 1923. In an early articulation battle, LSU refused to allow transfer of all of Normal's credits.[339]

Another of Roy's signature efforts was the unsuccessful attempt to keep a monopoly on teacher training. By 1923, Louisiana Polytechnic Institute and Southwestern Louisiana Institute both had teacher training institutes, though they had not gone through any official legislature procedures. Instead both had responded to the demand for better teachers.[340] Southwestern had organized its program by 1912.[341] In addition, there were programs at New Orleans Normal and several private colleges. Louisiana Normal fought this lack of exclusivity. After an initial legislative victory—the defeat of the Price-Johnson Bill, introduced to the Louisiana Legislature in 1914[342]—the other teacher-training programs were approved. After the Constitution of 1921, the State Board of Education adopted uniform curricula for all of the programs.

The maturity of Normal can be seen in its evolving standards of admission and faculty credentials. Before 1914, the minimum requirement for admission was the completion of the first half of 8th grade. In 1915, it increased to the completion of the 9th grade or second year of high school. By 1917, it was the third year of high school. In 1918, Normal required high school graduation which was the same as LSU and Tulane.[343] Faculty credentials generally reflect the quality of the teaching. In 1912, among Normal's 45 faculty members, there were no professors with Ph.D.s, 4 with Masters, 15 with Bachelors, and 26 with no degree. By 1928, among the 87 professors, 6 had Ph.D.s, 35 had Masters, 41 had Bachelors, and only 5 had no degree.[344]

A humorous look at a different era was President Roy's ongoing resistance to a new drink that was becoming popular in the South. For twelve years, Roy refused to allow Coca Cola to be served on campus. Finally, the company dispatched a chemist from St. Louis to make the case that Coca Cola was less harmful than coffee if drunk in moderation. Roy agreed to conduct a small trial run in a single dormitory so the effects could be determined. Around 1925, Roy finally allowed the beverage on campus.[345]

Louisiana Tech University (1894)

The Industrial Institute and College of Louisiana (later Louisiana Tech University) was established in 1894. The legislative act provided for the "'establishment of a first-class Industrial Institute and College for the education of white children of the State of Louisiana in the arts and sciences—through which they may acquire a thorough academic and literary education together with a knowledge of the practical industries of the age.'"[346] Classes began in September of 1895 with six professors and 202 students. As the only state college in north Louisiana, the entrance requirements were not stringent. Students had to be at least 14 and to read, speak and write "with tolerable correctness."[347]

The original instruction led to the Bachelor of Industry degree, though this was replaced with a "standard" degree—a bachelor's of science in engineering—by 1921. Also, the name was changed to Louisiana Polytechnic Institute after the Constitutional Convention of 1921.[348] Enrollment first passed 500 in 1901 and 1,000 in the 1930s.

University of Louisiana—Lafayette (1898)

The Southwestern Louisiana Industrial Institute (SLII) (later the University of Louisiana—Lafayette) was established primarily due to the efforts of State Senator Robert Martin. In the 1896 session, Martin introduced a bill for an "Industrial Institute and Academy." It was approved by the Legislature but vetoed by Governor Murphy Foster due to lack of funds. Martin felt the need for the Institute because of the dearth of educational opportunities. In Lafayette Parish, there was no high school and only 35 teachers in 29 public schools (with 1037 students), mostly at the elementary level. Also, there was no college in southwest Louisiana.[349]

Martin tried again two years later when funds became available. On July 13, 1898, Foster signed Act 162 creating the "Southwestern Louisiana Industrial Institute." [350][351] Lafayette beat out New Iberia and Scott in the competition to get the school, in part because it was in the geographical center of southwest Louisiana and had unusually good railroad facilities. [352]

Dr. Edwin L. Stephens became the first president at age 27. When the site for the SLII was chosen in 1900, it was "a sugar cane field that had been plowed and leveled" with "not a shade tree on the entire 25 acres."[353] The curricular emphasis was on practical education, including the study of telegraphy. [354] Stephens, an 1892 LSU graduate, instilled a system based on military discipline that persisted until 1910. [355]

The first session commenced on September 18, 1901, with 100 students and 8 teachers. Stephens had insisted on the completion of 8th grade as a requirement for admission. This did not sit well with the community. Sheriff Ike Broussard threatened that the SLII's buildings would be pulled down by a posse if admissions standards were not eased. Stephens did not relent. For the first few nights, the windows in the newly completed buildings were shot out by individuals hiding in the darkness. Stephens gave in and lowered the admissions threshold to the 6th grade, with the idea of gradually raising it.[356] In 1905, the school year was delayed almost two months due to a yellow fever epidemic. [357]

SLII essentially started out as a high school. In 1916, the school became a combination high school—junior college when completion of the 10th grade was required for admission.[358] The Constitution of 1921 designated the school a four-year college and moved it under the governance of the State Board of Education. The name was also changed to the "Southwestern Louisiana Institute of Liberal and Technical Learning." [359] It gained accreditation by the Association of Southern Colleges in 1925. From 1920 on, anyone with a high school diploma was eligible to enroll, and selective admissions were not implemented until the turn of the twenty-first century.[360]

Delgado Community College (1921)

While almost all of Louisiana's higher education institutions started as two-year colleges, the great majority eventually expanded their curricular offerings. The most notable exception was the establishment of what became Delgado Community College in 1921. As Louisiana's oldest existing two-year college by over forty years, the founding of the college gave a glimpse into what a two-year college was like in the 1920s.

In 1909, industrialist Isaac Delgado revised his will to leave money for a technical school. Like Paul Tulane twenty-five years earlier, Delgado was a successful businessman who saw the need not for liberal arts focus but for a more practical education designed for success in business. He died on January 4, 1912, and by 1921, the Isaac Delgado Central Trades School opened as an institution "for the free industrial training of boys who have finished at least the eighth grade in public or private schools, and for men of whatever educational qualifications. It is designed to educate and train boys and men in some useful trade and to prepare them to enter one of the trades as a finished operative immediately upon finishing the courses required."[361] There were few public trade schools in America and especially the South, so the opening was a celebrated event and "brought to New Orleans the honor of being one of the centers of practical trade education in America." [362]

There was great optimism about the value of higher education in this era. At the 1921 opening, a reporter from *The Times-Picayune* extolled: "'Go back to school! Here is your chance to stop drifting; here is an engine for your hull that will send you skimming through life's strongest eddies. Here is a future for you.'"[363] The article noted that Delgado was "the finest, most complete trades school in America, experts say—to officially open." [364] An interesting note was that the Electrical Department was the only class in which a text-book was used. [365] Also, fresco painting was featured in the curriculum. [366]

Continued segregation

The era also saw the continued development of a dual educational system for whites and blacks. Following the Supreme Court decision of *Plessy v. Ferguson* in 1896, higher education in Louisiana operated under the concept of "separate but equal." As the "flagship" institutions for whites and blacks, respectively, LSU and Southern came to symbolize educational conditions and possibilities in the state. Historian Raphael Cassimere, Jr., wrote that LSU became a "liberal arts school for the sons and daughters of white planters and businessmen" while Southern "was initially nothing more than a vocational school modeled after the more famous Tuskegee Institute." [367] In a trend that continued throughout the twentieth century, the state provided more resources to universities serving whites than to those serving blacks. At the beginning of the twentieth century, according to Cassimere, "[n]owhere, not even in other Southern states, was duality so clear, so unequal, so planned." [368]

Grambling State University (1901)

The roots of Grambling State University arguably began with the North Louisiana Colored Agricultural Relief Association Union (Relief Association), founded in 1896.

"The Relief Association" decided to establish an industrial school for the training of boys and girls and basic classes—probably in rudimentary reading—were taught from 1899 to 1901.[369] The school was called the Colored Industrial and Agricultural School of Lincoln Parish, and the Relief Association leased the old Allen Green store as a schoolhouse.

The Relief Association realized they did not have the expertise to properly run the school, so they wrote to Booker T. Washington at Tuskegee Institute for assistance.[370] In May of 1901, Washington called to his office a student named Charles P. Adams who was surprised when told: "'Some people in North Louisiana want a man to come there and build an industrial school for them and I have selected you to go, this being your graduation year.'"[371] Adams had already planned to attend Howard University to study law, but Washington countered: "'Tuskegee is educating men and women to stay in the South and do their work here. If you study law you will have to leave the South in order to practice it. The race needs your service right here in the South.'"[372] Adams was convinced and agreed to return to his home state of Louisiana.

On August 4, 1901, the Relief Association welcomed Adams, an imposing figure at six feet ten inches tall and weighing 300 pounds. He was 28 when he took over the school.[373] After Adams raised personal funds for the completion of a new building, the School opened in November 1, 1901, with two teachers in addition to Adams.[374] Adams was committed to providing an industrial education to the rural inhabitants of the area. He later defined an industrial education as "being steadfastly engaged in anything useful and honest; it meant being busily engaged in wholesome work, whether it be a farm, a teaching job, constructing a building, or operating a blacksmith shop."[375]

Adams' choice to offer an industrial education placed him on one side of a fundamental debate over the best way to bring African-Americans, especially in the South, into the educational mainstream after the end of the Civil War. Booker T. Washington, Adams' mentor, and W. E. B. Dubois differed on the best type of education. This debate is discussed more fully in Chapter Two.

Adams applied Washington's philosophy on industrial education, and the School opened with 125 students. The initial fee was $5 per month, but since most students could not pay in cash, they chose the barter of commodities such as potatoes, flour, and peas.[376] Friction, however, soon developed between Adams and the Relief Association which "became infiltrated with Baptist ministers."[377] The Relief Association wanted to convert the curriculum to religious instruction, while Adams wanted to keep it an industrial school. Also, the Relief Association wanted the school to be controlled exclusively by African-Americans, while Adams sought the aid of whites, even if that meant ceding some control. The friction escalated. In July 1905 while Adams was away, a top school official communicated that he had "been forcibly removed by gun-point" from the Colored Industrial and Agricultural School. The tensions culminated in a lawsuit won by Adams. Though he won the court battle, the conflict was too much for Adams, and he split off to start a new institution. The older school, which by this time was known as the Allen Green Normal and Industrial Institute, closed in 1929. [378]

Adams established the new institution, the North Louisiana Agricultural and Industrial Institute[379][380] (Institute), in 1905 in the town of Grambling. The town of Grambling had been named for P. G. Grambling, a white man, who leased the land that would become the town for a sawmill site. At the time, Grambling was not even considered a village.[381] People began moving to the vicinity of the school so their children could attend and these "migrants made up the nucleus of the town of Grambling."[382] The town grew along with the school, and the first official government of Grambling was formed on September 9, 1953.[383]

Adams was able to open the Institute when seven men, all friends, pledged funding for the new school. The enrollment for the first year was 152 students, with five of those being in the ninth grade.[384] From 1905 to 1912, classes extended through the first ten grades.[385] When the General Education Board, a national endowment fund, made visits in 1914, 1915, and 1916, its report noted that there were "'110 students, all elementary.'"[386] The rural nature of the location was evident by the fact that water was secured from hand-dug wells and drawn by hand in a bucket.

The Institute was originally classified as a private school. On July 6, 1907, Adams petitioned the Lincoln Parish School Board for operating funds, but the Board only provided a nominal amount. The Board passed a motion on July 30, 1913, which "approved the Grambling Colored School as an agricultural school"[387] and agreed to pay the salary of one additional teacher each year until 1918. In 1919, Lincoln Parish School Board accepted the school and renamed it the Lincoln Parish Training School.[388]

Southern University continuation

Southern University was established in 1881 in New Orleans, and its first few years were precarious. Some measure of stability was achieved under president Henry Hill who served from 1887 until 1913. The level of instruction increased and in 1893, the 4th and 5th grades were deleted.[389] The school greatly increased its prospects for success with the acquisition of federal aid in the early 1890s.

Southern University benefited, ironically, from the hardening system of racial separation in Louisiana higher education. An Agricultural and Mechanical Department was established in 1890, and Southern gained recognition as a Land Grant College with the Second Morrill Act in 1891.[390] The Second Morrill Act was enacted by the U. S. Congress as a way to bring benefits to African-Americans, just as the first Morrill Act (passed in 1862) had expanded higher education, mostly to the benefit of whites. To get the funds from the Second Morrill Act, states had to admit blacks to their land-grant colleges (established with the first Morrill Act) or provide separate institutions. Echoing the decision of most Southern states, Louisiana chose not to integrate its land-grant college, LSU, but to establish a "separate but equal" one. Southern University became the black, public, land-grant university in Louisiana.

Valera Francis, higher education historian, summarized that "public HBCUs [historically black colleges and universities] were, in essence, created in segregationist states to ensure separate and unequal higher educational institutions."[391]

The next major event was the 1912 move of the university from New Orleans to Scotlandville, just outside of Baton Rouge. Legislative Act 118 of 1912, signed by Governor Luther E. Hall on July 9, 1912, authorized the closing and sale of the campus in New Orleans.[392] It held its last commencement in June 1913 and reopened in Scotlandville on March 9, 1914.[393] The governor and other leaders thought the school was just serving New Orleans as a high school and that it should be more centrally located in a rural area. The move was supported by James H. Dillard, white President and Director of the Negro Rural School Fund, who became the namesake of Dillard University in 1930.[394] Private Straight University also favored the reduction in competition.[395] Another reason for the move was the influence of J. S. Clark, president of Baton Rouge College and of the Louisiana State Colored Teachers Association.[396] Clark was born Josiah Clark but renamed himself Joseph Samuel.[397] He was the most important influence in shaping the new Southern University.

Clark began organizing the University in September of 1913, at a time when "every tangible evidence and possession" was still in New Orleans.[398] The most pressing matter was a location for the campus. New Iberia and other locations were thrown out due to the presence of racial hostility.[399] Time was running out and the state faced the prospective loss of $50,000 in Morrill Act funds.[400] Land was acquired near Scotland plantation though the best building was a one story frame house with four bedrooms.[401]

With the campus secured, Clark built the university from modest beginnings. There were few college-level classes and the focus was on practical education.[402] The Morrill Act funds provided a strong agricultural base. Booker T. Washington visited in April of 1915. J. S. Clark led the school until his resignation on January 1, 1938.[403] His long tenure was exceeded by that of his son, Felton Grandison Clark, who succeeded him.[404]

Combined Topics—Important Elements

In addition to the fundamental topics of LSU, Tulane, and the dual system of higher education, important secondary elements also developed during this time period. Seven currently-existing religious colleges were founded. Higher education for women was established. Finally, football programs were instituted and generated a passion that consumed colleges and fans.

Religious Colleges

During the era, seven still-existing religious colleges were founded. Not surprisingly given the French and Spanish heritage of the state, five—Loyola University, Xavier University, Our Lady of Holy Cross College, Our Lady of the Lake College, and St.

Joseph's Seminary College—were Catholic institutions. The other two—Louisiana College and New Orleans Baptist Theological Seminary—were founded as Baptist colleges, reflecting the Protestant influence of the Americans that streamed in after the Louisiana Purchase. Nationally, the establishment of religious colleges has a strong tradition—going back to Harvard and Yale. In addition to the surviving colleges, there were many religious colleges at the time that subsequently closed.

Loyola University was founded as Loyola College in 1904 and originally consisted of three years of high school and two years of college. It is Catholic, and more specifically Jesuit. The roots of the School go back to the 1849 establishment of the College of the Immaculate Conception. Jesuits first came to Louisiana on Iberville's second expedition. From almost the beginning, Bienville and the other leaders of New Orleans had hoped for a Jesuit college. In 1763, the Jesuit order was banned from the French colonies. When restored, the Bishop of New Orleans implored the Jesuits in France to send representatives to the city. In 1837, seven Jesuit priests arrived and chose a spot in St. Landry Parish—as better for a college than the "fever-ridden city" of New Orleans. By 1849, College of the Immaculate Conception opened its doors.[405]

Loyola College opened for classes in its current Uptown New Orleans location—near Tulane University—in 1904. In 1911, there was a reorganization of the two Jesuit colleges with the College of the Immaculate Conception educating secondary students from both, and the college-level students all going to Loyola. The College of the Immaculate Conception subsequently closed. On July 10, 1912, the governor signed the legislation for the college to be renamed Loyola University. Graduate programs were initiated in 1914 with a School of Law and a School of Dentistry (phased out by 1971, then absorbed by LSU Medical Center). [406]

Our Lady of Holy Cross College was founded in 1916 as the "College Department" of the Academy of Holy Angels High School, run by the Marianites of Holy Cross. Act 257 of the Louisiana Legislature, passed July 6, 1916, allowed the high school to confer college degrees, and the "College Department" operated as a two-year teacher-training program. The name was changed to Holy Cross Normal College by 1924, though the name change seems to have been officially recognized on September 8, 1931.[407] The state governmental oversight process was extremely informal by modern standards. It seems that the College had been issuing teacher-training credentials—with authorization from the governor's office—several years before the state official in charge was aware of the fact. The College was granted four-year college status with a July 6, 1938 letter from the State Board of Education. [408]

St. Joseph Seminary College, a private four-year liberal arts college, was established in 1890 by the Benedictine Monks of Saint Joseph Abbey. [409] Xavier University, at first a high school before adding a university division, was founded in 1915 by the Sisters of the Blessed Sacrament, a Catholic religious community dedicated to the education of American minorities. Of the nation's 103 historically-black colleges and 222 Catholic colleges, Xavier is the only one that shares both characteristics. Xavier has been noted for its Doctor of Pharmacy program since 1991.[410] Our Lady of the Lake College was officially established in 1990, though it grew out of the tradition of the Our Lady of the Lake School of Nursing, founded in 1923. The four-year college was sponsored by the Franciscan Missionaries of Our Lady, North American Province. Its primary curricular mission is the training of health-care providers.[411]

Louisiana College, a Baptist college, was founded in Pineville in 1906, though its roots arguably go back to the mid-1800s. Mt. Lebanon University was founded in 1852 by the North Louisiana Baptist Convention as a men's school. Keatchie Female College was founded in 1857 by the Grand Cane Association of Baptist Churches as an all-women's college. Both schools came under the control of the State Baptist Convention in 1899. An anticipated railroad did not get built, and the two colleges did not gain traction.[412] They were both closed and, in 1904, the Baptist Convention began looking for a suitable site for another college. Pineville was chosen due to its central location and fewer mosquitoes. The first year opened on October 3, 1906, with 19 students and 3 faculty members.[413] A "Great Fire" in 1911 almost prompted a move to another location, but the facilities were rebuilt.[414] In 1923, Louisiana College gained membership in the Southern Association of Colleges and Secondary Schools, the only Louisiana college besides Tulane and LSU to do so at the time.[415]

The New Orleans Baptist Theological Seminary was founded as the Baptist Bible Institute in 1917 by an act of the Southern Baptist Convention. The Seminary opened with the ambitious goal of providing a "mission center in the ungodly city of New Orleans." An "impassioned editorial" favoring the creation of the school noted that a seminary in New Orleans "'would plant the Baptist cause in this city in a way that would immediately command the attention and the respect of all. It would be planting the siege guns at the enemies' gates.'" The first session was October 1918.[416]

Women's higher education

In the 1880s, a paternalistic view generally held that a woman's ideal role was taking care of the home and family. Extensions of this nurturing role were acceptable in the workplace, with jobs like nursing, teaching and secretarial duties. The fear was that many other occupations, such as politics, business and law, offended women's delicate sensibilities, and many were simply closed to female participation. Women did not get a guaranteed right to vote until 1920, with similar reasons cited. The fact that so many of the professions requiring collegiate training were off-limits to women contributed to the relative paucity of women in higher education. Historian John Dyer noted the prevailing view that whether "a woman could or should learn mathematics, science, and economics was debatable."[417] In Louisiana, Tulane, LSU and Normal provided early educational opportunities for women.

Sophie Newcomb College, part of Tulane University, played a pioneering role in women's higher education. The two main avenues nationally for women before Newcomb were to attend an all-women's college or to enroll in one of the few coeducational institutions. As a third alternative, Newcomb College was the first degree-granting women's college that was a "coordinate division" of a men's university. [418] This gave the advantages of both. Radcliffe College at Harvard University followed Newcomb as a coordinate division and granted degrees starting in 1894 (though it was technically founded in 1879). [419] Josephine Louise Newcomb set up the college in honor of dead daughter, H. Sophie Newcomb "for the higher education of white girls and young women." [420] The absence of co-education at LSU was a negotiating point for Tulane in its failed attempt to gain recognition as a state university in 1906. Tulane's side was strengthened by an appeal "made to the women of Louisiana to demand state aid for the Sophie Newcomb College so that the women students of the State might have equal opportunities with the men for a general education." [421] A prominent women's organization further noted that the "'State has done a great deal to provide the advantages of higher education to the boys of Louisiana. She has done nothing to provide these advantages for her girls.'" [422] While LSU had admitted at least one student, the public outcry likely hastened its coeducational efforts.

The credit for allowing women at LSU goes to President Thomas D. Boyd, designated the "Father of Co-education." Boyd admitted the first female student, Olivia Davis, in 1904, in an informal process that seemed to go against the Board's disapproval of the idea.[423] Davis was a relative of T. Boyd's wife and lived in their home. T. Boyd arranged for her to attend classes, then stated that "unless the Board forbade him to do so, he would admit women students to the University." [424] After allowing female students for a number of years, T. Boyd came to doubt the wisdom of co-education at LSU, saying that "'I have not lost faith in co-education but I have grown skeptical as to the complete success of co-education under such conditions as exist here at this time.'" [425] Historian Marcus Wilkerson noted that if LSU had acquiesced to the admission of women after a push in 1894, it is likely that Louisiana Polytechnic Institute would not have been established.[426]

Finally, Louisiana State Normal School was established primarily for female students.[427] A normal, or teacher-training, school fit society's dictates of women going into an acceptable, nurturing field. The rules at Normal were very strict for female students, much more so than for male students. Women could not—even with parental consent—spend the night away, though they could go to town on Wednesdays and Fridays from 3:00 pm to sunset. Female students could attend church services alone on Sunday in the day, but at night had to be accompanied by a faculty member. [428]

Football

Football was another important element of higher education established during this era. The place of football in university life has been constant and controversial since the establishing of football in the early 1900s. Faculty and other supporters of academics have argued the emphasis on football is misguided. They have deplored the diversion of funds and special treatment of athletes from the very beginning. On the other hand, football is a vibrant link to a common citizen of the state who will never benefit from a university's academics. Building a multi-million dollar cage for a mascot seems foolish if universities were strictly academic institutions, but of course they are not. A possibly more realistic view is that the common citizen agrees to give huge subsidies to state institutions of higher education because of the pride and camaraderie (and entertainment value) of the football teams. As will be seen in the next chapter, Huey Long understood this lesson.

The central place of football, especially in the South, had been established by 1915. Writing about Tulane, but describing much of the nation's universities, John Dyer wrote that

> [f]ootball had passed from the realm of pure sport, where young college men played a game on Saturday afternoons, to a potent factor in the life and reputation of the university. However much many faculty members deplored the fact that the university was being forced to supply large-scale entertainment for masses of people wholly uninterested in higher education, the fact still remained that the university, having once waded into the stream of intercollegiate football competition, found no escape from the ever-increasing current of the waters. [429]

The fervor for football has not abated with time. In the 1960s, Clark Kerr, likely the most important figure in higher education in the mid-twentieth century, famously joked that to be truly successful, a university president had to provide sex for the undergraduates, parking for the faculty, and football for the alumni.

LSU has historically had the best football team, especially in the last few decades of the twentieth century. The LSU football team played an important role in state higher education under Huey Long, and this will be detailed in the next chapter. LSU has a strong emphasis on football which has been accompanied by a passionate following of much of the state's population. A former Chancellor called athletics, mainly football, "the school's front porch" and another used the phrase "the window through which the nation looks at LSU." [430] The dilemma in many universities is how to balance athletics and academics, when as a recent chancellor pointed out, "the exploits and follies of the 500 athletes draw far more attention than what the other 31,500 are doing."[431] Is it the proper mission of a state university to spend many millions of dollars on a football team when at the same time claiming the academic side of the institution is woefully underfunded? What is the best mix to provide the most utility to the state's citizens who are providing the bulk of the tax-based subsidies? Whatever the answer, an identical debate has been going on since the turn of the twentieth century.

In the early days of football, Tulane University was a powerhouse. The first football game in New Orleans was played on December 25, 1888. A club team associated with Tulane played its first game on November 18, 1893, played an LSU club team a week later, and picked the colors, olive and blue, a week after that.[432] Tulane's rivalry with LSU was intense. Soon after the bitter legislative fight in 1906 over becoming a state university, perhaps a more intense controversy involved the eligibility of LSU football players. During LSU's championship seasons of 1907-8 and 1908-9, Tulane charged LSU with using "ringers" which were paid players, not typical students. The matter was never settled and all sports between the two schools were discontinued for several years. [433]

Tulane experienced great success between 1920 and 1940, going to a Rose Bowl and two Sugar Bowls. In 1920, the nickname "Green Wave" likely originated with E. Earl Sparling's song, *The Rolling Green Wave*.[434] In 1926, a stadium was completed that seated 45,000 (with temporary seats). By 1928, some faculty members charged that standards were lowered to allow better football teams.[435] In 1936, Tulane began awarding athletic scholarships. Most important, the overall record in the annual November games with LSU was 12-6-2 with Tulane ahead.[436]

By the 1950s & 1960s, Tulane's successful efforts to become an elite academic university had run counter to its football prowess. A faculty member noted: "'You can't have Ivy League academic ideals and successful Southeastern Conference football. The two are incompatible.'" [437] Though later to exit the Southeastern Conference, most years Tulane competed with Vanderbilt to see which would finish last.

The football program at Southwestern Louisiana Institute had two early brushes with fame. Christian Keener Cagle entered the U.S. Military Academy at West Point after attending SLI. While there, in 1929, he won the equivalent of the Heisman Trophy and was on the cover of Time magazine. Demonstrating a very different era, West Point had a rule: "'Cadets may not ride on bicycles, chew tobacco, nor have a horse, dog, wife, or mustache.'" Cagle secretly married the sweetheart he had met at SLI and had to leave with less than a month remaining before his graduation. [438]

An early SLI athletic director likely made one of the worst personnel decisions in the history of college athletics. After losing seasons in the mid-1930s, the football coach was reassigned to teaching. The field for his replacement was narrowed to two candidates, both former University of Alabama football players. Johnny Cain was chosen and had a decent record over the next six years before fading into obscurity. The rejected candidate, Paul "Bear" Bryant, went on to coach the University of Alabama and became one of the most successful coaches of all time. [439]

SLI's football program started around the turn of the century, but until 1921, it was considered a high school and played mostly high school opponents.[440] It competed at the highest collegiate level for about a decade but dropped Tulane and LSU from football schedule in 1931 "because of the many defeats suffered at the hands of these two powerful teams." [441] In 1939, SLI helped form the Louisiana Intercollegiate Conference which eventually counted as members Centenary, Louisiana Tech, Louisiana College, Southeastern Louisiana College and Louisiana State Normal as members.[442] All of the member institutions chose not to field football teams in the 1942-43 season to devote their energies to more urgent things during World War II.[443]

PART II

Formative Period of Higher Education in Louisiana: 1928-1972

In the period from 1928 to 1972, the contours of higher education in Louisiana were formed. Governors became the driving force in the development of individual institutions as well as higher education as a system. The vast majority of colleges and universities established the final form of their character—settling on the basic mission, length of study, location and other formative characteristics. Finally, higher education in Louisiana evolved from being a collection of disparate institutions with unique conditions to being considered a unified system with many parts.

The year 1928 was a line of demarcation that separated Louisiana history, and that of higher education, into two parts. Like the Civil War that divides American history, the explosion onto the scene of Huey P. Long changed Louisiana in a fundamental way. Huey Long dominated Louisiana with radical new ideas, and it is possible that only an assassin's bullet prevented his domination of the nation as well. While only his effect on higher education will be explored here, it can be argued that he had an equally formative influence on many other institutions in Louisiana life.

The modern history of higher education in Louisiana—from 1928 to 2004—is the story of three governors. Governor Huey Long's primary contribution to the history of higher education, beginning in 1928, was the introduction of the dominance of governors. He raised the powerful but hands-off approach of previous governors to a level of micro-managing not seen in national history before or since. He inserted himself into the smallest decisions at LSU and other universities and succeeding governors acted similarly, if not to the same extreme. While Long's impact was unmistakable, he dealt with colleges and universities on an individual basis. He did not really conceive of higher education as a system.

Governor John McKeithen, first elected in 1964, introduced the next fundamental change in Louisiana higher education, the "all-in-one" philosophy of higher education. He concentrated all educational missions—from developmental education to the awarding of Ph.D.s—in single comprehensive universities. Responding to the historic enrollment growth of the 1950s and 1960s, his tenure saw a proliferation of new degree programs, a building boom, and revenue increases. He made an ambitious, though largely unsuccessful, attempt to deal with higher education as a statewide system. His "all-in-one" philosophy still characterizes higher education into the twenty-first century.

Finally, in a change in philosophy that will be detailed in Part III, Governor M. J. "Mike" Foster, starting in 1996, introduced reforms that began to move the state away from the "all-in-one" system to one based on institutional differentiation. He instituted a governance philosophy that argued different educational missions could best be accomplished at colleges and universities uniquely suited to the task. For example, community colleges should handle developmental education while universities could best oversee graduate study.

On a national level, the contemporary history of higher education was also dominated by the growth and influence of public higher education. After World War II, higher education ceased to be the province of the elite and instead was infused in the masses. The number of people attending colleges and universities exploded in the 1950s and 1960s. The influx of students, in large part, attended public colleges and universities. With a few exceptions, like Tulane University, which gained national and international recognition, the non-public colleges generally concentrated on educational niches and lost much of their influence amidst the explosive growth of public higher education.

CHAPTER 4

1928 to 1944: Huey Long

Huey Long reshaped Louisiana in the period from 1928 to 1944, and along the way fundamentally changed the course of higher education. From simple educational beginnings, postsecondary education expanded and became more populist in outlook. Though relatively few new colleges were established, the nature of higher education was changed by the fact that governors became the driving force in reforms. Though LSU had already been the favored institution, Huey Long took the devotion to extremes that garnered national attention. From this time on, like governors, LSU occupied a central and powerful role in the state and state politics.

Governor dominance from 1928 on

First elected governor in 1928, Huey Long broke from the previous Bourbon Democrat traditions by using the power of the governor's office not for the benefit of the elite but for poor people, of which there were many in Louisiana. Historian Betty Field argued that the Long years "are often viewed as years when state aid to the needy began." [444] He concentrated on vital infrastructure developments to link the rural parts of the state with New Orleans and its markets by building hundreds of miles of roads. When Long became governor, only three major bridges existed in the state, and none crossed the Mississippi. [445] He remedied this deficiency. He paid for his programs by taxing the elite and industries, and the enmity of these groups matched in intensity the appreciation of average folk.

Huey Long also concentrated on improving public education at the elementary and secondary levels. Since Louisiana had the highest rate of illiteracy in the nation, Long had to start where the need was greatest. During his governorship, he increased spending on public education, most famously providing free textbooks. He also sought to improve adult literacy. [446] The Great Depression hit during the first few years of Long's tenure, and local governments turned to the governor's office for assistance in funding education at the local level. Long provided the assistance, which had the added effect of centralizing power further in his hands. At the beginning of his term, local parishes provided most of the public education money, whereas afterward, the state furnished sixty percent of the funds. [447]

The primary contribution of Huey Long to higher education in Louisiana was the muscular assertion of the power of the governor. Though he broke with the Bourbon Democrats over the recipients of gubernatorial power, he nonetheless shared and extended the belief in executive centralism. A Louisiana history textbook summarized that "Long cared little or nothing for civilities, much less for representative government." [448] Echoing the disdain for even the appearance of fairness that was seen in the 9,499 to 1 vote in four parishes for Murphy Foster in the 1896 governor's contest, Long managed an even more obvious display. Long's hand-picked candidate for governor in 1932, Oscar K. Allen, won St. Bernard Parish 3,152 to 0 against four opponents, even though registered voters in St. Bernard rarely numbered more than 2,500. Long himself gave the most famous example. When asked if he had read the state Constitution, Long replied "'I am the constitution in Louisiana.'" [449]

The tendency toward "executive centralism" present in French, Spanish and American Louisiana exploded onto a national stage in the larger-than-life persona of Huey P. Long. Long was notorious for assuming almost dictatorial control with disdain for parliamentary procedures. Historian Harnett Kane noted that, under Long, "Louisiana had spawned a weird, governmental monstrosity. Some called it 'America's Rehearsal for Dictatorship.'"[450] Kane continued that "during that period Louisiana citizens lost their liberties and their fundamental American rights. The right of free elections was wiped out, and absolute control was seized by the leader of one political faction." [451]

Once Huey Long set the precedent of a powerful governor, his successors took up the mantle. Twentieth century Louisiana history was replete with stories of examples of executive centralism, usually in a negative light. Jeff Crouere, a political commentator, offered a succinct overview when he wrote that Louisiana is divided into politicians and everyone else. Louisiana politicians have been given special treatment and regarded as almost royalty. Crouere contended that Louisiana's "antiquated political system" was responsible for creating this double standard. [452]

Another telling example of Louisiana's colorful political history comes from *Vision 2020*, the strategic planning document published by the state government. This official publication unapologetically noted the "lingering perception that Louisiana remains a 'Banana Republic' with self-serving governmental leaders who lack the political will to enact and sustain fiscal and socioeconomic reforms that will facilitate broad-based economic growth and prosperity." [453]

While the historical legacy of executive centralism arguably provided the foundation, Huey Long took it to a higher level. One of the principal sources of power of the Louisiana governor's office was a well-accepted dominance of the governor over the Louisiana Legislature. Huey Long took the dominance to an extreme when he had installed in his office a device that could change the votes of legislators on bills.[454] The dominance has lessened somewhat since that time, but contemporary governors still retain an inordinate sway. John Maginnis, a political journalist, wrote that upon taking office in 2004, Governor Kathleen Blanco, "ordained" the leaders of the State Legislature and thus established control like previous governors.[455] She was even able to strip a member of his committee chairmanship for not voting her way on an issue.

Another source of gubernatorial power lies in the outsized control over state finances and patronage opportunities. Political scientist Ed Renwick argued that an important source of power is that the budgetary process has historically been dominated by the governor despite formal control by the legislature. This capability of distributing the spoils of the office has been crucial.[456] Renwick also noted that historically, state land leases, and the oil revenues associated with them, have been used as rewards for politically allied constituencies. Renwick summarized that "[t]hree facts of Louisiana life—oil, low taxes, and centralized government—the latter two, legacies of Longism, provide the foundation and columns of support for the Mansion and the formidable power it houses." [457] Renwick also pointed out the significant appointive power of governors. In 1968, the 1,425 appointments, for example, were an important source for political patronage. Louisiana Senate confirmation of the appointments has rarely been an obstacle. The appointment power was reduced by the 1974 constitution but remained considerable. [458]

The flip-side of strong governors is the populace's acquiescence to this power. Historians David M. Landry and Joseph B. Parker, in an overview of the culture of Louisiana, argued that people in Louisiana tolerate and even expect corruption and inefficiency because they "look upon politics as entertainment, and they want their politicians to amuse them." [459] The reasons for this tolerance are mostly attributed to the unique culture of Louisiana, the "Latin tradition of tolerance" that arose from the political-cultural origins of "a unique mixture of Mediterranean, Anglo-Saxon, and Afro-American values."[460] The French, Spanish, and a later large population of Italians all shared a distinctly Catholic culture that was comfortable with a centralized, hierarchical political structure. Following the American takeover after the Louisiana Purchase, a top official gave the following assessment of this French-Spanish upbringing: "'the display of wealth and the parade of power constitute their highest objects of admiration.'" [461]

The cultural tolerance was muted under the military occupation of Reconstruction but resumed with the Bourbon Democrats and exploded to the fore under the "dictatorship" of Huey Long. In a poetic manner, Hodding Carter explained the willingness of the people to overlook some of the overtly corrupt excesses of Long when he wrote that the

> first factor was that, after two hundred years, the people of Louisiana were ready and waiting for a messiah who would translate their needs into accomplishments. Theirs was the ground swell of the little people, a people undisturbed by his tactics as long as they got the roads, the free bridges, the hospitals, the free school books, the public works; as long as the men whom he pilloried and broke and banished were identified with the leaders of the past, bumbling representatives of an

indifferent, negative ruling class. The little people shrugged at graft because of their certainty that there always had been graft of a kind. This time, whatever the politicians skimmed off the top, they were getting theirs too. And they were getting something else. Revenge. A fantastic vengeance upon the Sodom and Gomorrah that was called New Orleans. A squaring of accounts with the big shots, the Standard Oil and the bankers, the big planters, the entrenched interests everywhere. Huey Long was in the image of these little people. He talked their language. He had lived their lives. He had taken them up to the mountaintop and shown them the world which the meek would inherit. [462]

The actions of Long were splashed across the front pages of the nation's newspapers and seemed exotic. In addition, Ed Renwick noted that low taxes combined with relatively high spending by government contributed to Louisianans' tolerance of corruption. [463]

The tendency to enact governmental changes by constitutional amendment is a unique feature of governing in Louisiana that contributes to the executive centralism. The Public Affairs Research Council (PARC), a non-profit public policy institute, noted that most states "use a constitution for basic rights which is meant to have permanence, and use statutory law for the details of government that are subject to frequent change. Louisiana generally uses the Constitution for both." [464] Mark Carleton wrote that no "other state has had as many constitutions (eleven) as Louisiana, and probably no other state has amended its recent constitutions as often as Louisiana—the 1921 constitution alone, for example, was amended 536 times within fifty-one years." [465] By 1970, the effect of the numerous changes was government by constitutional amendment. PARC noted that some states have constitutions unchanged for 200 years, but Louisiana was on its 11th constitution, and the 1921 Louisiana constitution initially had 49,200 words but became "the second longest constitution in the world at 255,500." [466] After voters finally rebelled by defeating all 53 amendments on the ballot in 1970, the 1974 revision shortened the constitution to less than 35,000 words.

Huey Long and the succeeding governors stamped the personality of Louisiana government, so it is important to give a roadmap of their tenures. H. Long changed the direction of politics, government and education when he served as governor from 1928 to 1932 and continued his dominance of state politics until his assassination on September 10, 1935. [467] Henry C. Dethloff argued that "[n]o single governor has shaped modern Louisiana political and social development so much as Long has." [468] Long was noticeably moderate on the race issue, unlike most governors in the South at this time. In contrast to the Bourbon democrat elite where "popular government had been more façade than reality," Long fashioned a new bloc of small farmers, laborers, rising urban business interests and African-Americans. [469] With populist policies such as providing textbooks, charity hospitals, and roads to the powerless, Long's popularity rose to a national level. Before his assassination, Long was viewed as a rival to Franklin D. Roosevelt in the 1936 presidential election. Long had a mixed legacy and was viewed as either "one of America's classic demagogues or dictators" or "a great democrat and mass leader" or both. [470]

Huey's successor, Alvin O. King, was governor for about six months as a result of the curious political battle between Long and his original lieutenant governor, Dr. Paul Cyr, after Long was elected to the U. S. Senate in 1930 but chose to remain governor simultaneously. [471] Oscar K. Allen was governor from 1932 to 1936. Long completely dominated Allen's administration, and "critics called the new executive a puppet, a weakling, a rubber-stamp governor." [472] A famous story was that while Allen was signing Long-approved documents, a leaf blew in and landed on his desk. "Taking no chances, Allen signed the leaf." [473] James A. Noe was governor briefly in 1936 after the death of Allen. [474]

Richard W. Leche was governor from 1936 to June 26, 1939. [475] Until Edwin Edwards, Leche was the only Louisiana governor to be imprisoned. After becoming governor with no wealth, he was heard to remark: "'When I took the oath of office I didn't take any vow of poverty.'" [476] Leche was the most notable convicted participant in the "Louisiana Scandals" of 1939-40, a series of federal indictments issued for governmental corruption. He served ten years in a federal penitentiary. Leche's time in office was noted by "the permanent stigma of being incurably corrupt, venal, and untrustworthy." [477] After Leche's disgrace, his lieutenant governor, Earl Long, became governor for the first of three non-consecutive terms. [478]

An illuminating example of how the nation viewed Huey Long (and thus Louisiana) can be found in the pages of the *New York Times*. In a series of articles during H. Long's time in the national spotlight, the image of a micro-managing, populist dictator emerges. In an article headlined "Long Still Seeks New L.S.U. Coach," the reporter noted that "Huey Long looked in all directions today for some one to fill the shoes of Captain Lawrence (Biff) Jones who resigned last night as head football coach at Louisiana State University after a dispute with the Louisiana dictator." [479] The article was straightforward and did not find anything amiss—at least in an overt way—with the governor of a state so closely managing the minute affairs of a state university.

A lengthy article entitled "Huey Long Gives His View of Dictators: He Says That They Have No Place in America And Denies That He Himself is One" is replete with damning statements and backhanded compliments. Responding to H. Long's comment that *Dr. Jekyll / Mr. Hyde* was the greatest book ever, the reporter noted that "one could understand his liking for the theory of a dual personality. It permits him to do so many contradictory and extraordinary things." Commenting on the national view of H. Long, the reporter wrote that there "are many men of intelligence in Washington who think that Long is a dangerous person, that he has gathered behind him and is consolidating the forces of unrest and unhappiness for his personal aggrandizement." Describing H. Long from a state-level perspective, the reporter continued that in "New Orleans they call Long a dictator. When he charges into the State, surrounds himself with a bodyguard, and calls out the troops, he has all the aspects of a Hitler driving to a meeting of the Reichstag to have the rubber stamp of approval put upon his acts." [480]

Finally, an article entitled "Long Usurps Rule At State Capital" discussed a legislative attempt by H. Long to take over a neighboring parish. The article noted that "[t]urning from his capture of the city of New Orleans to a new objective of political conquest, Senator Huey P. Long announced today plans to subjugate the parish of East Baton Rouge, a citadel of his foes, and make it the seat of his 'imperial' government through legislative act." The reporter also referred to H. Long as "Louisiana's political potentate." [481]

Institutions shaped by governors, especially by Huey Long

Higher education historian John Thelin wrote that the era from 1920 to 1945 in national higher education was marked by a "wave of campus-building" which greatly increased access and showed that the nation was "edging toward a commitment to mass higher education." [482] Before 1920, college had been a rare experience reserved for the elite. An increasing number of high school graduates increased the number of college aspirants. In 1917, less than five percent of eighteen to twenty-year-olds attended college, but by 1937, the number was fifteen percent. College and university campuses were greatly expanded to satisfy this increasing number of students, and a more populist view of higher education came to replace the previous elitism. [483] Huey Long's Louisiana exemplified this national trend.

LSU continuation

The most extreme example of governor involvement in higher education in the twentieth century—in the state and likely the nation—was Huey Long's involvement with LSU. Previous governors had shown favoritism to LSU, but Long took it to a new level. Harnett T. Kane noted that education "at the state's largest school became an instrument of the dictatorship, a unique implement whose utilization has no parallel in American university records." [484] Long personally got involved in coaching the football team and organizing the band. Huge patronage payments were directed to all aspects of the university.

H. Long transformed LSU into a more impressive institution of higher education. Kane wrote that from "small, moderately impecunious Southern institution, L.S.U. became bigtime, bedecked with everything that one protector, then another, could give." [485] Michael Kurtz and Morgan Peoples wrote that the "building of LSU into a major regional university had been one of Huey Long's proudest accomplishments, and the Kingfish had led the people of Louisiana in their admiration for the institution." [486] H. Long personally took control of major and minor decisions and treated LSU like any other governmental department that he controlled. [487] In 1928, when Long became governor, LSU had 1600 students. Under H. Long and his immediate successors, the student body reached 8500. [488] Long's dedication was real, and on his deathbed, "his last words were said to have been: 'I wonder what's going to happen to my poor boys at L.S.U.'" [489]

H. Long used LSU as a generator of patronage. The director of a department might return from summer vacation and find a new group of faculty members appointed without consulting him. [490] At one point, over fifty percent of LSU students were on some kind of payroll—"an all-time record for an American college." [491] Students were hired for campaigning and other uses, and the patronage turned out to be a comparatively inexpensive investment. [492]

Several examples of Huey Long's excesses were notable. Huey appointed Dr. James Monroe Smith to be the president of LSU. Kane called him "totalitarianism's strawboss" and Huey said of Smith: "'There ain't a straight bone in Jim's body. But he does what I want him to, and he's a good president.'" [493] Smith was under no preconceptions about his role and said that "'[w]e're living under a dictatorship now, and the best thing to do is to submit to those in authority.'" [494] In the Louisiana Scandals, the series of corruption trials, it came out that Smith had used university funds to speculate in stocks, bonds and commodities at a loss of over $500,000. [495] After fleeing to Canada, but later surrendering and returning to Louisiana, Smith served time in a penitentiary. [496]

Huey was insistent that LSU compete effectively on a national level, and his many construction projects demonstrated this. He authorized the construction of a swimming pool at LSU. As construction was nearing completion, Long entered and asked "'This the longest anybody's got?'" When told there was one on the West Coast that was ten feet longer, he had the pool stretched to exceed it. [497] In 1930, Huey created the LSU Medical School in New Orleans. [498]

Huey used the football team to bring the national spotlight to LSU and himself. He especially wanted to beat Tulane University because he had been prevented from getting a law degree there. He took a hands-on approach—to the point of calling plays and leading the band at halftime. He also offered state jobs to players who scored touchdowns. [499] After LSU lost a football game by one point, Long had a bill introduced into the Legislature to outlaw the point after touchdown. [500]

Huey appreciated the exploits of football star Abe Mickal. Long decided to award Mickal by appointing him to a senatorial vacancy, despite the fact he was under 21, was a native of Mississippi and did not live in the appropriate parish. Mickal declined, so Huey started a draft Mickal movement. When a critical letter by an undergraduate was published in the school paper, Long had 4000 copies of the paper destroyed. Huey said of the paper's editor: "That little bastard. I'll fire him and all his family.

This is my university. Nobody is going to criticize Huey Long on his money." [501] Also, the student journalists were expelled. [502]

Activities involving LSU contributed to corruption charges against Richard Leche after Long's death. Hodding Carter described Leche by writing that "his morals [were] as flaccid as his body. [503] Leche built over thirty buildings at LSU, including an agricultural center that was larger than Madison Square Garden and had the largest copper roof in the world. [504] The federal government probed the corruption surrounding LSU anticipating the use of tax fraud charges as with the mob, but the Louisiana politicians had the gall to report their income from graft on their federal income tax returns. The federal government found other charges. [505]

Another major figure in the Louisiana Scandals was LSU Building Superintendent "Big George" Caldwell. Amidst the Great Depression, he had mahogany stables that featured gold name plates on each stall.[506] His home which would have cost about $45,000 at typical market prices had bathrooms with golden fixtures. Caldwell managed all this and more on a salary of $5000 to $6000 a year. [507]

The Louisiana Scandals with LSU at its center resulted in 52 indictments against 149 individuals and 42 organizations. [508] Glen Jeansonne noted that "Louisiana has a sordid history of political corruption reaching back to the days of Bienville, but perhaps never before or since has corruption hit such an all-time low as in 1939." [509] It also resulted in three suicides and a total loss to the state of $100 million.[510]

Louisiana Normal continuation

Like at LSU, governors exerted a great deal of control over Louisiana State Normal College. In office since 1911, Normal President Victor Roy's resignation was orchestrated by Huey Long soon after his election in 1929. Historian Marietta LeBreton deemed this maneuver "an unprecedented gubernatorial interference with the state educational institutions."[511] Roy had given money to H. Long's opponent in the election. Roy met with Long about the rumor that he would be removed for not voting for Long, to which "Long reportedly quipped, 'Doctor, as a matter of fact you guessed wrong in the primary election, didn't you?'" Roy replied: "'Yes, Governor, I suppose I guessed wrong.'" [512]

Soon after gaining office, Long befriended T. H. Harris, State Superintendent of Education and gained control of the State Board of Education. Previously, the State Board had been somewhat independent of the governor, but H. Long used his status as ex-officio member to change that. Roy's days were numbered.[513] Technically, Roy was never asked to resign, but he felt it was best for him and the school not to buck H. Long. The State Board voted to accept Roy's resignation—6 for, 3 against, and 2 abstained. The three members that voted no explained they felt that "President Roy's removal represented gubernatorial usurpation of board power and feared the disastrous effect on Louisiana's education system of such executive interference."[514]

Generally, H. Long preferred to keep such machinations out of the public eye. The details on Roy's forced resignation were afforded only because the incident was included in the famous "round robin" impeachment charges unsuccessfully brought against H. Long in 1929.[515] When Roy left on June 30, 1929, Louisiana Normal was the 12th largest teacher training institution in the nation.[516]

Once H. Long gained control of the State Board of Education, the presidents of the state colleges and universities had little protection against the whims of the governor. One president opposed H. Long's interference and protested to him that the "'State Board of Education is my boss.'" H. Long simply replied: "'Who the hell do you think is the boss of the State Board of Education?'"[517]

William White Tison succeeded Roy but he too "ran afoul" of H. Long. The cause of the disaffection was likely intertwined with the national rivalry between H. Long and Franklin D. Roosevelt. Tison had twice worked closely with the Roosevelt administration, and this worked to his detriment.[518] Long considered himself a strong possibility to win the next presidential election. He ridiculed the aristocratic bearing of Roosevelt and unsubtly published a book entitled *My First Days in the White House*. Roosevelt responded in kind, including the cutting off of $10 million of Public Works Administration funds targeted to Louisiana.[519]

In 1934, Tison was replaced by A. A. Fredericks, "a very astute, pro-Long leader who was a combination of politician and educator." Fredericks was simultaneously the Louisiana Normal president and a State senator, "an unusual position even in Louisiana."[520] Fredericks oversaw an expansion of the campus's buildings and programs. By 1941, when he was removed by a politically unsympathetic governor, Louisiana Normal "had a modern physical plant and multifaceted programs of study."[521]

H. Long was assassinated in September 1935, and it then fell to new governor Richard W. Leche to use state jobs to favor his allies and punish his enemies.[522] An early target was Linus A. Sims, a Louisiana Normal professor who had campaigned against a Leche-sponsored candidate. Sims claimed his firing was political, and President Fredericks simply responded: "'I'll get fired if I don't fire you.'"[523]

As part of a protest over his firing, Sims brought up the Southern Association of Colleges and Secondary Schools (SACSS), an accrediting body which frowned on too much political control of a school. Without SACSS approval, other colleges in the nation would not accept transfer credits from Louisiana Normal. As early as March 1935, SACSS had investigated Louisiana Normal on charges that H. Long was running the college. The college was exonerated then but put on probation for academic deficiencies.[524] Sims threatened Fredericks about possible repercussions of his firing with SACSS. Fredericks replied: "'We don't care what the Southern Association says, . . . you should know that the school people of Louisiana do not run the schools. They are run by the politicians and they don't know anything about the Southern Association and they don't give a damn about it—and if they knew we were members they would make us get out.'"[525] The college lost its SACSS accreditation after a lengthy investigation, though it was eventually restored in 1941. Before Normal, Sims had been the first president of Hammond Junior College.

Southwestern Louisiana Institute continuation

The Southwestern Louisiana Institute of Liberal and Technical Learning (SLI) also experienced political control by governors in the 1930s. Dr. Edwin Stephens, long-time president, retired in January 1938 and denied that any political pressure caused him to do so. [526] He died less than a year later.[527]

Stephens was succeeded by Lether Edward Frazar who had close political ties to Governor Richard Leche. Historian Florent Hardy wrote that there was "no doubt that Frazar's political connection with the powerful Long faction of Louisiana aided his appointment." [528]

When Leche normalized relations with Franklin Roosevelt, the New Deal federal largesse once again flowed to Louisiana. Frazar was a close friend of state education superintendent T. H. Harris and became administrator for $2 million in federal Public Works Administration funds that he directed toward SLI.[529]

Despite the building boom in just two short years, Frazar resigned shortly after Sam Jones won the governorship in 1939. His resignation was voluntary. Showing that Louisiana politics was sometimes more important than family connections, Hardy noted that Frazar "knew that he would have been fired by the anti-Long administration of Governor Jones even though Frazar and Jones were cousins."[530] As a state legislator, before taking over the presidency, Frazar had co-authored the bill that led to the Teacher's Retirement System. After his resignation, he was appointed as Chairman of the Louisiana Highway Commission by Governor Earl Long, in his brief tenure after the resignation of Leche.[531] He went on to become the president of McNeese State College in 1950, and stayed there until his election as Lieutenant-Governor under Earl Long from 1956-1960. He died on May 16, 1960. [532]

Lincoln Parish Training School continuation

Lincoln Parish Training School benefited from the political involvement of H. Long. [533] President Charles Adams backed Long in the 1928 race for governor, and this paid great dividends. Though African-Americans were disenfranchised in Louisiana, they had some influence, and there "were 'favored' blacks who benefited from special connections with influential whites." [534] In a discussion with Adams, H. Long "spoke of Booker T. Washington and the excellent work being done at Tuskegee Institute." [535] H. Long was impressed that Adams had studied under Washington.

The passage of the bill to make the Lincoln Parish Training School a state institution showed the anti-democratic leanings that Long brought to the governorship. The original bill was introduced by H. Long but was defeated by the opposition of Superintendent of Education T. H. Harris who, as part of a long-running feud with Adams, tried to block the Training School from becoming a state institution. Harris continued to oppose Adams and the Training School, either because of personal reasons or because "Harris was an overzealous supporter of Southern University and felt a school in North Louisiana would interfere with the operation of Southern University." [536] The day after the bill was defeated, H. Long made a personal appearance on the floor of the legislature to push the bill through.

With H. Long's intervention, the bill passed. With Act Number 160, the Lincoln Parish Training School was renamed the Louisiana Negro Normal and Industrial Institute. Long signed the bill on July 16, 1928, and the school became a "state normal and industrial school for Negro youths."[537] An additional year was added to the curriculum to train elementary teachers for small rural schools, and the school first became regarded as a junior college.[538]

The unequal nature of the segregated system can be seen in a comparison with a college established as a state institution around the same time. Just after the establishment of the Louisiana Negro Normal and Industrial Institute, Southeastern College in Hammond became the seventh college placed under the state Board of Education. By 1932, the Board recommended appropriations of $45,000 for Southeastern and $20,000 for Louisiana Negro Normal. The salary of Southeastern's president's was $4,500, while Adams' was $1,500.

Charles Adams was forced into retirement in 1936 at the age of 62, probably because of the loss of political pull after the assassination of Huey Long. Without the support of Long, Adams became the target of a "vindictive" T. H. Harris. [539] Two reasons were given for Adams' forced retirement. First, Adams only had the equivalent of a high school education, and by 1936 advanced degrees were the "passports for leadership in Louisiana educational institutions of higher learning." [540] Second, Adams allegedly misappropriated funds. The Great Depression led to a revenue decline at Louisiana Negro Normal, and Adams had a laissez-faire attitude toward administration and bookkeeping. In addition, Adams had hired close relatives, so there was an question of nepotism.[541]

Adams was replaced by Ralph Waldo Emerson "Prez" Jones who was associated with Grambling from 1926 to 1977, 41 of the 51 years as president. Jones first came to Grambling as a teacher. He believed that a man as large as Adams would not hire him at 120 pounds, and he was correct. Adams had not intended to offer Jones the job and "had indeed been expecting a larger man." Jones stayed around to see if he would get the position. Adams gave it to him and wanted him to coach the football and baseball teams, form a band, and to teach biology, chemistry, physics, and math. On June 15, 1936, Jones, the only professor with a masters' degree, became president. [542]

When Jones took over as president, Louisiana Negro Normal had 120 students and 17 faculty members. In 1939, a third year of college work was added. In 1940, the college was authorized to become a four-year college, offering a B.S. degree in elementary education.[543] In 1943, the biggest issue was the fact that there was one well for water, and if it stopped working, Jones would have to close the school. Within a few years, a back-up well was authorized. Also, since the college had increasingly been referred to as "Grambling," Jones sought an official name change. With Act

Number 33, signed on July 4, 1946, the name of the college officially became "Grambling College of Louisiana." [544] Grambling was involved in the integration movement in the 1950s and the Civil Rights movement in the 1960s, and these will be covered in later chapters.

Southeastern Louisiana University (1925)

Hammond Junior College (later Southeastern Louisiana University) was founded before the political upheaval of Long's governorship, but it soon became enmeshed in the machinations. Its fortunes suffered under H. Long but prospered under Leche.

The story of the College began in January of 1925 when T. H. Harris, the influential State Superintendent of Education, was quoted as considering a junior college system in the state. [545] Linus Arthur Sims, the principal of Hammond High School, immediately sought to rally the community behind such a college for, among others, the "sons and daughters of strawberry farmers."[546] The College opened its doors on September 14, 1925, about nine months from Sims' original vision, with 40 students. [547]

For several years, the College maintained a close association with the public secondary school system. Sims was both president of the College and principal of Hammond High School. Also, the College occupied two rooms and a janitor's closet at the high school. [548] The close association with a high school was emblematic of the in-between nature of junior colleges—halfway between high school and college. As late as the 1960s in Louisiana, two junior colleges were founded on high school campuses and were called "Thirteenth and Fourteenth grades." At least since the 1970s, if not before, junior colleges have been more associated with college life than that of high school.

Hammond Junior College became Southeastern Louisiana College in 1928, under the auspices of the State Board of Education. The 1928 Legislature saw heated debates over a way to accommodate the enrollment growth at the College. One of the local legislators, Tom McKneely, showed his passion when he "took off his coat and offered to whip any member who voted against the bill." The measure passed.[549] Also, the College might have been the only entity that benefited from the catastrophic 1927 flood that inundated much of the central part of the country. Hunter Leake, a New Orleans attorney, had bought a weekend home in Hammond. The 1927 flood made him think his home was prone to flooding—even though it was a once in a century occurrence—and he wanted to unload the property. The college bought the property in 1927. [550]

Under H. Long's governorship, the downside of favoritism directed toward LSU was the neglect (or worse) shown to other emerging colleges, including Southeastern Louisiana College. H. Long vetoed an appropriations bill that would have placed the College on firm financial footing. While he did not publicly state a reason for the veto, some leaders thought it was because H. Long wanted the money for LSU. Historian Ronald Harris argued that "many believed that Long's crusade to build LSU into a nationally recognized 'flagship institution' came at the expense of the smaller colleges and, in the long run, proved detrimental to higher education in the state.[551] LSU president James Monroe Smith attempted a legislative takeover of Southeastern before his indictments rendered him ineffective. [552] Also, Hodding Carter, a newspaper editor who challenged Long, wrote that the "Long machine intended to punish the Hammond area into political submission, perhaps even by removing the college to a new location." [553] In the Spring of 1933, Sims was forced out of the presidency in response to his political activities. He took a faculty position at Louisiana Normal. [554]

Following H. Long's example at LSU, Governor Richard Leche tried to build a power-base by advancing Southeastern Louisiana College from humble beginnings. In 1936, Leche vowed to "make Southeastern his jewel, much as Huey Long had done at Louisiana State University, in Baton Rouge. Leche had a vision for Southeastern, and it was grand."[555] Leche took advantage of the federally-financed New Deal building programs to complete several significant building projects. The scandals leading to his resignation prevented Leche from fully fulfilling this promise.

University of Louisiana at Monroe (1931)

Another college that was hurt by the politics of the era was Ouachita Parish Junior College (later the University of Louisiana at Monroe). The College opened on September 28, 1931 and was under the governance of the Ouachita Parish School Board for the first three years. [556] In 1934, the Legislature brought the College into the state's authority as the Northeast Center of Louisiana State University. [557] In 1939, the Legislature authorized the transfer of all properties to LSU, and the College became the Northeast Junior College. [558] It stayed as part of LSU until 1950 when it gained four-year status, becoming the Northeast Louisiana State College, and was transferred from the LSU Board of Supervisors to the State Board of Education. [559]

The College was originally headed by arguably the most important scholar in the history of two-year colleges, Clyde Cornelius Colvert. In 1931, the 32-year-old C. C. Colvert arrived to a "half-completed building . . . with cotton stalks still standing in front of it." Despite 460 incoming students, a faculty had yet to be hired.[560] He not only solidified the operations of the College, he also assisted in the development of other state junior colleges and developed an innovative curriculum.

Colvert moved the curriculum of the two-year college away from the exclusively academic transfer classes and added courses in home economics and agriculture. He also encouraged more adults to attend and started night classes. He was not able to accomplish too much reform because of "the poverty of the community and the political power of hostile Louisiana State University." He accepted a political compromise to place the college directly under the control of LSU.[561] Colvert noted that about seventy-five percent of the students at the junior college were not fit for pre-professional training and yet were in a junior college trying to attain this training.

Despite the progress, Colvert fell victim to the political eddies swirling around the state when a "new state political organization in Louisiana that was jailing many of his political allies threatened to undercut both Colvert and his college."[562] In October of 1944, after working a full day at the College, he and his wife drove to Austin, arriving at 3:30 a.m.[563] He established what became the Community College Leadership Program at the University of Texas at Austin, a program that greatly influenced two-year college development through the twenty-first century.[564] He became the first full-time professor in two-year college education in the nation[565] and directed the program until January 1, 1971.[566] The Community College Leadership Program trained a large percentage of the two-year college leaders throughout the rest of the twentieth century, including Dr. Walter Bumphus, the president of the two-year college system in Louisiana as of 2004.

Tulane continuation

Being a private institution did not spare Tulane University the wrath of Huey P. Long. The most notable example was H. Long's interference with the Tulane Medical School. Dr. Edward William Alton Ochsner, appointed to be the head of the department of surgery, unintentionally incurred H. Long's disfavor over a letter he wrote to a friend that mildly criticized the "politicization" of Charity Hospital. The letter was stolen from his coat in the hospital and delivered to H. Long. In September of 1930, H. Long stated that "'Ochsner must go.'"[567]

H. Long used the attack on Dr. Ochsner and other actions to damage the prospects of Tulane. Historian John Dyer suggested two reasons for the enmity. First, Tulane had refused to grant H. Long an honorary degree. Also, the Tulane Board of Administrators consistently opposed him, and Board-member Esmond Phelps, general counsel for the *Times-Picayune*, was a particularly effective thorn in his side.[568] H. Long's devotion to LSU was the most likely overriding reason, and a close advisor summarized that "'Huey was determined to make L.S.U. a great medical school and as long as he was Governor of our state he was determined to do so even though it may work a hardship on Tulane and particularly Dr. Ochsner, who, in his opinion, had given Tulane's Medical School a tremendous amount of prestige.'"[569] Ochsner's removal was the last major event of political interference for Tulane, and the Tulane and LSU schools of medicine learned to cooperate, especially after 1949.[570]

Tulane's unpleasant interactions with H. Long further cemented a move away from a mass-education mission and towards an elite, liberal-arts institution. In the 1930s, the faculty submitted a communication that outlined the strategic goals of the university. Though couched in general terms, a reference to H. Long was unmistakable, when they wrote that the

'South . . . must be rescued from the demagogue; it must preserve and develop its own contributions to the culture of the nation; and the exodus of southern youth of promise must be stopped. If these ends are to be attained . . . southern universities that are genuine intellectual centers must be developed.'[571]

They further refined the anticipated mission of the university, based on the above-stated general goal, when they wrote that

'Tulane should not and cannot compete with its sister institution [Louisiana State University] in mass education, which should remain the obligation of the State, but should produce a select and higher type of scholarship to furnish that intellectual leadership which the South so sorely needs.'[572]

The suggestion was that Tulane must be an endowed university. Coming full circle from the 1906 attempt to be designated a state university and receive state funds, by the 1930s Tulane had embraced its private-college status and finalized that part of its character.

Institutions not really shaped by governors

While most colleges and universities were intricately connected to politics during the 1930s, two seemed to escape the notice of the governors in Baton Rouge. Perhaps because they were new and fairly small, both Dillard University and Lake Charles Junior College were established with comparatively little state-level political interference.

Dillard University (1930)

Dillard University, a private historically-black institution, was formed in 1930 from two predecessors established during Reconstruction, Straight University and New Orleans University. It was named for James Hardy Dillard, a white man, who was a former Tulane professor and served as a trustee for both predecessor schools.[573] The school opened with a new physical plant in September of 1935.

The most prominent figure in the founding of Dillard was Edgar B. Stern, a white New Orleans philanthropist. Stern's involvement in Dillard demonstrated the complexities and contradictions of race relations in the South before the Civil Rights movement. On the one hand, Stern dedicated thirty years of work and frustrations to the University, when he had the means to live a life of leisure. He was absolutely devoted to the institution. On the other hand, he believed in views that, though decidedly moderate by contemporary standards, would be deemed racist by a later generation.

Stern was the prime mover behind the 1930 merger and played an active role until his death in 1959. He bridged the two contentious denominational boards, occasionally becoming so frustrated that he threatened to resign.[574] When classes began, the president was often absent, and Stern took a hands-on role of management.

He attended faculty meetings, spoke to the students, and supervised the campus beautification which he also financed out of his own pocket.[575] Despite ample business and charitable opportunities, Dillard was his primary activity.[576]

Stern believed in many aspects of the color caste system in the South, including segregation. In addition to his good works at Dillard, he often challenged the mores of society. In 1932 New Orleans, a black woman could be invited into a white home, but she could not be made guest of honor. The Sterns made Marian Anderson, famous black singer, the guest of honor at a party in their home, despite the possibility they would lose many friends.[577] At times, Stern also reflected the worst of New Orleans society. When he was on vacation, he wrote to a colleague: "'Confidentially, . . . one of the many things that have tremendously appealed to me here in my present state of mind is the fact that I have not seen a negro [sic] since I arrived. If I did,' he continued, in jest, 'I almost believe I would call him a d—n nigger just to show that I am on vacation.'" [578] Stern described the often contradictory pulls when he said that "he felt like the circus performer who rode two horses with a foot on each 'only in this case contrary to circus practice, the horses are not carefully matched in color; one horse being white and the other black.'" [579]

The merger of Straight University and New Orleans University was initiated by Stern and others in the hope of having one outstanding black university as opposed to two marginal, underfunded ones that competed with each other to the detriment of both.[580] Much to Stern's surprise, upon approaching the two respective governing boards, both agreed to support the merger if they "'could get together on an honest-to-goodness university basis.'" [581] The eventual merger was a difficult decision because each institution had devoted professors, students, alumni and supporters, and in essence, the merger resulted in each giving up its unique identity. [582]

The Board of Trustees' deliberations over the first leader of Dillard demonstrated the complicated racial situation of the time. The race of the president, as well as his comportment in social situations, could determine the viability of the university. Stern himself gave the reason for the sensitivity when said that "New Orleans was a rather conservative city . . . and great care must be taken 'in our relations with the white community if we are to maintain the good will that up to this time, I believe, we have established with them.'" [583] Stern realized that it was the white community that would provide the funds to support a successful university.

Stern played a leading role in the selection process and suggested that race had little to do with the administrative effectiveness of the president. He had been impressed with black administrators at Tuskegee as well as a white administrator at all-black Fisk University. However, Stern argued that the race of the president mattered greatly in social situations. He assumed that if the president was black, the Dillard faculty would have to be all-black as well. It was unacceptable to have a black president in an executive position over white faculty. On the other hand, a white president could make for complicated social situations. Stern had heard that the wife of the white Fisk president had danced with black faculty members at a party. Stern, commenting on this situation, said that "'the day the wife of a white president of Dillard does this, you will find me among the missing trustees of this institution.'"[584] Another variable was whether the president should be from the north or the south.

After several months' indecision, the Board chose Dr. Will Alexander, the southern, white director of the Commission on Interracial Cooperation.[585] Like Stern, Alexander believed in the "separate but equal" approach to higher education, but both shifted their positions by the 1940s and came to oppose segregation.[586]

Alexander was in place for the construction of the main campus that began in 1934. The Great Depression had hit after the initial merger, but fortunately, the General Education Board was able to make up for non-paid pledges and construction proceeded. Bad relations among the denominational boards of the original two universities almost stopped construction. The Methodists were not able to honor their pledges, so the Congregationalists thought they should not have to either. The Congregationalists agreed to pay, but it led to further strains between the two.[587] Classes began in September 1935. Alexander was often absent, so Stern took on most of the administrative tasks.[588] For a while, students seemed to have more loyalty towards their respective predecessor colleges.[589]

In 1936, William Stuart Nelson became the first black president, relieving Stern of some of his duties.[590] In part because the white community "remained suspicious of or indifferent to the school," Stern became disillusioned with Nelson by 1939.[591] Stern favored his protégé, Albert W. Dent, who became Dillard's second black president in 1941. The combination of Dent running the campus and Stern stabilizing the finances proved to be enduring. In addition to providing a firm foundation of stability for Dillard, the working relationship led to a softening of Stern's advocacy of segregation.[592]

McNeese State University (1939)

Lake Charles Junior College (later McNeese State University) was founded in 1939 for three reasons, none of which had to do with governors or state politics. First, the local parish government wanted a school. Second, the Southwest Louisiana Cattleman's Association needed an exhibit area for livestock shows and rodeos. Finally, federal funds were available through Public Works Administration for public facilities.[593] In the 1938 bond issue to raise construction money for the school, a series of editorials "emphasized the services that would be provided by the Arena far more than they proclaimed the virtues of a junior college." [594] The bill establishing the college passed both houses of the legislature in June of 1938 and was signed by Richard Leche on July 6. [595]

As initially conceived, Lake Charles Junior College had been intended to be under LSU administration.[596] The first class opened on September 11, 1939, with 140 students. Joseph Farrar, later to become the president of Louisiana State Normal College, was the first dean. By the fall of 1940, the name was officially changed to

"John McNeese Junior College of Louisiana State University."[597] John McNeese, born July 4, 1843, had been superintendent of Calcasieu Parish Schools and was an important figure in state education.[598] In the fall of 1946, following tough times of low enrollment during the World War II years, the "John" was "quietly" dropped from the name.[599]

CHAPTER 5

1944 to 1964:
Earl Long, the GI Bill & Integration

From 1944 to 1964, Earl Long stood out as the most important figure in Louisiana higher education, even though he was not as powerful as brother Huey. The dramatic enrollment growth in higher education sweeping the nation after World War II did not lead to fundamental changes in Louisiana's approach to colleges and universities. Instead, these changes came to Louisiana after the 1964 election of Governor John McKeithen. The dramatic changes spurred by the 1954 *Brown v. Board* decision did affect Louisiana, and Earl Long was at the center of attempts to rationalize integration with Louisiana's "dual system."

Two other trends impacted the prospects for higher education in the succeeding decades. First, Louisiana had greatly decreased its illiteracy rate. Functional illiteracy as a percent of the population over 25 years old had gone from 35.7% (1940) to 21.3% (1960)—and it fell further to 13.1% in 1970. Despite the improvement, Louisiana still maintained the highest illiteracy rate in the South.[600] Second, in the decade after World War II, industries developed to take advantage of South Louisiana's abundant supplies of gas, petroleum, and sulphur. [601] These industries contributed to an increase in state revenues that later constituted an "oil boom," providing ample funding to colleges and universities up through the early 1980s.

GI Bill & fundamental national changes

The era after World War II was one of startling change and growth in American higher education. The G. I. Bill, which provided benefits to servicemen returning from World War II, was the prime mover behind this growth. One of the most important government programs in American history, the G. I. Bill allowed access to higher education to non-elite Americans. A whole generation of middle and working class families (and their descendants) gained the upward mobility afforded by a college degree. In other words, the G. I. Bill "democratized" higher education. Though outside the scope of this book, the G. I. Bill also "democratized" home ownership by providing affordable home loans. Into the twenty-first century, the percentages of Americans who attend college and own homes exceed any other country by significant margins. Historian George Vaughan aptly summarized that the Bill "helped break financial and social barriers for millions of Americans who had served in World War II." [602]

The G. I. Bill, also known as the "G. I. Bill of Rights" and officially known as the Servicemen's Readjustment Act of 1944, was established by Franklin D. Roosevelt on June 22, 1944. Roosevelt had two significant worries as World War II wound down. The first was the prospect of unrest caused by the large numbers of demobilized soldiers. After World War I, many military veterans could not find jobs and descended upon Washington, D. C., to pressure President Herbert Hoover to move up the timetable on promised pensions. This so-called "Bonus Army" was dispersed by the military and proved a great embarrassment. [603] Even worse, in Europe, civil strife among demobilized soldiers was a significant contributor to fascism.[604]

The second worry was how to move from a wartime to a peacetime economy. The established trend called for a recession following a war. Compounding the problem was the prospects of millions of young men coming home from the War to seek employment at precisely the time when industries laid off workers as they ceased manufacturing for the military. [605]

Roosevelt and congressional leaders hoped that the G. I. Bill would take care of both problems. Servicemen received a reward that allowed them to increase their skills and financial prospects. Also, the time spent in college delayed their entry into the workforce by two to four years. By that time, it was anticipated that the economy would have recovered, and jobs would be available.

In reality, every industrial competitor was seriously hurt by the War while America's economy became a colossus through war-time production. America boomed after the War and did not suffer the anticipated serious recession. Fortuitously, the G. I. Bill provided trained managers and engineers in the sufficient numbers to feed the needs of the modern American economy. America—and the new college graduates—reached a level of prosperity never seen before.

The democratizing effect of the G. I. Bill was stunning. In 1940, about 11% of Americans had graduated high school, and about 5% had college degrees. [606] Between 1943 and 1946, college enrollment doubled.[607] By 1947, the 1.6 million veterans represented 49% of all students, with 60% enrolled in science and engineering classes.[608] By 1956, 2.2 million veterans had gone to college, 3.5 million attended technical schools, and 700,000 received off-campus agricultural instruction. Over the succeeding decades, access to college was extended to other groups, and it increasingly became a middle-class expectation. By 1990, 14 million Americans were in college, and about 20% had a college degree. [609] In 2000, 24% of Americans had a college degree. Also, the monthly stipend that accompanied the college expenses was more money than many of the veterans—who had grown up during the "dark days" of the Great Depression—had ever held in their hands. [610]

The democratizing effect of the G. I. Bill on home ownership was also important and worked hand-in-hand with the higher education advances to bring an unprecedented level of prosperity to the American middle class. In 1940, about 33% owned a home, but by 1949, the figure was 60%. These homes were largely built in the suburbs of large cities, and thus the G. I. Bill was arguably responsible for suburbanization. William Levitt, the real estate developer who revolutionized homebuilding with a factory-like assembly-line system, built houses to conform exactly to the G. I. Bill mortgage payments. The homeownership also provided advantages to the country beyond the creature comforts to the individual. Levitt was prescient on this as well and contended that "'[n]o man who owns a house and lot can be a Communist. He has too much to do." [611]

Earl Long

The major higher educational achievements of the immediate post-World War II era in Louisiana belonged to another Long. Like Huey, brother Earl Long was a populist and "vigorously identified with social-welfare legislation." [612] E. Long demonstrated the considerable power of the governor when it came to higher education, but unlike Huey, the extremes of behavior were toned down. Like most governors, E. Long was devoted to LSU, but he did not interfere with its operations. [613] At the secondary level, he also increased funding for free lunches, improved vocational schools and equalized the salaries of white and black teachers. [614]

Earl Kemp Long was governor from 1939 to 1940, from 1948 to 1952 and from 1956 to 1960. A flurry of reform activity in higher education occurred in E. Long's terms while a lack of activity occurred in the interceding governors' terms. Jimmie Davis was governor from 1944 to 1948 and 1960 to 1964. Contributing relatively little to higher education, he was best known for his theme song of "You Are My Sunshine," for being a country singer inducted into the Country Music Hall of Fame, and for appearing in movies while governor. [615] Robert F. Kennon, governor from 1952 to 1956, instituted a strong state civil service system that decreased the power of the governor. [616]

Though enrollment increased, Louisiana did not experience explosive growth in higher education as a result of the G. I. Bill, for several reasons. First, as a result of Louisiana's educational history, the college enrollment was very small to begin with. Second, a large portion of the available jobs did not require higher education. In addition to the agricultural jobs in the mostly-rural state, the booming oil sector provided well-paying jobs on rigs to high school graduates. The availability of low-skilled jobs that afforded a middle-class lifestyle allowed "many parents and high school graduates to regard higher education as superfluous." [617] This view minimized the popularity of higher education until after the "oil bust" of the 1980s. Finally, higher education was still seen as a luxury to the vast majority. Historian Alfred

Delahaye noted that, especially in rural areas, "[g]rown men and women, in the dominant view of the day, should be working or keeping house, not sitting in a classroom." [618] Louisiana had to wait until the "baby boom" generation came of age in the 1960s to experience dramatic enrollment increases.

There were exceptions. Southwestern Louisiana Institute had a large enrollment increase from returning veterans. By October of 1946, SLI had 3,243 students, of which 1,783 were veterans. The college had to turn away 1,250 prospective students. SLI became the largest college in the state. [619] Joel L. Fletcher, president from 1941 to 1966, faced the considerable difficulty of accommodating such a large increase without a corresponding increase in appropriations.[620] Southeastern Louisiana College also saw an enrollment surge in the Fall of 1946. At the time, Southeastern did not have a formal application process, and potential students simply showed up and sent in their transcripts later. The G. I. Bill enrollees overwhelmed the system which resulted in "near chaos."[621]

A number of statewide policies affected higher education during this era. The most important development was the requirement of the completion of a 12th year to qualify for a high school diploma. Before this Department of Education mandate in 1949, most high schools ended in the 11th grade. This change all but curtailed freshman enrollment the 1949-50 year. Louisiana was one of the last states to mandate this 12th year.[622]

The Communist Scare symbolized by Joseph McCarthy also affected Louisiana higher education in the 1950s. All state employees, including at colleges and universities, had to take loyalty or non-communist oaths. Also, the state mandated the completion of a one-credit course called "Democracy versus Communism." [623] This course was not removed as a graduation requirement until the 1973-74 year at Nicholls State University.[624] Finally, in 1961, the state mandated a 4.0 grading system for all of its colleges.

Nicholls State University (1948)

Francis T. Nicholls Junior College (later Nicholls State University) was established in 1948 to respond to the needs of the sugar industry and to provide qualified teachers. The shortage of workers across the so-called sugar belt in Louisiana was so intense during World War II that German prisoners of war worked on the plantations.[625] Modernization of the sugar industry called into question the type of training that might be needed after the war, and the Junior College was intended to be integral to the process.[626]

During the War, Robert O. Moncla, Superintendent of Schools in Lafourche parish, responded to the growing importance of junior colleges in the state and nation.[627] In the 1930s, LSU had taken over Ouachita Parish Junior College and McNeese Junior College, and Moncla considered a similar relationship. In the lead up to the establishing act, the local legislator learned of developing opposition. He spent $700 stocking a Baton Rouge hotel room with the finest brands of liquor before giving the key to some opponents of the junior-college bill.[628] The bill passed.

The junior college was named in honor of Francis Redding Tillou Nicholls, a Bayou Lafourche native.[629] Nicholls entered West Point at age 16 and later rose to the rank of brigadier general in the Confederate Army. In addition to being a prisoner-of-war, he was twice wounded. He lost his left arm at the Battle of Winchester in Virginia. A year later, he lost his left foot at the Battle of Chancellorsville. Making light of his injuries, Nicholls told an aide that if he fulfilled his goal to be a judge after the war, "'it would always be said of me that I was a 'one-sided judge.'" [630] He went on to serve two terms as governor, 12 years as chief justice of the Louisiana Supreme Court and another six years as Associate Justice.[631] In his first campaign as governor, it was said that the Democrats ran "all that was left" of Francis T. Nicholls.

Francis T. Nicholls Junior College opened its doors to students on September 23, 1948.[632] The site was part of the Acadia Plantation, once owned by Jim Bowie of the knife and Alamo fame.[633] Charles C. Elkins, formerly director of the Remedial Reading Bureau at LSU,[634] was the first dean, and upon arrival, he found "'an abandoned rice field on the left and right, cane stubble out front along with johnson grass—and an African jungle in the back.'"[635] Most students arrived on school buses as all of the surrounding parishes provided free bus transportation.[636]

The Junior College's relationship with parent LSU was decidedly mixed from the beginning. Historian Alfred Delahaye noted that LSU regarded Nicholls as a "financial burden" and "'treated the junior college like a stepchild.'" [637] General Troy H. Middleton, after returning from the European theater in World War II, was the LSU comptroller and a very influential official (who later became president). [638] He regarded junior colleges as a drain on the main campus and bluntly spoke of his "disdain" for them. [639] Middleton agreed with a May 1946 *Life* magazine article that noted that the "'junior college has always been the runt of the United States educational litter.'" [640] On a positive note, LSU blessed the beginning of a football team at Nicholls, hoping it would be a farm team. LSU provided hand-me-down purple and gold uniforms.[641]

A vestige of the historical creole-Anglo dispute was seen in this culturally non-Anglo stronghold. Delahaye noted that the original faculty members at Nicholls "tended to be Protestants who knew little about the area dominated by Catholics, Cajuns and cane." [642] In a 1963 presidential search, school and community leaders noted their preference for "a Catholic Cajun" and were delighted when Vernon F. Galliano became the first Catholic president in the state-board system.[643]

Nicholls suffered a spate of bad luck in its early years. In just its second year, the state instituted the additional fourth year of high school, thus eliminating most of the potential incoming freshman class. In its third year, the Korean War had begun and many potential students had chosen to serve in the military. In the fall of 1950, enrollment stood at only 190. By 1951, there were rumors of closure due to the ongoing Korean War, but the school stayed open.

By 1956, Nicholls was strong enough to make the leap to four-year college status. Spearheading the advance was State Senator A. O. Rappelet, a good friend of E. Long, who was known for his "trademark white suit, dark sunglasses, and white cowboy hat." [644] Delahaye detailed his influence when he wrote that when "Earl Long was governor, if Rap[pelet] wanted something that had merit, it was a done deal." [645] Senate Bill 424 gave the four-year status, bestowed the name "Francis T. Nicholls State College" and transferred the college from LSU to the State Board of Education. In the face of possible opposition, Earl Long had stated that "he was determined to see the legislation through." [646] Long signed the bill on July 11, 1956.

The move to four-year status was somewhat risky, since the prestige and guidance from LSU helped solidify Nicholls' position. Nicholls lost its ROTC program and had to reapply for accreditation on its own standing.[647] Most faculty members saw the move as bad in the short run though good in the long run. They recognized the change as a political, not academic, decision. [648] The transition was successful as Nicholls received its accreditation in December of 1964, retroactive to 1958 when first four-year degrees were added. [649]

Other notable happenings at individual colleges

In addition to the establishment of Nicholls, a number of other notable things happened at Louisiana colleges and universities. Louisiana State University at Alexandria was established as a two-year college in 1959. Intended as a commuter college to prepare students for entry into LSU, the first students registered in September of 1960. LSU at Alexandria became a four-year college in 2001.

Tulane took the next step to becoming an elite regional university by emphasizing graduate education. Top educational leaders and foundations realized that the South was far behind in providing high-quality graduate studies. In 1950, Southern universities had 1/3 of the nation's population but awarded only 1/12 of the doctorates. As Southern students left to get advanced training, many never returned and the South was "constantly being drained of its top research and teaching scholars." [650] With the assistance of top foundations such as the Carnegie Corporation and the General Education Board, Tulane developed as a premier center of graduate studies, along with universities such as Duke, North Carolina, Texas, and Vanderbilt.[651] Also, by the 1960s, the Tulane School of Medicine had become nationally recognized, particularly in the areas of tropical medicine and public health.

Political interference also continued to influence higher education. At McNeese Junior College, local legislators first tried to get four-year status in early 1950. When that bill was defeated, another was introduced that deleted any reference to four-year status, but simply requested a name change to "McNeese State College" and a shift from LSU to the State Board of Education. [652] It was obviously a legislative ploy, but it worked. Earl Long signed into law on July 1, 1950, and the formal separation from LSU came on July 17, 1950. [653] A failed lawsuit over this maneuver indicated "that the establishment of the [college] had been purely political, and that Louisiana had too many four-year colleges."[654] Lether Frazar was first president of McNeese State College, but retired when he ran for lieutenant governor on the Earl Long ticket in 1956. His successor, Wayne Cusic, did not have a doctorate like three of the other five candidates, but he was Governor Robert Kennon's brother-in-law. He officially became president in October of 1955.[655]

Integration

The most important higher education issue of the era—in Louisiana and the nation—was the integration of colleges and universities that occurred after the *Brown v. Board of Education of Topeka, Kansas* Supreme Court decision in 1954. Governed by the "separate but equal" precedent of *Plessy v. Ferguson* in 1896, a dual system of segregated education had been instituted in Louisiana and across the South. While primarily concerned with elementary and secondary education, the *Brown* decision also called for integration of higher education.

With a few exceptions, southern leaders generally resisted the integration of state universities. A famous instance was Alabama Governor George Wallace's "Stand in the Schoolhouse Door" at the University of Alabama to prevent a handful of black students from attending. The resistance often turned into violence, rioting and death, as happened when James Meredith integrated the University of Mississippi.

Integration also created uncertainty for the historically-black colleges and universities (HBCUs) which previously had a virtual monopoly on black students. As white colleges provided competition, a question arose about the proper mission of HBCUs in a post-integration environment. Echoing Washington and Dubois at the beginning of the century, a new debate arose concerning the best path to a college education for African-Americans.

In Louisiana, integration was fought in a determined but peaceful manner. Resistance to integration was popular with the voters of the state, and most politicians used it as a basis for winning office. Once in office, legislators and other officials consistently used obstructionist tactics to thwart the implementation of integration decrees. Thus, Louisiana was one of the most segregated states. For example, by 1950, New Orleans was the only large city in the South with no black policemen.[656]

The primary vehicle for the segregationist tactics was the Joint Legislative Committee to Maintain Segregation, chaired by state senator William M. Rainach of Claiborne Parish. This Committee devised the strategy for forestalling integration.[657] Soon after the *Brown* decision, the Legislature offered Constitutional Amendment 16 which was designed to circumvent the federal mandates. It passed by a margin of more than five to one. In Plaquemines Parish, the home to the state's most famous segregationist, Leander Perez, the margin was forty-eight to one.[658] The legislators realized that it was unwise to pass laws that overtly contradicted federal integration decrees. Thus, they adopted a series of measures that accomplished the same thing but were designed not to incur the wrath of the federal government.

While the Legislature passed segregationist laws in the mid-1950s, the administrators at public colleges and universities in Louisiana found themselves in a difficult position. The 1954 *Brown* decision was clear that integration should proceed, and a federal court had nullified Louisiana's segregation laws in 1955. However, as state agencies, the institutions also had to follow the orders of the people higher in the chain of command. To disobey the legislature or an official at the State Board of Education might lead to serious consequences from state officials or even the local sheriff. The uncertainty was compounded by the process where the state legislature quickly erected some type of racial barrier, and the federal court in New Orleans just as quickly countermanded the law.[659]

The most telling example of the attempts to circumvent integration in higher education was the so-called "certificate of eligibility." Act 15 of 1956 decreed that a person needed a certificate "attesting to academic eligibility and sound moral character" in order to register for classes at a state university. This certificate had to be signed by the parish superintendent of education and principal where the individual completed high school. The signed document was then presented to a university's registrar as a first step in the admittance process. Theoretically, it was possible for a black student to obtain a certificate, but in practice, local officials withheld the necessary signatures. The difficulty for university administrators was that by accepting a black student without the certificate of eligibility, they were on record for favoring integration. In turn, this act violated state laws "forbidding acts that assisted or promoted racial integration," which made the administrator subject to dismissal, or even criminally guilty.[660][661] The NAACP brought suit against the practice, and the federal courts found the requirement unconstitutional.[662] Act 15 was not officially rescinded by the State Board of Education until April 3, 1965.[663]

Once all of the court challenges had been expended, Louisiana institutions of higher education were integrated peacefully but reluctantly. The integration of Northeastern Louisiana College exemplified the typical experience. An Associated Press report of June 1964 noted that there were no incidents of violence. However, College President George T. Walker put out the following statement: "'I deeply regret the decision of the federal court that we must admit Negroes . . . . We are compelled to obey the injunction. As has been done in the earlier cases of institutions under the control of the State Board of Education, we will work with Negro enrollees in as good grace as is possible under the circumstances.'"[664] Despite the begrudging nature of the statement, Walker took the necessary steps to make sure the integration was peaceful and orderly.

Most of the colleges were integrated by the late-1950s; however, vestiges of segregation persisted. On November 14, 1960, State Superintendent of Education Shelby Jackson declared that public colleges and universities be closed for a "holiday" that coincided with the federal mandate of the integration of public K-12 schools in New Orleans.[665] As late as the mid-1960s, a law was on the books that made it illegal for an athletic team from a white Louisiana college to play an opposing team that had a black player. This was obviously unconstitutional and was not universally adhered to. [666]

University of New Orleans (1956) & Southern University at New Orleans (1956)

The establishment of Louisiana State University in New Orleans (LSUNO) (later the University of New Orleans) in 1956 constituted Earl Long's greatest impact on higher education. E. Long fully used the power of the governor's office. Also, the opening of LSUNO served as an important, but relatively little-noticed, event in the segregation battles of the time. Earl Long acted progressively for the time in taking steps to ensure that the university was racially integrated and that there was no violence associated with its opening.

In his 1956 campaign, E. Long promised to establish a branch of LSU in New Orleans. New Orleans, by far the largest city in the state, did not have a single public four-year university. The establishment of a campus would allow residents who could not afford the room and board in Baton Rouge to attend college. The powerful LSU lobby had long blocked similar legislation for fear it would hurt enrollment at the main campus. The story of the establishment then became a fierce battle of political heavyweights eventually won by E. Long. [667] After his death, Dr. Homer Hitt, LSUNO's first chancellor, praised Long's successful efforts "'despite the opposition of the New Orleans press, the Chamber of Commerce, and City Hall.'" [668]

E. Long was not necessarily committed to integration as a moral issue, but he knew that the federal courts would not allow the opening of a legally segregated university. To minimize any potential disruptions, E. Long had the Legislature also authorize a branch of Southern University at New Orleans (SUNO) within a few miles of LSUNO. Long intended for African-American students to attend SUNO and white students to attend LSUNO, thus maintaining de facto segregation amidst the de jure integration. This was a continuation of Louisiana's "dual system" of segregated higher education.

While no white students attended SUNO, over 200 black students joined over 1000 white students in registering for LSUNO. Historians Michael Kurtz and Morgan Peoples summarized that "without meaning to, Earl Long had established the first public, state-supported university in the Deep South that admitted all students without regard to race." [669] Other Southern universities, including in Louisiana, had technically integrated previously to LSUNO, but only on a token basis.

The opening of LSUNO had the potential for racial violence as the White Citizens Council and other segregationist organizations planned to interrupt the registration process. E. Long made his presence known at the opening and spoke about the educational benefits. With a large contingent of state troopers, he also made it clear he would respond to any violent demonstration. Kurtz and Peoples contended that "[b]ecause of Long's actions, the first fully integrated public university in the Deep South held its first year of classes without a single incident of racial violence, and in ensuing years, LSUNO continued to maintain its academic integrity and an integrated student body." [670]

E. Long was able to avoid the national headlines of violence surrounding integration. He was not so fortunate in other areas. His political battles led to mental strains, and the resulting irrational behavior was played out in the national press.[671] E. Long was better known for consorting with stripper Blaze Starr—meriting a movie in which he was portrayed by Paul Newman—and other foibles than for his admirable success in helping to integrate Louisiana higher education.

Earl Long was also responsible for an additional chapter in the story of segregated higher education in Louisiana, the establishment of SUNO. It is a curious development where E. Long could be lauded for increasing integration in Louisiana higher education (with LSUNO), while at the same time increasing segregation with the creation of an all-black SUNO.

The establishment of SUNO was emblematic of the controversy over the purpose of HBCUs in the era of legal integration. After the 1954 *Brown* decision, their proper role was in question. In 1947, black institutions educated 85% of the nearly 75,000 black students.[672] The debate had first arisen in Louisiana with the establishment of Southern University in the Reconstruction era. At the time, the hardening of segregation rendered the debate moot, but the *Brown* decision brought it to the fore. Though a complex issue, the debate was simplified to a crucial distinction: were HBCUs anachronisms that delayed true integration, or were they needed cultural assets uniquely capable of educating African-Americans?

SUNO's authorization in 1956 made it the first HBCU established after the *Brown* decision and thus an early focus of the controversy. Valera Francis, SUNO historian, wrote that the founding "sparked heated debate" as "many in the Black community saw this as a means of perpetuating separate facilities for Black students for the specific purpose of keeping them out of the recently opened Louisiana State University of New Orleans."[673] Three prominent African-American organizations— the United Clubs, Inc., the Studs Club, Inc. and the Frontiers of America—sought to block the construction of the university. [674] Four Southern University officials were at the SUNO groundbreaking, but did not comment. B. A. Little, University Auditor, later said: "'We respectfully broke ground for this school we did not want during the days of segregation. We didn't want SUNO because we didn't think it was necessary at the time.'" Francis summarized that it "appeared that no one in the Negro community wanted the university, not even the parent body." [675]

While the lack of violence surrounding the opening of LSUNO was commendable, E. Long's clearly intended to maintain segregation in higher education. The establishment of LSUNO and SUNO only a few miles from each other was part of the often-used "separate but equal" strategy in the state. Francis wrote that while no violent incidents were reported at LSUNO, nonetheless "considerable racial tension permeated the opening." [676] Despite the dictates of the *Brown* decision, the LSU Board of Supervisors declared: "'This board wishes to point out that any Negro student whose enrollment is forced upon this university, enters as an unwanted matriculant.'" [677]

A little over three years after the September 4, 1956 Extraordinary Session that established SUNO as a branch unit of Southern University, SUNO held its first day of classes on a fully segregated basis. It began with 158 students and a faculty of 15. [678] A vote of the legislature on November 8, 1960 ensured that SUNO did not have autonomy but remained a branch unit of Southern University. In January of 1964, Virginia Cox Welch, a white woman, filed a lawsuit that eventually opened up SUNO to all races. Grambling also was the target of an integration suit which was brought as a test case. [679] In 1975, following the provisions of the Louisiana Constitution of 1974, SUNO gained a measure of independence and became a free-standing unit of the Southern University System.

Due to the close proximity of the universities and the circumstances of their founding, the idea of a merger between LSUNO and SUNO has been suggested on at least three occasions. The first was in 1969, and the Urban League of Greater New Orleans was in favor of it. [680] Merger talk resurfaced in 1971, when the Louisiana Coordinating Council for Higher Education, the statewide governance board of colleges and universities, suggested it. [681] Finally, the idea was brought up again in 1992. [682] All tries at a merger failed. In general, it seemed that HBCU administrators and alumni preferred to maintain the separate institutions, while the African-American community probably did not.

Response at HBCUs: Grambling & Southern

The period of integration was a time of mixed prosperity for the other public HBCUs in Louisiana, Grambling and Southern. In general, the colleges saw a significant increase in appropriations from the state at the beginning of the 1950s. State leaders anticipated that by greatly improving the facilities and degree offerings at black colleges, the "separate but equal" approach would be more plausible, and integration could be forestalled. In the midst of integration, activism and protests consumed much of the attention, as the "trial run" of the Civil Rights Movement was played out on the campuses. The end of integration brought uncertainty, as many of the best black students opted for more prestigious universities, and the HBCUs were forced to compete for the first time for the remainder.

Grambling College of Louisiana experienced decades of limited state funds. This changed around 1950 when it received appropriations to commence a whirlwind of building activity on the campus. As more blacks tested segregation by applying to all-white universities, the Louisiana legislature and Louisiana State Board of Education adopted the strategy of improving HBCUs to allay the integration controversy. [683] This contributed to growth, and the enrollment surpassed 2,000 for the first time in 1956-7. [684] Two years later, Grambling was reorganized from "an over-emphasis on teacher education," and in 1974, the newly named "Grambling State University." added a Graduate school. Navigating integration fairly smoothly, Grambling was not able to avoid the upheavals of the 1960s, as will be discussed in the next chapter.

Southern University faced the typical state response of higher appropriations in the establishment of the Law School. In an early salvo in the integration battle, Charles Hatfield, a black man "'who was otherwise apparently qualified,'" applied for admission to LSU Law School just after World War II, following a Supreme Court decision.[685] The State Board met in September of 1946 to discuss the plan for an alternate Law School at Southern University. Despite the usually glacial pace of such matters, the School was established and funded within six months. Governor Jimmy Davis reported an appropriation of $40,000 for its immediate opening.[686] The dual system remained intact.

White college response

The first successful attempt at integration involved the LSU law school in 1950. The court battles of the early civil rights movement were led by the NAACP. Until 1950, the strategy had been one of "equalization" in the sense of accepting the "separate but equal" doctrine and pushing for improvements at black facilities. This changed with the U. S. Supreme Court decision of *Sweatt v. Painter*. The University of Texas Law School was forced to admit Herman Sweatt, despite the nearby black Texas Southern University Law School. [687] This victory caused the NAACP to shift its strategy away from equalization and toward integration. The first Louisiana test case in line with the integration strategy was for admission to the LSU law school. Blacks were admitted in 1950.

The *Sweatt* case dealt only with graduate and professional schools, so undergraduate integration of LSU came almost a decade later. President Troy Middleton summarized the official stance when he stated that "'LSU welcomes all the support it can get from those sincerely interested in preserving segregation." [688] A. P. Turead, Jr., the son of the famous civil rights lawyer, was technically LSU's first black undergraduate. [689] The LSU Board of Supervisors appealed his admission, and his registration was cancelled while the case was in litigation. By the time a federal appeals court had upheld the admission, Turead had transferred to Xavier because he felt lonely and isolated on the LSU campus.[690] The case, which began in 1953, ended with the court-ordered entry of the first black undergraduate attendees to LSU in 1958. [691]

The other white colleges simply followed the dictates of the appropriate governmental body, generally in a non-violent manner. At first, they followed the policies of the segregationist state legislature and Board of Education and prohibited blacks from registering. When the legal challenges became final, the colleges followed the legal orders of the courts and accepted black students.

Individual colleges and universities fit the general pattern of non-violently deferring to the controlling legal authority. Southwestern Louisiana Institute was the first of the State Board of Education institutions to be integrated. On July 18,1954, the Shreveport federal court ruled SLI must integrate, which responded to a January 8th lawsuit by four potential black students. [692] [693] On July 22, John Harold Taylor became the first black student to register. The process was interrupted with state laws, like the certificate of eligibility, but SLI was permanently integrated by 1957. [694] McNeese State College had a slight wrinkle to the process as it had to overcome the provisions of its 1950 establishing legislative act which explicitly stated it was a college for white students only. [695]

Francis T. Nicholls Junior College was the last to integrate, and it was promoted to independent, four-year status amidst the controversies of integration. As a branch campus of LSU, there was a spillover of the great attention garnered on the main campus, though Nicholls essentially had to follow the lead of LSU.[696] Nicholls was in a staunchly Catholic area, so Archbishop Joseph Francis Rummel's "strongly worded" pastoral letter that called segregation "morally wrong and sinful" influenced the process. [697]

The main defense against integration was that its establishing stated the college was created "for the education of white persons of the State of Louisiana." [698] At the trial concerned with integrating Nicholls, President Galliano reminded the sitting federal judge, Judge Robert A. Ainsworth, Jr., that he had overseen the act designating Nicholls a segregated school when he was speaker pro tempore of the Louisiana Senate. [699] As it turned out, both sides considered the hearing a "charade" as the outcome was predetermined in favor of integration, and main parties on both sides had lunch with the judge at the Playboy Club after the court session. [700]

As a private, university, Tulane faced a unique problem surrounding integration which involved its historical uncertainty over being a quasi-public institution. Unlike most state universities, Tulane embraced integration from the beginning. The first formal step took place a month before the *Brown* decision where Graduate School faculty recommended a formal exploration of the issue. After the May 1954 *Brown* decision, faculty groups began to work for a full implementation, though with an abundance of caution and a division of opinions. [701] The chief impediment was the limitations of the charter, establishing act and bequest of Paul Tulane—all explicitly limiting admission to white students.[702] Tulane's legal advisors said that only a court opinion could facilitate integration. The Tulane Board thus favored integration, but faced the conundrum of fulfilling either "its responsibilities as trustees to honor the conditions of the gifts made to them" or a desire "to take account of changing social and economic conditions that had developed since the time the gifts were made." [703]

The milquetoast solution was a statement that said: the "Administrators of the Tulane Educational Fund . . . voted that Tulane University would admit qualified students regardless of race or color if it were legally permissible." [704]

A federal court opinion was handed down in September of 1961 that had a decidedly double-edged meaning for Tulane. On the one hand, Federal District Judge J. Skelly Wright laid the legal foundation for Tulane to integrate. His decision noted that Tulane was "in effect a state agency" because a "private college often does the work of the state in the place of the state." He held that "Tulane was so impressed with public interest that it was amenable to the term of the Fourteenth Amendment and could not restrict its admission to whites only." [705] The ruling should have been welcomed, but it had a further connotation that Tulane considered insidious.

Unlike in 1906 when it fought for state appropriations, Tulane ardently held to its private university status in the 1950s. If it was declared a quasi-state agency, then it might lose part of its independence and financial advantages. When Wright was promoted to the Court of Appeals, Tulane asked the next judge for a stay of the decision, and a new trial was set. At its conclusion, Judge Frank Ellis stated that

> Tulane could voluntarily admit Negroes, since it would be unconstitutional to compel discrimination. He also held that Tulane was not so significantly impressed with a public interest as to be amenable to the Fourteenth Amendment, and that by the same token Tulane could not be compelled to admit Negroes. [706]

The slightly bizarre opinion satisfied Tulane's paradoxical requirements. One week later, Tulane was voluntarily desegregated by the Tulane board, and the university was integrated in spring of 1963.

A postscript on the contentious integration battles was the transformation of LSU President Troy Middleton. In the 1950s, Middleton had resisted the overtures of extreme segregationists like Rainach and Perez, but he had remained a convinced segregationist. He ardently fought integration in the courts. However, with the passage of the Civil Rights Act of 1965, integration became the law of the land with the legitimacy of the broad-based political process. The *Brown* decision was often seen by some Southerners as a handful of judges imposing an unpopular edict. Middleton had been a general in World War II and took seriously his oath to defend the country and its laws. He explained that the "'Civil Rights Act is a law; to violate it would be to violate my oath. I shall never do that.'" Middleton devoted his retirement years to promoting racial equality in Louisiana.[707]

CHAPTER 6

1964 to 1972:
John McKeithen & the Baby Boom

The contemporary state of affairs in public higher education in Louisiana was established in this period. The bulk of the credit goes to John McKeithen who oversaw a formative period of higher education development in his tenure as governor. McKeithen created an "all-in-one" approach that became the status quo in public higher education in Louisiana at least until 2004. Universities served widely variant missions and included forms of instruction that ranged from developmental classes for students not ready for collegiate-level classes all the way up to doctorate-level graduate education. Reacting to this approach as wasteful and inefficient, M. J. "Mike" Foster instituted a different higher education philosophy when he became governor in 1996.

John J. McKeithen, a protégé of Earl Long, was governor from 1964 to 1972. He was generally known as a reformer, and his election "marked an end, for better or worse depending upon one's perspective, to the bifactional politics that characterized Louisiana elections from the time of Huey Long." [708] In general accounts of his administration, the most notable occurrence was a controversy with the Mafia where thirty-nine state, parish and local officials were under indictment after a Mafia probe. McKeithen was not personally implicated. [709] The Superdome was also built under his watch. According to Valera Francis, higher education historian, McKeithen was also noted for displaying "a unique brand of statesmanship that set him apart from other Southern governors of the period. Louisiana was spared the racial turmoil experienced in other states primarily because of McKeithen's leadership."[710] Finally, the historical power of the governor was intact in McKeithen's terms. For example, in 1964, the governor of Louisiana appointed more people to office than any other governor except New York's.[711]

All-in-one philosophy—driven by enrollment increases

John McKeithen's role in Louisiana higher education is difficult for an historian to assess. On one hand, several factors indicate he had profound influence. The current state of public higher education was fundamentally shaped during his time in the governor's office. As governor, he maintained the considerable power that had historically accrued to the governor in governmental affairs in general, but especially in higher education. Finally, no other individual or institution is prominent in the literature for impacting Louisiana higher education at this time. The most obvious inference is that he can be credited with the reorganization of higher education in the "all-in-one" model.

On the other hand, his role in higher education is not listed prominently—if at all—among his notable achievements. This historian could find no full-length biographies on McKeithen and even the extended commentaries failed to mention higher education as being an important component of his governorship. In a New York Times obituary article, Edward Renwick, Loyola University political scientist, cited four major accomplishments, none having to do with higher education (or education).[712] More telling, McKeithen himself does not rank statewide higher education reform as among his notable achievements in the interviews that he gave.

The transformation of higher education under McKeithen came in response to the drastic enrollment increases as a result of the "baby boomers" reaching college age. In Louisiana, the student body population more than doubled between 1960 to 1970.[713] Enrollment at public institutions of higher education jumped from 46,000 in 1961 to 107,800 in 1971, a 134%, increase.[714] In the decade covering most of the 1960s, the number of students at Nicholls State College increased by 573%.[715] The scramble to provide enough professors and appropriate facilities generally came with insufficient resources. As the curricular programs, especially at the graduate level, grew to meet demand, McKeithen realized the need to have some type of statewide coordination of the growth.

The "baby boom" generation is the moniker for the historically large number of births from 1946 to 1964. Uncertain times often cause couples to defer having children. In America, the economically tumultuous Great Depression of the 1930s had been followed by 100,000s of young men heading off to uncertain fates in World War II in the 1940s. When the war ended in 1945, the newfound security and prosperity resulted in an energetic reversal of the putting off of families.

The proliferation of births overwhelmed institutions at every stage of their development; their progression resembling a python swallowing a pig. At first, there was an extreme shortage of obstetric facilities. When the generation first started turning six, scores of elementary schools had to be built to accommodate their numbers. Their entering of retirement age has brought on the impending bankruptcy of the government retirement system. As envisioned in the 1930s, Social Security is built on the system of part of the withheld pay of workers going immediately to retirees. As the baby boomers were in their working years, the system was flush. As the leading edge reaches retirement age in 2008, a surfeit of workers will make giving the promised benefits unworkable. More pertinent to this story, in the mid-1960s, the baby boomers reached college age, and they wrought great changes in higher education in Louisiana and the nation.

A fundamental change in higher education that accompanied the baby-boomers to college was the exchanging of "students' rights" for the previously accepted doctrine of *in loco parentis* ("in place of a parent"). Before the late 1960s, college authorities had acted in place of parents and established strict guidelines for "reasonable and appropriate" behavior both on and off campus.[716] The restrictions on activities were draconian by later standards, especially for female students. Students began asserting their rights in a direct challenge to *in loco parentis*. They argued that they were adults who had contracted with the university for education. The university was thus a service provider, not a parent. This led to a relaxation of controls on behavior. The 1974 Family Educational Rights and Privacy Act (FERPA) went further by limiting even parents' rights. For example, parents had no right to information on the academic progress of the students. [717]

The most prominent response in the nation to the great increase in students was the pioneering efforts of Clark Kerr in the state of California. In an approach that came to be known as the "California Model," Kerr set up three levels of higher education that were differentiated by mission. The highest level encompassed the most selective research universities. The middle level had regional universities that specialized in teaching undergraduates. The third level comprised open-access two-year colleges that offered remedial classes and served as a conduit to the higher levels. This approach was the basis for Mike Foster's reforms after 1996— in response to McKeithen's "all-in-one" approach—and will be discussed in detail in Chapter Eight.

McKeithen took a different approach and expanded offerings at currently existing colleges and universities. In a burst of reform activity, McKeithen upgraded colleges to universities, added high-level graduate programs, established new colleges and created a new statewide governance body.

The most emblematic action of McKeithen's "all-in-one" philosophy was the upgrading of six colleges to university status in 1970. McKeithen followed a national trend that saw the upgrading of colleges to universities for several reasons. A name change arguably aided the recruitment of students and faculty because of the added prestige. Also, with "university" on a diploma, graduates looked better to potential employers. Finally, the institutions had more of an advantage in the competition for private and federal grants.[718] The six universities of 1970—Louisiana Tech University, McNeese State University, Nicholls State University, Northeast Louisiana University, Northwestern State University, and Southeastern Louisiana University—joined the University of Southwestern Louisiana which had been promoted to university status in 1960. Nicholls was almost a university in 1968, but McKeithen vetoed the bill, only so it could be promoted under the auspices of the new statewide governance body.[719]

Another telling feature of McKeithen's "all-in-one" philosophy was the authorization of five universities to offer doctoral degrees in 1967. Doctoral degrees are considered the highest level of knowledge attainment. They bring great prestige to the professors and students, but they are extremely expensive for a university to offer. In the California Model, Kerr strictly limited the awarding of doctoral degree to the highest tier of universities, due to their great expense. At a meeting in late 1967, the State Board authorized doctorates for many of its universities. [720][721] The institutions authorized the doctorate in 1967 were Louisiana Tech University, McNeese State University, the University of Southwestern Louisiana, Northeast Louisiana University, and Northwestern State University

Also under McKeithen, five two-year colleges were established. Unlike with Kerr in California (with over 100) and much of the rest of the nation, Louisiana deliberately chose to establish very few academic two-year colleges, generally called "community colleges." Only the institution that became Delgado Community College existed before 1964. The lack of community colleges can be ascribed to two main developments. First, most typical community college academic functions like developmental education and the freshman/sophomore level transfer classes were performed at the university level. Second, most typical vocational functions were performed at the vocational-technical colleges that were separate and did not offer an "academic" mission.

The five two-year colleges established by McKeithen represented varying missions. LSU—Shreveport was established as a two-year college in 1964, and the first classes began on September 21, 1967. In 1972, it was promoted to four-year college status. Two of the colleges served mainly as feeders to their respective universities. LSU—Eunice became a two-year school in 1964, and ground-breaking ceremonies were held in May 1966.[722] Southern University at Shreveport was also established in 1964 and opened on September 19, 1967. [723] Finally, the institutions that became Bossier Parish Community College and Elaine P. Nunez Community College were established in 1967 as pilot programs that added Thirteenth and Fourteenth Grades to secondary school systems. The establishment of the colleges in Shreveport fell into the familiar pattern of dual institutions for whites and blacks. LSU—Shreveport and Southern University at Shreveport, both originally two-year colleges, are ten miles from each other. Currently, 16 miles separate Southern University at Shreveport and Bossier Parish Community College.

An illuminating example of McKeithen's governship can be seen in two interviews he gave to LSU professors in which he defined his impact on the state and on higher education. In response to the interviewer's query of his "most lasting achievements as governor," McKeithen cited the industrial complex in the New Orleans area and improved race relations.[724] Though higher education was notably absent in his short list, the governor did remark that he was "prouder of the new colleges and universities I helped to build instead of that Superdome." [725]

McKeithen followed the historical trend of strongly favoring LSU. A proud LSU alumnus, McKeithen said that, as governor, "I think we had a real love affair," and that I went into the governor's office "with a burning ambition to help the university every way I could." [726] The interviewer questioned whether, as a LSU graduate, he would be deemed impartial, and McKeithen responded

> No, sir, the thing was I didn't care. Louisiana State University is our state university and a great university and I didn't care what people thought. They could like it or lump it. I guess you could put it like that. I was fair to the other colleges and universities . . . . [T]hese other colleges universities, they can't compete with LSU, anyway. They know that. With that in mind, I just went on about my business. I said, 'Well shucks, if they don't like it, it will be just too bad.' [727]

Despite the strong affection, McKeithen said that he never interfered with the LSU Board of Supervisors and that he maintained a respectful distance in official day-to-day matters.[728]

The establishment of higher education institutions in the Shreveport area gave an insight into McKeithen's informal method of decision-making. He said that he needed the "support of the people" and that, regarding the university system, Shreveport felt "greatly abandoned." He cited this as the reason for the "Eunice thing" and the "Shreveport thing," presumably the colleges established there. [729] Also, regarding the genesis of the Shreveport Medical School, McKeithen noted that "Edgar Hull recommended that we build a new medical school and he said, 'Shreveport is the place to build it.' I didn't ask him why. I had that much confidence in him and respect for him. I said, 'Well, if you feel like it we will do it.'" [730] Hull was a medical professional that McKeithen placed among the two or three people he most respected.

McKeithen's rapid rise in the political establishment came courtesy of Earl Long who chose McKeithen as a floor leader, despite his status as a young and new member of the Legislature. McKeithen noted the beginning of their professional relationship when he said that

> I didn't know Mr. Earl [Long]. He didn't know me from Adam when I came down here. Mr. Earl had known my mother in Texas . . . . Mr. Earl more or less adopted me. My mother never boasted about her relationship with Mr. Earl . . . . He'd speak real kind of her; he said 'Your mother was the best dancer and the nicest girl I ever knew.' She was in tight with Earl Long in the last four years. [731]

In a telling example of the power of the governor and the informal nature of the legislature, McKeithen said that he and E. Long typically would meet "for about thirty minutes and make up the state budget." [732]

Protests of the 1960s & 1970s

The turmoil on college campuses nationwide did not spare Louisiana in the 1960s and 1970s. Violent unrest generally sidestepped the white colleges in Louisiana. McNeese State was notable for being the only public college in the state, and possibly the nation, still trying to enforce hair regulations in the 1970s. [733] Historically-black campuses were not so fortunate, witnessing a series of protests that culminated with the death of two Southern University students in 1972. McKeithen is often credited for tamping down the racial protests that engulfed the nation during the late 1960s. A Louisiana history textbook contends that McKeithen's "most lasting accomplishment . . . came in the area of race relations."[734]

While previous Louisiana governors inflamed issues of race and integration to get elected, McKeithen sought peaceful coexistence, especially in higher education. Nonviolent responses to protests exemplified his approach. At Grambling, a student uprising occurred on October 25, 1967. About 800 students, representing 20% of the student body, resigned from the school in protest over "neglect of the academic program in favor of athletics." [735] Willie Zanders, student government president, said that like "many Southern Negro schools, Grambling is unable to produce the sort of atmosphere conducive to learning that the Southern Negro so desperately needs. That, basically, is the problem, and that is our complaint." [736] McKeithen worked with Grambling President R. W. E. Jones to quell the protest, and the students were expelled. At SUNO, McKeithen also successfully assisted in a protest at the request of the president.[737]

Events at Southern University mirrored the national Civil Rights Movement—both the non-violent, civil disobedience approach of Martin Luther King in the early 1960s and the separatist Black Power movement of the early 1970s. J. S. Clark was succeeded by his son, Felton Grandison Clark, in 1938. F. Clark served until 1969, and, according to historian Charles Vincent, "[d]emonstrations and sit-ins occupied a great portion of [his] and the administration's energy and talent." [738] Baton Rouge had taken an early and prominent role in the Civil Rights Movement, instituting a bus boycott that preceded the more famous 1955 Montgomery Bus Boycott by a couple of years. Vincent noted that the "Southern University student demonstrations from 1960-1962, were closely connected with the on-going drive for civil rights throughout the South, and the integrationist thrust." [739]

F. Clark personally opposed segregation and felt the best approach was its gradual eradication as educational levels increased among blacks. However, he took the demonstrations as personal attacks upon his leadership and sought to preserve the University. He was willing to expel student demonstrators, even though this measure satisfied the all white State Board of Education. [740] In March of 1960, there was a sit-in at a department store in Baton Rouge and a full-scale boycott of classes, when about 1500 students went to the Capitol in an orderly demonstration.[741] Clark carried out the State Board of Education directive that the protest leaders be expelled. In response to a

December 1961 protest, Clark closed the University, and when it reopened he required all students to re-register in order to weed out "trouble makers." Lawsuits lasted for several semesters with most students eventually gaining readmission. [742]

The more serious incident came under Clark's successor, George Leon Netterville, Jr., who, with exception of one year at Baton Rouge High School, had attended Southern University from 6th grade through college graduation. [743] Netterville was president during the Black Power movement, which, according to Vincent, was "characterized by an unwillingness to submit to any delay in recognition of black rights and a demand to have black studies taught." [744] A May 1969 demonstration on the Southern campus ended without violence even though National Guard troops and local police officers were called out to maintain order. [745] Demonstrations in 1972 did not meet such a peaceful end.

The protests that led to the deaths of two students on November 16, 1972, began over a month earlier as an effort to remove a white psychology teacher. Student demands escalated to a call for a new president and a black board of supervisors.[746] A group called Students United was formed and organized the ensuing protests. In late October, the group, with upwards of 6,700 people, marched five miles to the State Department of Education, intending to meet with the Superintendent. When he was out of town, they went another block to the State Capitol. Their demand to meet with the new governor, Edwin Edwards, was granted. In a ten minute meeting with six student leaders, Edwards promised to "work" for the students. [747]

About a week later, after having asked for Netterville's resignation, the students met en masse in the campus gym. Netterville responded by closing the University and ordering the students out of the dormitories. [748] Similar protests were happening across the state. SUNO students demanded the resignation of the president and other structural changes. At Grambling, the call for the resignation of the president escalated into small-scale destruction of property that necessitated the arrival of 200 State Police to the campus. Order was returned after the dismissal of several students. [749] Southern reopened on November 6, and Governor Edwards created a Blue Ribbon committee to monitor the situation.

On November 16 at 4:00 am, four Southern students, all members of Students United, were arrested. When the word got out, other students sought to obtain the release of the arrestees. Student United members assembled and decided to question the President about the arrests. Netterville apparently agreed to go downtown to see about the arrested students and left the campus. At Netterville's request, fifty-five sheriff's deputies and thirty state troopers arrived on the campus. They fired tear gas to disperse the crowd, and in the confusion, two students were killed by a shotgun round. [750] A report on the matter concluded that an unidentified sheriff's duty officer had fired the fatal round. [751] Governor Edwards closed the Southern campus, declared a state of emergency in Baton Rouge, and called the National Guard to the campus.[752] The Southern campus was eventually reopened in January of 1973. [753]

LCCHE—1ˢᵗ attempt at centralized governance / History of governance

McKeithen's reforms—the promotion of so many institutions to university status, the addition of so many doctoral degrees, and the establishment of five two-year colleges—had two major results. First, the "character" of the colleges and universities had been more-or-less established. For about another quarter of a century, there would be no more changes in mission, in locations, nor would there be the establishment of a college (with the exception of vocational-technical colleges). Louisiana colleges and universities continued to serve students and the state in a business-as-usual mode.

Second, in response to the proliferation—seemingly uncoordinated—of new programs at the individual colleges and universities, the focus of governors shifted to the governance of higher education as a whole. The existing governance institutions—the State Board of Education and the LSU Board of Supervisors—were more concerned with the details of running the colleges and universities under their respective control. McKeithen wanted to establish another organization that was concerned with long-range strategic planning and made sure the state's resources were used efficiently. In theory, this body dealt with strategy while the others operated a more operational level. McKeithen established this body—the Louisiana Coordinating Commission on Higher Education (LCCHE)—in 1968. Due to political resistance, it was not successful, but it established the framework for the creation of the Board of Regents in 1974. Before detailing the LCCHE, it is first necessary to look back at the history of state-level coordination of higher education in Louisiana.

Prior to 1921, the five public institutions of higher education each had a separate board of trustees or supervisors appointed by the governor or the State Board of Education. Each board considered only the interests of the individual institution. A 1942 *Louisiana Educational Survey* found that these boards were essentially "political bodies" that abdicated the bulk of their responsibilities to the institutions' presidents.[754] The Constitution of 1921 created two overall governing boards—the LSU Board of Supervisors which administered LSU and the State Board of Education which administered eight state institutions of higher education.[755] The new State Board of Education took office on January 1923.

In the 1930s, Huey Long turned the two boards into captive institutions of the governor's office. He hand-picked the successor to the retiring LSU president in 1930, and he routinely interfered in the affairs of the other state colleges as well. Before H. Long, the boards were obviously influenced by political considerations, but they did not seem to be overtly controlled. Historian T. Harry Williams noted that, in response to a college president saying the State Board—not the governor—was his boss, "Huey retorted with 'who the hell do you think is the Board's boss?'"[756]

By the early 1950s, higher education had grown enough so that the State Board of Education wanted to coordinate the governance of colleges and universities in the state that were outside of the LSU system. In 1953, the Board established "uniform curricula" across all of its colleges.[757] The attention of the State Board was not squarely on the matter of higher education because its purview included all public education—colleges, elementary schools, junior high schools, senior high schools and trade schools. The only exceptions were LSU and Delgado Trade School, which was controlled by the city of New Orleans.[758]

The 1940s and 1950s saw a series of studies and recommendations for a statewide governance organization, but none of the efforts came to fruition. Legislative Act 38 of 1946 established a study of public education and concluded that "'the problem of coordination of all education in the state is ACUTE!'"[759] Act 415 of 1948 called for the establishment of a state coordinating council on education. Its provisions were never carried out "due basically to the inability of the existing boards to work together to achieve over-all coordination of their activities." Funding was withdrawn in 1954 and the Act remained in effect until the 1968 creation of the LCCHE.[760] In 1954, the Louisiana Commission on Higher Education was created and charged with a comprehensive study of higher education. The Commission agreed with early studies that there was a lack of statewide coordination that needed to be remedied.[761] A 1958 legislative report recommended the creation of a board of regents for all state colleges.[762]

By 1968, the inertia surrounding a statewide governance body had been overcome, and the LCCHE was established. The growth in higher education of the McKeithen years caused statewide leaders to realize the importance of some type of coordination. In 1845, there were two public institutions of higher education; in 1900, 4; in 1945, 10; and by 1970, there were 21.[763] From 1966 to 1968 alone, six were established, three each in the LSU system and the statewide system.[764] Also, a 1968 survey on higher education noted that Louisiana was "top heavy with specialized, professional and graduate schools and lacking in a strong junior college and technical school base."[765] In 1968, the citizens voted 287,353 to 252,657 on a constitutional amendment for the creation of the LCCHE.[766]

Implemented on April 3, 1969, the main purpose of the LCCHE was to prevent "unnecessary duplication" in higher education.[767] The governance body had the authority to approve all new degree programs at public colleges and universities in the state with the exception of the LSU-administered schools. McKeithen hoped to reorganize the statewide higher education governance system in a more rational way. The wording of the Constitutional amendment summarized:

> In order that unnecessary duplication might be avoided and the resources of the state devoted to Higher Education might be better utilized, a Council to provide the leadership which such coordination requires should be established to end that the State of Louisiana may achieve excellence in the Higher Education of its youth through the efficient and effective utilization of all available resources and facilities.[768]

The seemingly straightforward and noble goal met the intransigence of the existing higher education boards and their member institutions. The LCCHE failed to fulfill its role as an effective coordinating body.

Despite its promise, the LCCHE faced constitutional and statutory limitations which constrained its ability to enforce compliance. Basically, the LCCHE was a "planning coordinating and advisory agency" that had no authority to enforce management decisions. The State Board of Education, the LSU Board of Supervisors, and the Legislature all had to voluntarily comply with its policy decisions. The LCCHE lacked sufficient sanctions to rein in uncooperative groups. According to historian Rochelle Nash, the constitutional and statutory limitations caused the LCCHE to be "unable to become the driving force in Louisiana higher education that its creators envisioned." [769]

One lasting positive effect of the LCCHE was its adoption of the 1972 *Master Plan Toward Balanced Growth in Louisiana Post-high School Education: Quantity and Quality.*[770]

Succeeding governors continued the precedent of creating Master Plans as the primary vehicle to outline their plans and goals for higher education. The LCCHE remained in place until the 1974 Constitution created the Board of Regents to take its place.

Historical primer on two-year colleges

With the surge of activity by McKeithen, the age of character-building for four-year colleges was over. The majority of colleges had achieved their final university status, graduate programs and locations. McKeithen concentrated his reform efforts on the academic side of higher education. The next thirty years were devoted to the development of two-year colleges. McKeithen's immediate successor, Edwin Edwards, seemed to believe that the path to educational success in Louisiana depended upon vocational-technical colleges, not academic universities. Mike Foster, governor in 1996, put his faith in community colleges. It is important to take a step back and sort out the differences in educational philosophies and missions of the included institutions of higher education before moving on.

The definition of four-year colleges and universities is generally clear—institutions with programs of postsecondary instruction that take about four years to complete for a full-time student and end with a Bachelor's Degree. Often, these institutions offer further instruction that results in a Master's or Ph.D. degree. A "college" is generally a small institution that features a single subject area—for example a liberal arts college with a single "College of Arts & Sciences" and no other areas. A "university" is generally an institution that encompasses two or more individual "colleges." For example, a university might have a "College of Arts & Sciences," a "College of Education," a "College of Engineering," and a "College of Business." Usually, only universities offer graduate degrees. Of course there are numerous exceptions. Also, an average student might now take five or six years to earn an undergraduate degree. Within the general public and academic community, however, a basic description is understood and agreed upon.

In contrast, the definition of a two-year college involves a thicket of overlapping missions and purposes. This lack of clarity has resulted in a bewildering array of names—junior college, community college, comprehensive community college, vocational college, technical college, vocational-technical college, technical community college, 13th & 14th grades—and the list goes on. In order to understand the nature of two-year colleges, it is important to offer a brief historical primer of their development.

The first pre-cursors to modern two-year colleges were called "junior colleges," with the first established in 1901. At a time of extremely low college attendance, they were seen as a bridge for unprepared students. Walter Crosby Eells, an influential thinker writing in the 1930s, first examined the four "commonly recognized functions" of the junior college.[771] The first is the "popularizing function" which is often equated with the process of "democratization." The second is the "preparatory function" which equates to the idea of transfer to a four-year college. The third function, called "terminal" by Eells, closely corresponds with what came to be called the "vocational-technical" function of two-year colleges. The fourth was the "guidance function" which has generally gone under the same name in later history.

The popularizing function described the then revolutionary fulfillment of higher educational aspirations by allowing a greater stratum of society to attend a junior college. Eells defined the "popularizing function" as giving "the advantage of college education of a general nature to high school graduates who could not otherwise secure it for geographical or economic reasons; and to give similar benefits to mature residents of the community."[772] He felt the junior college should be the "people's college" and available to all Americans. He felt it should provide higher educational opportunity for the "mass of high school graduates who can't, won't, or shouldn't become university students."[773] One of the principal barriers in the popularizing function noted by Eells was the geographical barrier. He wrote that long distance is a strong deterrence to college attendance.[774]

The preparatory function described what contemporaries referred to as the "junior division" of university study, the first two years. Eells wrote that the "preparatory function" of junior colleges was to "give two years of work locally, equivalent to that given in the freshman and sophomore years of standard universities, which will adequately prepare students for upper division specializations in the university." [775] This transfer function has become the mission most synonymous with two-year colleges in the mind of the public.[776]

The terminal function has come to be identified with the vocational nature of two-year colleges where students terminate their schooling in two years, generally in preparation for the workforce. Eells defined this "terminal functional" as giving "specific preparation by vocational courses for specific occupations on the semi-professional level, qualifying students who finish them for immediate place in a definite life occupation." [777] The vocational offerings of a two-year college have generally been associated with trades like carpentry and welding.

The final function, of guidance, has been a central part of two-year colleges since this era. Eells wrote that the guidance function "assumes a scientific interest in the individual traits and ability and the personal welfare of young students, in training them to think, in organizing their studies effectively, in supervising their teaching, and in making the college experience of each profitable to him to an optimum degree." [778] Over the twentieth century, two-year college students have generally been less prepared than their four-year college peers in academic, social and emotional areas upon entry into college. The guidance function has helped two-year college students gain the needed skills in academic and non-academic areas.

Since Eells' writing in 1931, the core functions have remained the same, though additional missions have been added. W. D. Breneman and S. C. Nelson, writing in 1981, noted two additional missions. First is remedial or developmental education intended to bring deficiently-prepared students up to a collegiate level. Second is the availability of non-degree classes and community service activities. This includes courses geared toward leisure activities, like yoga, or courses that are vocational in nature but don't require enrolling in a full program, like a real estate exam preparation course. [779]

The difficulty in reconciling many of these varied (and sometimes contradictory) missions has been explored by many of the leading thinkers on two-year colleges. Blocker, Plummer, and Richardson contended that the "two-year college is probably more diverse in defined functions, programs, clientele, and philosophical bases than any other educational institution in existence." [780] Thomas Diener noted that "[o]ne reason the junior college in the United States has been difficult to understand is that it has taken on so many forms of sponsorship and control." [781] Gregory Goodwin continued that "[c]onfusions resulting from various names for community-junior colleges is a reflection of the complexity of the overall movement, not merely a case of faulty terminology." [782]

PART III

Contemporary Higher Education in Louisiana:
1972-2004

Before exploring this contemporary age of Louisiana higher education in detail, it is necessary to discuss a factor it shares with the earlier time—the recurrent theme of low educational attainment. In the distant past of French and Spanish domination and the Civil War, Louisiana lagged on measures of literacy. In the more recent times, the standard of measure has changed to "low educational attainment," but the underlying deficiency has remained constant. Put simply, the people of Louisiana have not emphasized the role of education as much as the nation.

What are the implications of this path? For most of American history, the lack of a college education has not been a barrier to a relatively prosperous life. Up to 1900, less than 5% of Americans attended college and a liberal arts education of Latin and Greek did not promise a lucrative existence in a largely agrarian economy. Even as attendance surged through the 1970s, a majority of individuals could comfortably support a family without a college degree. Towards the end of the twentieth century, however, society changed, and the skills implicit in a higher education became increasingly necessary to garner the advantages of a middle-class lifestyle. As international economic changes pushed increasingly more unskilled and low-skilled manufacturing jobs to other countries, the prospects for a hard-worker with a high school degree or less became diminished.

Louisiana has been able to weather the low level of educational attainment in the past. At the turn of the twenty-first century, however, American businesses are increasingly reliant on skilled workers. As a consequence, it has been difficult for the state to attract business due to the lack of trained workers. In turn, the lack of economic prosperity has resulted in a low ranking in many quality-of-life indicators. Louisiana's historical lack of emphasis on education has become a significant impediment to the progress of the state.

It is important to take a brief break from the history and look at the end result of Louisiana's twentieth-century educational journey. The *USA Today* reported that Louisiana was 48th in the nation in the rankings of the percentage of residents 25 and older with high school diplomas in 2002.[783] Also, the state has poor national rankings in the areas of adult literacy and high school dropouts. [784] Louisiana's official long-term strategic-planning document, *Vision 2020*, starkly admits that the state has a "system of public education that has not imparted to its students the skills and training necessary for many to qualify for or retain advanced, technology-based jobs in a globally competitive job market." The state's overall educational deficiencies, of course, correlate to the state's deficiencies in higher education.

So what are the causes of the low educational attainment? It is not ignorance of the problem or ambivalence about the importance of education to individuals and society. The leaders of Louisiana recognize that education is an important element in the lives of the state's citizens. *Vision 2020* acknowledged that the "right to a good education is fundamental to our democratic society. No human being should be denied the right to participate fully in the free enterprise system because of the lack of education." [785]

The exact cause is a complex and thorny issue, and in the end it might be unknowable. In working with society in general, it is often beyond the scope of a history to answer questions of cause and effect. That being said, it seems apparent that the poverty of the state is at least a contributing factor. Louisiana has historically been a poor state. In 2001, Louisiana ranked 45th in the nation in per capita personal income.[786] Also, Louisiana consistently has one of the highest percentages of people living in poverty.[787] According to *Vision 2020*, this high poverty rate results in "large numbers of citizens who are not benefiting sufficiently from or contributing sufficiently to Louisiana's economy."[788] In conjunction with the "large pockets of chronic poverty," many adults are outside the workforce because they do not have the education and skills to compete in a modern economy.[789]

A related contributing factor is Louisiana's poor record of funding for education. Besides the obvious factor of general poverty, four additional factors have contributed to the poor funding. First, the state has a high rate of attendance at private and parochial schools,[790] which tends to de-emphasize the support for higher taxes to support public schools. Second, the large rural population has been "said to be leery of change in general and to have had a limited interest in pursuing educational change."[791] Third, property taxes, a typical way for funding much of the cost of education, are especially low, and governors who have tried to increase them have been punished by the voters. In general, the average citizen has benefited from "generous" government services without a heavy tax burden usually required to pay for them.[792]

A final factor in the poor funding for education is that traditional funding sources have been reduced in the last two decades of the twentieth century. Historically, from the end of Reconstruction to 1928, Louisiana was governed by the economically conservative Bourbon Democrats with a low tax and low spending philosophy. From 1928, when Huey Long was elected, to the 1980s, the populist spending was mostly financed by oil revenues.[793] The "oil bust" of the mid-1980s caused an economic crisis, and the state has not recovered to previous economic levels.[794] An economic upturn in the mid-1990s and oil industry stabilization allowed a medium level of prosperity but there were fewer high-wage, low-skilled jobs.[795]

Adding to the complexity is that low educational attainment is both cause and effect of the poverty of the state. The state is relatively poor, in large part, because of the low educational attainment. The state has low educational attainment, in large part, because it is relatively poor. Breaking this vicious cycle is important to the future prosperity of the state and its citizens. As will be seen, the impetus behind reform activity in higher education in Louisiana at the end of the twentieth century rested on the attempt to break this cycle by improving the organization of higher education in the state.

CHAPTER 7

1972 to 1996: Edwin Edwards

Following the establishment of the "all-in-one" tenor to public higher education by Governor John McKeithen, the era from 1972 to 1996 was characterized by the dominance of Governor Edwin Edwards. Edwards served four terms and generally eschewed reform in higher education, with the notable exceptions of vocational-technical colleges and a reorganization of the state's governance system with a new constitution in 1974. Governor Buddy Roemer attempted but failed to reform higher education in the face of pervasive national social changes. This failure set the stage for Governor "Mike" Foster's successful reforms after 1996.

Louisiana experienced two major trends in the 1980s that fundamentally altered the economy, society, and higher education. An "oil boom" that lasted through the 1970s and early 1980s brought significantly increased revenues to the state. This translated into significant budget increases for the colleges and universities. It also provided economic prosperity and job opportunities for the graduates. A devastating "oil bust" beginning in 1983 leeched revenues from the state and resulted in severe cuts in higher education. Likewise, the state's economy declined precipitously and had not recovered its previous levels by the dawn twenty-first century. These two events influenced the parameters within which the governors of the era could operate.

The oil boom of the 1970s was a time of economic optimism for Louisiana. Since the days of Huey Long, the state had relied heavily on revenues generated from the oil and gas industry. Edwin Edwards instituted legislation that changed the way severance taxes on oil were calculated. Noting the continued presence of executive centralism, the measure was "duly passed by a compliant legislature." [796] Before the tax was based on volume, but Edwards changed it to be based on value. His timing was superb, and the state benefited from a historic increase in the price of oil. The price increased throughout the 1970s, and just between 1979 and 1982, the deregulation of crude oil produced nearly $1 billion in extra income for Louisiana. As sometimes happens with politicians, "[s]uddenly flush with money, Louisiana saw its spending mushroom." [797]

The abundant prosperity for over a decade magnified the fall from the oil bust beginning in 1983. In the early 1980s, significant new sources of oil were developed in the North Sea and in Alaska. Also, the Organization of Petroleum Exporting Countries greatly increased production of petroleum products. These factors contributed to a worldwide glut of oil and gas. With supply up, the price fell, and local production plummeted. Additionally, Ronald Reagan deregulated gasoline which cut the price of a gallon of gas from $1.30 to $1.00 in one month. In 1982, oil was $35 per barrel. By 1986, the price had declined to $11 per barrel. The principal sources of Louisiana's revenue dried up.[798]

The economic effect of the oil bust was devastating. While the rest of the nation enjoyed prosperity, within three years, a major depression hit Louisiana. Unemployment rose and wages declined. The energy industry laid off tens of thousands of workers. From 1983 to 1989, Louisiana had the highest unemployment rate in the nation with a net loss of 170,000 jobs. As people "voted with their feet," the state suffered a net population loss in the 1980s.[799] By at least 1995, the economy had not recovered to pre-1983 levels.[800] The effect on higher education was equally severe. With the decline in state revenues, public colleges and universities saw their budget cut significantly eleven times in four years.[801]

Edwin Edwards dominates the era

Edwin Edwards dominated the era in Louisiana and rose to national fame as a flamboyant figure. He was governor from 1972 to 1980, from 1984 to 1988, and again from 1992 to 1996. When Kathleen Blanco was elected governor in 2004, she was the first Louisiana governor in almost thirty years who did not follow Edwards into office. The Constitution of 1974, that replaced the much-amended Constitution of 1921, is often considered his signal achievement.

Like Huey Long with charges of dictatorship and like Earl Long with episodes of mental instability, Edwards gained national infamy. Federal racketeering charges involving governmental corruption made Edwards "a figure of national notoriety."[802] In February of 1985, Edwards was named in a 51-count federal indictment, though he was never found guilty of the charges. He was the subject of many other allegations. Edwards was eventually found guilty of corruption charges and began serving time in a federal prison starting in 2002. U. S. Attorney Jim Letten summarized that Edwards represented "the legend of the Louisiana politician who is above the law, who is too smart, too good looking, too quick, too clever to be caught by authorities, a legend that has cost us in Louisiana in terms of loss of investment, of jobs.'"[803]

The historical power of the governor in Louisiana was intact during Edwin Edwards' terms. He was renowned for abusing his political power, as evidenced by his conviction on corruption charges.[804] Perhaps befitting the power of the position, the 1983 campaign between Edwards and David Treen featured expenditures that "likely translate into the highest spending per voter for any governor's race ever conducted in the United States." [805]

Two examples showed Edwards' involvement in higher education. The first involved the overturning of a reform instituted in the administration that preceded Edwards'. Governor Roemer had created a state watchdog post to follow up complaints about government wrongdoing by Louisiana citizens. He chose Bill Lynch, "a crusty former investigative reporter for the New Orleans *Times-Picayune* and a 35-year observer of Louisiana's wheeler-dealer style of politics" to fill the post. The result was several high-profile investigations of abuses at Louisiana universities. [806] After his election, Governor Edwards issued an executive order that precluded Lynch from investigating the state's institutions of higher education. Lynch was quoted as saying that he believed "the order was issued due to politics." [807]

A second example involved a direct appeal to a governance body. In an earlier Edwards' term, the Board of Regents had voted to terminate some programs in an attempt to reduce "unnecessary duplication." Edwards removed five members of the board during the 1987 gubernatorial campaign, and after the new Regents were seated, "Governor Edwards made an unprecedented appearance before the board and asked it to reconsider the terminations, and they were rescinded." [808] Kerry P. Davidson, deputy commissioner for the Board of Regents noted that this "was the last time the regents forced any institution to terminate a program.[809] A Louisiana history textbook aptly summarized that during "his four terms as governor, Edwin Edwards would demonstrate on numerous occasions that a strong chief executive still had many powers with which to run the state the way he wanted." [810]

In the realm of higher education, Edwards had a curious approach where he accomplished some significant reforms yet seemed to have a disinterest (or worse) toward the academic goals of colleges and universities. He had two far-reaching reforms. First was an expansion of Louisiana's vocational-technical colleges. Second was a major reformulation of the higher education governance system with the Constitution of 1974.

Vocational-technical Boom (including early history)

Given the oil boom economy, Louisiana in the 1970s had a high demand for vocational-technical skills. The surging petrochemical industry provided a large number of "well-paying, low-skill roughneck jobs in the oil patch." A high-school graduate could find a job that provided a middle-class lifestyle. With the addition of the skills of a trade such as welding or pipefitting, a lifelong career with a good salary and benefits was feasible. If the goal was getting a good job or "workforce development" (from the state's perspective), then it arguably made more sense to avoid an academic path while concentrating on acquiring vocational-technical skills. In the long run, this emphasis contributed to an increased illiteracy rate and low high school and college graduation rates and became a problem when the nature of jobs changed in the late 1980s. In the short run, low-skilled workers could reach their financial goals without an academic education. [811] It was in the boom years of the vocational-technical occupations that Edwin Edwards expanded Louisiana's vo-tech colleges.

Leading up to the critical 1973 legislation that greatly expanded the vo-tech colleges, there was a debate over the direction of higher education. Should state revenues be directed primarily to four-year colleges and universities that prepare a small minority of Louisiana's citizens for leadership positions? Or should most state revenues be directed towards helping the majority of citizens—who likely will not graduate from a four-year school—get as much education as possible to be qualified for a semi-skilled job or to excel at a low-skilled job?

In the oil boom years of plentiful low-skilled jobs, many citizens and public officials argued that the emphasis on the college-bound segment of the higher education population was unwise when only 13% of students who entered first grade went on to graduate from a four-year college. The educational system should be re-oriented towards vo-tech and career education which was "aimed at retaining more youth in school and making all youth socially and financially independent insofar as their ability permits."[812] Edwards agreed and instituted a reform program, eventually costing about $200 million, that was enacted to correct two major deficiencies in the Louisiana system. The first was the "the lack of occupational skills which has deterred Louisiana's economic growth." The second goal was "the lack of an educational alternative for those who did not want to go to college." [813]

Before detailing Edwards' reforms, it is important to consider the nature of vocational-technical colleges (vo-techs). Put simply, are vo-techs "real" colleges? They provide a curriculum that teaches skills beyond the level of high school but generally short of an academic college level. This in-between nature of vo-techs, which persists to the present, has limited the amount of prestige attached by the academic community and the public. [814] The debate had not been decided in Louisiana, as of 2004. The vo-techs are included among the state's community college system, which indicates recognition of their "academic" status. However, a Board of Regents document used two separate terms "higher education" and "postsecondary education" in order to "distinguish the traditional degree granting two- and four-year institutions from the campuses of the Louisiana Technical College (LTC)."[815] The LTC is a single college that comprises the state's vo-tech campuses. This indicates a "less-than-academic" status. The outcome of the debate will likely be important to Louisiana in the twenty-first century, but in the 1970s, vo-techs had a rising importance to the state.

Edwin Edwards' first two terms witnessed a massive expansion of vo-tech colleges. The first of the vo-tech colleges, originally known as "Trade Schools," was established in Bogalusa in November of 1930. The second college was established in Shreveport in 1936. Five more colleges—in Winnfield, Crowley, Lake Charles, Opelousas, and Natchitoches—were established with the passage of Louisiana Legislative Act

14 in 1938. Three more colleges were established in the 1940s. Between 1950 and 1957, seventeen more colleges were added as a result of the Vocational Education Act of 1946. [816] From 1958 to 1973, only six vo-tech colleges were established leaving a total of 33.[817] As a result of Edwards' legislation passed in 1973, there would be 52 colleges by 1982. The total included 8 regional institutes, 19 area colleges and 25 branch colleges. Of the total, 10 were new colleges that replaced existing ones, 22 represented new construction, and the remainder were refurbishments of existing colleges.[818]

Leading up to the reforms enacted by Acts 208 and 209 of the 1973 Legislature, the vo-tech system was in poor shape. In an analysis, the Public Affairs Research Council (PARC) noted that though Louisiana was one of the first states to initiate vo-tech schools, it had fallen far behind. The programs provided in the schools were "unplanned, uncoordinated and underfinanced" and "hardly anyone knows what programs exist, where they are located, what they are doing, and what they plan to do." [819] PARC cited that a basic weakness in the system was that Louisiana had "failed to develop a philosophy for vocational-technical education." [820] Also, the vo-tech facilities were seen as "dilapidated and overcrowded." [821]

Despite the significant investment, PARC found that the resulting vo-tech system was not very effective due to the inadequate administrative system. Oversight of the colleges was split between the State Board of Elementary and Secondary Education (BESE) and the State Department of Education (SDE). BESE hired the directors of the colleges, while SDE was responsible for implementing board policy. In effect, this meant that BESE could set policy but it could not hold the SDE accountable for implementing it. In staffing, BESE had no say in the selection of the state vo-tech administrative staff, while the SDE had no direct control over the directors. [822] The result of this bifurcated organization was that BESE and the SDE "made little, if any, improvement in collecting and processing vo-tech data necessary to plan, budget, manage and evaluate vo-tech schools and the programs they offer." [823] It also created an adversarial relationship between the two organizations. Only a small portion of the students finished the programs. [824]

The curious result was that Edwards enacted far-reaching reforms but almost purposely allowed them not to work effectively. It seemed that there was some other purpose for the reform other than working towards some type of learning outcome. Having many unconnected fiefdoms in many communities all over the state offered a plethora of patronage possibilities which might be part of the explanation.

1974 Constitution—the Board of Regents & *Master Plans*

The Constitution of 1974 is another example of an action by Edwards that significantly impacted higher education in the state yet, ironically, seemingly demonstrated Edwards' lack of interest in higher education. On the one hand, the Constitution set the fundamental governance structure for public higher education that was in place as of 2004. On the other hand, higher education issues were discussed on the 84th to 87th days of the Constitutional Convention of 1973, a schedule that indicated a relatively low priority.[825]

In the lead-up to the Constitution of 1974, voters were given two choices in the reorganization of statewide higher education governance. The first was a single statewide planning and coordinating board—later termed a "superboard." An amendment was proposed to make the State Superintendent the Chief Executive Officer of both the statewide Board of Elementary and Secondary Education (BESE) and the Higher Education Board. This alternative was rejected because of the "massive concentration of power it would have placed in the hands of one single individual." [826]

The second alternative, which was adopted, featured a four-board system consisting of three management boards—the Board of Supervisors of Louisiana State University, the Board of Supervisors of Southern University and the Board of Trustees for State Colleges and Universities with one statewide planning and coordinating agency, the Board of Regents. [827] The Boards were officially recognized by Article VIII of the 1974 Constitution of Louisiana, and were implemented by Act 313 of the 1975 Legislature. In addition, BESE had the responsibility for overseeing vocational-technical education at the high school and college level.

The Board of Regents adopted *The Master Plan for Higher Education in Louisiana* in December of 1977 to outline the intended direction of higher education. The Board of Regents was granted more extensive control than the LCCHE.[828] With a few modifications, this basic governance structure is still intact as of 2004. Also, succeeding *Master Plans* have remained the principal expression of the Louisiana's long-term strategy for public higher education.

Segregated education & The Desegregation Lawsuit

During the era, a federal lawsuit responded to the state's long and consistent history of segregated higher education. The lawsuit was initiated in the early 1970s by civil-rights groups. It wended its way through the legal system before finally ending in 1994 with the approval of "broad changes aimed at desegregating the state's colleges." [829] The lawsuit influenced the actions of every governor through 2004 and likely will affect future governors as well.

The national context of what became the Louisiana desegregation lawsuit (as well as many others across the nation) began in 1964 when Lyndon Johnson signed the Civil Rights Act. The Act, prohibiting discrimination based on race, color, or national origin at all colleges and other entities that receive federal funds, provided the basis for the federal enforcement of integration in higher education. Federal oversight of states' efforts in desegregating public institutions of higher education increased greatly when a federal appeals court ordered the U.S. Department of Health, Education, and Welfare (HEW) to take a more active role in the late 1960s. [830]

Another seminal national development occurred in 1992 when the U. S. Supreme Court agreed to hear a case that originated with the father of a student at historically-black Jackson State University in Mississippi. The Supreme Court increased what states needed to do to remove the vestiges of segregation and ruled that "states must reform all policies that perpetuate segregation 'to the extent practicable and consistent with sound educational practices.'" [831] In the case, *US v. Kirk Fordice* (but commonly known as *Fordice)*, the decision basically said that states could encourage desegregation by making sure that historically-black and white institutions that were near each other did not offer "broadly similar" academic programs.[832] As of 2004, eleven states have technically moved beyond the past segregation and have plans that "generally call for more programs and facilities at historically black colleges, increased diversity in student bodies at predominantly white and historically black institutions, and unique missions for each institution to eliminate duplicate programs, some of the last vestiges of 'separate but equal.'" [833]

In Louisiana, the desegregation lawsuit had a long and varied history that impacted the higher education decisions made by governors over its twenty-six year run. In 1969, HEW determined that Louisiana had a system of separate public colleges for African-American and white students which was a violation of federal anti-bias laws. [834] In 1974, the U. S. Justice Department sued the state of Louisiana for "maintaining a segregated university system and spending more money on programs and facilities at predominantly white colleges than at historically black colleges." [835] For the next seven years, the case went through the courts.

In September 1981, a Consent Decree was filed in the settlement of the long-standing lawsuit. While the State denied the charges, it nevertheless settled the case before a trial. The State of Louisiana was bound through December of 1987 by the following provisions:

1. Implementation of intensified other-race student recruitment by all institutions;
2. Expansion of developmental education offerings for under-prepared students;
3. Increases in informational activities designed to inform the public of available Higher Education opportunities;
4. Scholarships for African-American graduate and professional students; and
5. Regular dissemination of lists of college-bound students who take certain standardized tests. [836]

Among the other provisions was the mandate to assist Southern University at Shreveport to develop into a comprehensive community college. [837]

A curious irony of the Consent Decree involved Grambling University. The Board of Trustees, the governance body for the public universities not affiliated with LSU, was one of the targets of the lawsuit. Grambling was the only historically-black university in the Board of Trustees. Thus, Grambling was essentially a target of the Consent

Decree for promoting segregation when the unequal conditions had been to the detriment of the University and its students.[838]

In 1988, after the expiration of the Consent Decree, Federal District Judge Charles Schwartz, Jr. and two other judges issued a ruling that Louisiana had been engaging in illegal segregation and ordered a series of changes to revamp the higher education system to promote more integration.[839] The order was based on a report commissioned by the court. Paul R. Verkuil, president of the College of William and Mary, was appointed a special master in 1988 and asked to evaluate desegregation efforts and develop an integration plan. The plan he produced was more far-reaching than the remedy in the 17 other states that had been subject to desegregation orders. In those other states, most plans had been limited to requiring new recruitment programs at predominantly white colleges and mandating facility improvements at historically black colleges. Verkuil, however, proposed "a new governance system, a revamping of the missions of most state colleges, and the introduction of admission standards." [840] The judges accepted the plan and ordered the state to carry it out.

In 1990, Judge Schwartz withdrew this earlier ruling. A federal appeals court ruling on a Mississippi desegregation case (which eventually became *Fordice*) had outlined a basis for determining whether or not a state had successfully desegregated. Since Louisiana was in the same judicial district, the standards also applied. Louisiana had met the standards.[841] The issue was then put up for consideration of the U. S. Supreme Court. When the Supreme Court ruled that it lacked jurisdiction to determine the matter, the case then had to be taken up again in a federal appeals court. This ended the hopes for a quick solution and left the desegregation plans in a legal limbo. Since more challenges would assuredly be forthcoming, the governor indicated that he "did not know whether he is legally obligated to abide by the plan, or whether it would be politically astute to do so." [842]

Judge Schwartz disagreed with the findings of the Mississippi case, but he had no choice but to go along with the findings. He still believed that a major reorganization was needed and desegregation could only be achieved by combining the three governance boards into a single one.[843] He argued that "enrollment patterns or discrepancies in financial support for white and black colleges were signs of illegal segregation." [844] This standard was rejected by the Mississippi decision.[845] Governor Buddy Roemer, who will be discussed later in this chapter, embraced the plan as well—since it generally fit with his "superboard" proposal, though he denied that the state was operating a segregated system.[846]

The legal issues of the desegregation case continued under Edwards' final term as governor from 1992 to 1996. In 1992, the U. S. Supreme Court issued *Fordice*, which settled college desegregation issues. As discussed earlier, the decision basically said that states could encourage segregation by making sure that historically black and predominantly white institutions that were near each other did not offer "broadly similar" academic programs.[847]

In December of 1992, the Board of Regents approved a desegregation plan to overhaul the governance system in Louisiana as an effort to avoid an expected mandate from the federal courts. Federal Judge Schwartz had given the state a chance to come up with the one he ordered in 1990. [848] The proposal featured an overarching Board of Governors that would function as a "superboard." Underneath that board would be a "Board of Supervisors" to oversee LSU, Southern University's Baton Rouge campus, Southern's law center, LSU's law, medical and agriculture centers, and the University of Southwestern Louisiana. A "Board of Trustees" would govern the remaining ten four-year colleges. A "Board of Community Colleges" would govern all of the two-year colleges. [849]

Another key component of the plan addressed the requirements in *Fordice*. The plan sought to "force campuses where 90 per cent of the students are of one race to undertake aggressive recruitment efforts for 'other race' students." [850] This situation applied to historically black Grambling, Southern at Baton Rouge and SUNO as well as predominantly white Southeastern Louisiana Univ., LSU at Baton Rouge and LSU at Alexandria.

In January of 1993, a federal judge issued an order that approved the "superboard" idea,[851] and in March he refused to delay this earlier order.[852] Later in March, a federal appeals court blocked the desegregation order. Had the appeals court not acted, Louisiana officials would have been forced to begin the establishment of a "superboard" by April 23.[853] By January of 1994, a federal appeals court had thrown out the desegregation order and ordered Judge Schwartz to reconsider the entire case. At the time, African-American students made up 7% of enrollment at LSU, and white students 8% of Southern University.[854]

The proposed new trial was delayed to give the various constituencies a chance to come to an agreement.[855] An agreement was approved by a federal court in November of 1994. The agreement took effect in January of 1995 and was popular because it left "Louisiana's historically black and predominantly white public colleges open as separate institutions." [856] Governor Edwards supported the result and had actively encouraged a settlement, especially since the idea of a "superboard" was shelved. A hint that the issue was not completely settled; however, was voiced in the note that since Edwards had announced his retirement after that year, "some in Louisiana wonder if his successor will want to take the settlement back to the drawing boards." [857]

In 1995, the State of Louisiana finally entered into a final Settlement Agreement that ended the desegregation lawsuit. In general, resources and programs were allocated to predominantly African-American institutions to help achieve a reasonable parity, a push was made to eliminate duplicative programs, and recruitment efforts of minority students were stepped up at all universities, but especially at LSU and Southern University.

A major part of the Settlement Agreement was the creation of Baton Rouge Community College under the governance of the LSU and Southern University Board of Supervisors in a Joint Management Board configuration. [858] The college was established on June 28, 1995, and was "created as a racial mixing tool."[859] The college opened its doors on August 20, 1998. Reporter Mary Owen summarized the significance of the action, when she wrote that in "a state with a racial history as tortured as Louisiana's, the opening this month of Baton Rouge Community College represents something of a breakthrough." [860]

In a 2004 postscript, an analysis on the impact of the Settlement Agreement after a decade showed unpromising results. John Laplante, capitol bureau chief for *The Advocate*, wrote that "Baton Rouge's two universities remain about as segregated as they were nearly a decade ago, when state officials agreed to spend more than $120 million to erase all traces of the old policy of racial separation in Louisiana higher education."[861] In the fall of 2003, one of eleven students at LSU was African-American, compared to one of twelve in the fall of 1995. This represented only a slight improvement. In the fall of 2003, one out of fifty students at Southern University was white, compared to one of thirty in the fall of 1995. This represented increased segregation. James Caillier, who participated in the negotiations as president of the predecessor to the University of Louisiana System, said: "'We were perpetuating the status quo,' and everyone knew it."[862]

Roemer's instructive failures

Two governors broke up the three separate tenures of Edwin Edwards. David Treen was governor from 1980 to 1984 and was Louisiana's first Republican governor in the twentieth century.[863] He had a relatively uneventful tenure, including in the area of higher education, and his efforts were hampered by financial problems in the state that resulted from the oil bust's "financial nightmare of shrinking revenues." [864] The second governor, Charles E. "Buddy" Roemer III, planned ambitious reforms in higher education, but these reforms were thwarted. Because he was reacting to important national trends, however, his failures were instructive.

Though not successful in pushing through his most far-reaching ideas, Buddy Roemer was not reticent in using the power of his office to affect higher education. One example was Roemer's involvement in the 1990 search for a new president of Northeast Louisiana University. The Board of Trustees for State Colleges and Universities was charged with the search, but Roemer publicly backed a political ally even before the current president had officially announced he was going to step down. Roemer told reporters that State Sen. Lawson Swearingen "'would do a great job'" and downplayed the stated requirement for a doctorate since Swearingen did not have one.[865] Faculty members indicated that "the entire search process was a farce." [866] Sammie W. Cosper, the state's commissioner of higher education, said that it "'certainly looks like everything has been arranged.'" [867]

In his term from 1988 to 1992, Roemer highlighted education reform as a top goal. Upon his election, it was noted that educators hailed the victory as a sign that the state was "finally committed to improving education." [868] He declared that educational reform would be one of the defining issues of his agenda.[869] He was considered one of the "bright lights" in referring to governors who sought to improve educational efforts. [870] He took on the reform of the secondary educational system as well as that of higher education.

Roemer's secondary educational reform efforts were primarily based on teacher accountability issues.[871] The measures met widespread opposition and Roemer basically lost the publicity battle as well as the support of the legislature and teacher unions. Roemer antagonized teachers by linking pay raises to "a program of intensive evaluation of classroom performance." [872] Spencer J. Maxcy and Doreen O. Maxcy argued that, despite Louisiana's poor showing in education, "the Roemer Revolution was marked for failure from the start." [873] This failure was due to the political power of educators and their professional associations. They concluded that this failed reform ultimately led to Roemer's failed reelection bid. Roemer lost his re-election bid to Edwards, "long a friend of the teachers' organizations." When he got into power, Edwards "pulled the teeth out of the assessment movement." [874]

When Roemer took office, he was met by a series of challenges that had long plagued higher education in Louisiana. In designing a reform, he had to consider the following questions:

* How can the state end racial segregation?
* How can it compete nationally, even though its populist tradition has led its universities to adopt the lowest common denominator as their educational standard?
* How can a state whose natives joke about living in the 'northernmost banana republic' work toward a new level of fiscal and political responsibility? [875]

In outlining his policy pronouncements, Roemer said: "Higher education is the engine that will pull our economy. Otherwise, all we can do is compete with Singapore on a per-hour basis. If we can't be cheaper than the rest of the world—and we shouldn't try—we have to be faster, smarter, more flexible, more trainable." [876] He was labeled a reformer who sought to improve academic quality, reduce duplication of programs and increase faculty salaries. [877] Higher education was a higher priority to Roemer than it had been in previous administrations.[878]

The centerpiece of Roemer's higher education reform efforts was the creation of a "superboard" to simplify the governance of colleges and universities in the state. He proposed eliminating the three governing boards that existed at the time and transferring their authority to the Board of Regents. He argued that this would increase efficiency and was the easiest way to eliminate duplicative programs."[879] He also favored the establishment of a community college system[880] and the raising of admissions standards at what should be more selective universities. In pursuit of this latter goal, he quipped that to "'go to LSU, you're going to have to have more than a beating heart. You'll have to have a living brain.'" [881]

Roemer met stiff opposition from all sides over the "superboard" proposal as his efforts "increased already bitter divisions in this populist Gulf Coast state."[882] He antagonized virtually all of academia with the proposal. [883] Supporters of the predominantly white institutions charged that the Governor was simply seeking to control all of higher education.[884] Many of the universities felt they would lose power to the Governor's office or to the state's flagship institution, Louisiana State University, if they did not have their own board, and had other reasons for opposition.[885] David Duke, a state legislator and former Ku Klux Klan leader, rallied opposition to the plan by "accusing the Governor of shifting the tax burden from big business to people in the working class." [886] Louisiana's Legislative Black Caucus also led opposition to the plan because it would eliminate the Southern University System, the only historically black system in the country. [887]

Roemer failed to gain enough support for his superboard proposal, and this failure, in part, led to his unsuccessful re-election effort. A reporter for The Chronicle of Higher Education noted that the "stymied campaign to eliminate Louisiana's multi-board structure is perhaps the only blot on Governor Roemer's record." [888] He had successfully passed two balanced budgets and passed an omnibus education bill in only 18 months, among other successes. He was also not the first to fail at establishing a single-board system. In fact, he was a delegate at the 1973 Constitutional convention where multi-board and single-board options were put forth in an effort "to eliminate the Jim Crow provisions in the Louisiana Constitution.[889] At the time, he opposed the multi-board choice, but it was enacted.

The history of superboard attempts before Roemer had been equally unfruitful. As early as the 1930s, a report from a prominent educator had indicated the need for a single board with "'a centralization of responsibility for planning and management of state education.'" [890] Numerous attempts to institute such a board were consistently defeated. In the process of the 1968 LCCHE establishment, a superboard was expressly rejected by the LSU Board of Supervisors and the State Board of Education. State superintendent of education, William Dodd, "served notice" that he was prepared to fight any attempt to create what he termed a "superboard." [891] This was the first use of the term that this writer found.

In his re-election effort, most voters approved of Roemer but thought he lacked leadership ability after he lost "key fights over restrictive abortion legislation and his plan to reorganize the governance of the state's higher-education systems." [892] His switch from the Democratic to Republican Party also contributed to this perception. He had placed a high priority on reforming education in Louisiana, but according to Susan E. Howell, UNO Survey Research Center Director, 42% of the voters said that economic issues were most important and that "'[e]ducation as an issue is irrelevant.'" [893] In 1991, Roemer finished third in the open primary election behind Edwin Edwards and David Duke, with only the top two vote getters advancing the general election.

Roemer's lack of success reflected national trends / Stage set for Foster

Roemer's reform attempts were made in response to a fundamental shift in the national economy that reshaped the underlying philosophical basis for higher education. Though Roemer was not successful, Mike Foster responded to the same realities when he initiated fundamental reforms when he became governor in 1996. It is important to delve into the fundamental changes since they explain many of the succeeding actions.

The local conditions in Louisiana that gave impetus to higher education reform was the sharply diminished revenues as a result of the oil bust of the mid-1980s. The deficits in the state revenues led to the collapse of a series of college and university budgets. Also, the resulting contraction of the petroleum industry, upon which the economy was overwhelmingly dependent, led to a skyrocketing unemployment rate and an exodus of skilled workers and professionals. This oil bust left Louisiana of the 1990s in the unenviable position of having comparatively low revenues, high unemployment and a poorly educated workforce. [894]

The timing of the oil bust was especially bad because it came at a time of fundamental change in the nature of employment throughout the nation. In the preceding generations, it was quite possible for an individual without a college education to get a well-paying job that allowed a middle-class lifestyle. As improved technology and increased international trade conditions became insinuated into the American economy, however, the availability of high-salaried unskilled or semi-skilled jobs decreased rapidly. Employers placed a premium on highly educated workers. Businesses were increasingly willing to relocate to states that offered educated workers—and to shun states without them. An educated workforce became a key determinant in the overall financial condition of a state's population, offering significant monetary and non-monetary benefits. Success in higher education increasingly became an important indicator of the future prosperity of individuals, communities, and states.

The change in the nature of employment was the result of a complex series of factors. Globalization caused transformative changes on the American economy in the 1980s and 1990s. The end of the Cold War coincided with the development of far-reaching new technologies and led to an increase in international trade and communications. This set the stage for the out-migration of low-wage, unskilled jobs to cheaper Third World factories. Additionally, new technologies increasingly eliminated low-wage jobs in the United States. The result was a demand for "well-educated workers who understood mathematics, science, and technology and were prepared both to exercise individual initiative and to work in teams." [895]

Prior to the 1990s, unskilled workers could support their families via other roads than higher education, primarily in many manufacturing fields. In the 1990s, the new information economy began limiting the alternate choices so that higher education was increasingly the main avenue for a good job. [896] Education beyond high school became almost a necessity for a middle-class lifestyle. Patrick Callan, higher education scholar, summarized that if "opportunity is broadly defined as the chance to participate fully in society, higher education has become the only road to opportunity for most Americans." [897] He continued that for individuals, some postsecondary education has become a "virtual prerequisite for full participation in the economic, civic, and social benefits of our nation." [898] Also, states and communities needed a college-educated population to compete in the global economy.

Callan noted that two groups of Americans did not benefit from the gains of the last twenty-five years of the twentieth century. Individuals with only a high school education saw flat real income growth, and individuals who had not completed high school saw a decrease in real income. On the other hand, individuals with some college education or higher had an increase in real income as well as an increasing divergence from the lower-educated group. In 1975 the annual income of a worker with a bachelor's degree averaged 1.5 times that of a high school graduate. By 1999, the advantage had increased to 1.8 times. Compounded over a lifetime, these differences in educational level represent average lifetime earnings of $1.2 million for a high school graduate, $1.5 million for those with some college education but no degree, and $2.1 million for bachelor's degree holders. [899]

Nationally, it was governors—not higher education officials—who responded to the pressing problem. Employers could not find enough prepared workers and had to spend time and money educating what workers were available. Businesses complained to state officials who then began to question the cost and quality of high school and postsecondary education. Sensing a political need and opportunity for improving the quality of education, policy analyst Diane Ravitch noted that "governors, state legislators, and business leaders pressed for higher standards in the schools." [900]

This national reform movement swept higher education in the 1980s. J. Wade Gilley, scholar of higher education, argued that the 1980s witnessed a fundamental change in the leadership of higher education, specifically a shift as the driving influence in changes from the presidents of colleges and universities to the governors of states.[901] As the underlying economic environment changed, and college presidents were seen as unresponsive, governors felt the need to do something. This prompted increasing control over higher education by so-called "new governors" who believed that greater educational attainment of a state's citizens was the key to overcoming serious economic and social problems. [902]

When Ronald Reagan became president in the early 1980s, he sought to trim the power of federal government. This shifted more power to the states. Coincidentally, a group of governors elected in the mid-1970s "leaped at the opportunity to confront social and economic challenges." Compared to the past, these governors assumed a strong arm in state affairs. Concurrently, American higher education started to witness a shift from federal intervention to state control. University presidents were "confused, even hurt" at the lack of communication as the governors took more control over higher education. [903]

These "new governors" believed that higher education could play a key role in economic competitiveness as the type of available jobs shifted from low-skilled manufacturing to high-skilled, technology-oriented jobs. Economic indicators had become the most important measuring stick for governors, so they felt the need to act. Perceiving stonewalling from unresponsive higher education administrators, governors began to generate "their own ideas about the role of colleges and the curricula they should offer." [904] The governors were "action-oriented" and often constrained due to term limits. This resulted in an urge to institute significant changes quickly. They relied more on governmental advisors than educational officials.

In a 1986 survey[905] sent to all governors, 29 of 32 responding governors said education was the top priority. The same survey indicated that governors did not rely on higher education officials for advice about reforms. The stage was set for governors to take control of educational reforms without much input from college presidents. Gilley summarized that the "overall survey results clearly indicated that a rift exists between governors and college presidents, a breach that poses a serious problem for colleges and universities in the 1990s." [906]

This shift of control to governors was noted in the national context of having college presidents playing the largest role in higher education decisions. In Louisiana, with an already strong role for governors, the effect was magnified. Roemer attempted to harness the trends in the 1980s, but he was unsuccessful. Mike Foster fit the pattern almost perfectly when he became governor in 1996.

After Roemer failed to advance past the 1991 primary, Edwin Edwards defeated David Duke to become governor—taking office for his fourth term in 1992. Interestingly, political pundits generally agreed that Roemer would likely have defeated either of the two in a head-to-head election. In higher education, Edwards departed from the reform mentality the 1980s "new governors." He was more reactive and cognizant of the political importance of the higher education establishment and how it could be used to further his political base. Edwards indicated his priorities with a telling quotation when he said: "'[w]e need, in my judgment, to quit forcing everybody to get ready for college.'" [907] In looking back at the final Edwards term, a reporter summarized that despite his achievements, "some would say the money was spread too thin and there was not enough emphasis on promoting and supporting higher education as an economic development engine, as most other states elected to do." [908]

In the inherited controversy over Roemer's "superboard" proposal, Edwards was clearly against a consolidation of the governance boards. In large part, Edwards had been elected with the support of black voters.[909] Since proponents of Southern University[910] and many civil rights groups opposed the "superboard" idea, Edwards also opposed the plan. State Sen. Cleo Fields said the single board would hurt Southern by eliminating the system, and that "Mr. Edwards was a strong supporter of Southern University during his terms as governor, from 1972 to 1980 and 1984 to 1988. And Mr. Edwards has told black leaders that he is still committed to strengthening Southern." [911] Milton Womack, a member of the LSU System Board of Supervisors said that "Mr. Edwards has always been good for higher education—particularly the black colleges." [912] A reporter for The Chronicle of Higher Education commented that during Edwards' previous terms, "he was a strong supporter of higher education in general and historically black colleges in particular." [913] As in his earlier terms, Edwards favored the interests of the independent vocational-technical schools, and opposed a statewide consolidation of the governance of two-year colleges in the state. He was labeled "a populist who favors an expansion of vocational-school programs." [914]

CHAPTER 8

1996 to 2004: Mike Foster

In 1996, Governor Murphy Jame "Mike" Foster, Jr. began a series of reforms intended to replace McKeithen's "all-in-one" approach to higher education. Foster's philosophy opposed the idea of having universities fulfill the range of missions from developmental education to doctoral studies and instead advocated a strict differentiation of missions. The most significant reform was the diverting of underprepared students, especially those needing developmental education, away from universities to two-year colleges. Foster, the grandson of 1890s governor Murphy J. Foster,[915] pushed through the creation of the Louisiana Community and Technical College System that brought together most of the state's two-year colleges in a single system. The two-year colleges would educate students displaced from universities by the final plank of his reform efforts—the raising of admission standards at many of the state's colleges and universities in 2005. At the heart of Foster's reform efforts was the assumption of the cost-effectiveness of the "California Model" of higher education governance.

California Model

Before delving into Foster's far-reaching reforms, it is important to discuss their philosophical basis, the "California Model." This organizational system for public higher education descends from the California Master Plan for Higher Education, adopted in 1960, instituted by Clark Kerr.[916] It had great influence on the organization of higher education nation-wide and made Kerr one of the most prominent voices on colleges and universities. John Douglas, historian of the California Model, argued that to "a degree unmatched by any other state in the twentieth century, California embraced public higher education as a tool of socioeconomic engineering, and with dramatic results."[917]

Under the 1960 Master Plan, there were three separate tiers of education in California. The highest, the University of California System, comprised universities that had the most selective standards. The next highest, the California State University System, was more regional in nature and had selective standards that were a notch lower. The lowest tier was composed of a wide-ranging system of open-admission community colleges. The idea was that as students proved their merit at one level, they could move up to the next.[918]

In this tripartite structure, each level was assigned a specific and rigid mission. The stated goal was "to decrease redundancy among the state's network of colleges and university campuses and to encourage public institutions to excel in their own sphere of responsibility." [919]

The missions of the three levels were clearly defined. The University of California (UC) system, the most elite tier, offered bachelor's, master's, and professional degrees, as well as the Ph.D. The UC universities served the primary research and public service functions and took minor responsibility for awarding teacher credentials. The California State University (CSU) system offered bachelor's and master's degrees, had primary responsibility for teacher credentials, and had only minor research and public service functions. Finally, the community colleges offered associate's degrees, provided preparation for movement up to the UC and CSU institutions, and also provided vocational and adult education. [920] Community colleges were "better able to screen and do remedial work and counseling than are the other segments." [921]

There were three interesting facets of the Master Plan. The first was that only the UC system would offer Ph.D.s, though some joint doctoral work, especially in the field of Education, was anticipated. [922] Also, the set-up purposely avoided a centralized governing board. [923] Finally, the Master Plan intended for higher education to be tuition-free. [924]

The Master Plan had a primary goal of increasing access to the non-elite in the state. Douglass wrote that the "innovation of the tripartite system is, in no small measure, a reaction to this constant desire to serve the expanding needs of a burgeoning population and economy—the efforts of an activist state government to shape the future." [925]

A secondary benefit of California's Master Plan was its cost-effectiveness. This was an important role in the rationale for the use of the tripartite system in Louisiana. One of the most important effects was the extremely efficient delivery of educational services. Basically, developmental education and general education could be provided at the low-cost community colleges, whereas the more expensive upper division classes would be given to already-prepared students.

Another important cost-saving attribute of the system was that the structure helped to rein in unneeded expansion. The rigid definition of the role of each of the segments "avoided the high cost of all four-year public institutions attempting to provide the same academic programs. The concept was to give each segment a distinct mission, that, when combined, would meet the needs of the people of California." [926] In other states, the self-interest of colleges and universities led to expansion that resulted in "a proliferation of doctoral and costly research programs." [927] Another reason for the success was that the Master Plan "clarified the role of the legislature in policymaking." [928] In other words, the legislature could not meddle in order to increase patronage possibilities.

In two important documents, the Foster administration outlined its philosophy toward higher education. First, *Louisiana: Vision 2020*, a long-term strategic plan created under the Foster administration, demonstrated the pressing need for education reform. The document argued that one of the "key ingredients for a vibrant 21st century economy" is a "skilled and educated workforce."[929] A way to gain this workforce is to "sharpen its focus on providing training and re-training for today's jobs as well as those of the emerging, knowledge-based economy." [930] It said that the "diffusion of education throughout our state is critical to our overall success. As Louisiana sets out to eradicate poverty within its borders, education must be at the heart of all strategies." [931] It continued that the "right to a good education is fundamental to our democratic society. No human being should be denied the right to participate fully in the free enterprise system because of the lack of education." [932]

The *Master Plan for Public Postsecondary Education: 2001 (Master Plan)* spelled out the specifics of how the general philosophy was to be put into action. The document contained the practical details of applying the theoretical "California Model" to Louisiana. The Board of Regents (BOR), the governance body that oversaw public higher education in the state, had recognized the low performance of higher education as well as its larger effect on society. The BOR argued that the primary impediment to the state's future was that most of the new jobs created over the next decade required a level of college education or training not present in enough of the state's citizens. [933] Reform proponents argued that if many citizens are unprepared for the workforce, the individuals and the state will suffer adverse effects.

Foster's Reforms

Governor Mike Foster was elected for two full terms, from 1996 to 2004, and epitomized the 1980s "new governor" idea of reforming higher education to assist economic development. He made higher education reform a centerpiece of his administration. Former Governor Roemer assessed Foster's tenure by saying that "'I give him high marks for education improvements. There is nothing more important that a governor can do in this state.[934] Jim Brandt of PARC said that education reforms "'have certainly been the highlight of his administration.'" [935]

The historical power of the governor's office was intact under Foster. One example involved a dispute with the actions of the Tulane University Environmental Law Clinic's activities. When the Governor perceived that the Law Clinic's *pro bono* legal representation interfered with the state's efforts to attract new industry, he threatened to pull the tax breaks enjoyed by Tulane. A reporter for the *Chronicle of Higher Education* wrote that this raised questions "about the role that law clinics play in their communities, and whether politicians have a right to interfere with that role." [936]

A second example of Foster's use of the power of the governor's office involved the appointment of Bobby Jindal to lead the University of Louisiana system. Foster nominated Jindal on the same day of his application and just a single day before the national search ended. A week earlier, the requirement for a Ph.D. had been dropped, possibly because Jindal did not have one. It was reported that the "fix is in to give the top job . . . to Gov. Mike Foster's 27-year-old boy wonder, as even the Governor admits." [937] This type of language did not seem to raise an outcry, indicating that the process was fairly usual.

Foster's ultimately successful higher education efforts benefited from a general agreement on the need for reform from the general populace. The mid-1980s "oil bust" led to an economic crisis—high unemployment and a poorly educated workforce. Oil prices did not recover, which changed the public's view of education. The public realized the vital importance of diversifying the state's economy. It was clear that a skilled work force was the key to attracting new businesses. Writing in 1990, prominent education leaders noted that the "'changing mood of the last decade, driven by a deep economic crisis, has now created a consensus that compels reform.'"[938] Edwards might have taken advantage of the consensus, but he was not reform-minded. Foster took up the charge.

Foster's first concerted attempt at higher education reform was a resurrection of the superboard idea. When he was elected, his position was not known. Publicly, he had been "vague" on the appropriateness of a superboard.[939] By February of 1996, it was announced that Foster's "advisers expect to recommend this week that the Governor propose a new Board of Governors to replace the four separate boards that now oversee Louisiana's public colleges." [940] Foster called a special session of the State Legislature to consider the proposal for the necessary approval. [941]

This push for a superboard engendered a great deal of opposition from constituencies in the state, as the earlier proposals had.[942] A law was passed that granted expanded authority to the Board of Regents to act as kind of superboard. The law gave the Board of Regents expanded powers over the state's higher-education budgets, programs, and planning, including the authority to confirm the selections of chancellors and presidents by the state's three university systems." [943] In January of 1998, state court judge Kay Bates signed an order blocking the legislation pending the outcome of lawsuit over its constitutionality.[944] The superboard plan was eventually dropped after Foster could not win the support of the Legislature.

Two-year College System

After the failure of his superboard plan, Foster turned to the establishment of a key missing piece of the California Model, a community and technical college system. His major higher educational accomplishment was the establishment of the Louisiana Community and Technical College System, a new system that combined most of the two-year colleges in the state.

Before Foster's direct role is considered, for proper context, it is important to look back at the history of the earlier attempts to create a community college system. The idea for some type of statewide reorganization of Louisiana's community and technical colleges long preceded the successful creation of the two-year college system. In the 1976 and 1984 Master Plans, the BOR had expressed the need for a community college system. [945]

During Roemer's term, an ambitious but failed reform effort was symbolic of his overall record. Roemer unsuccessfully attempted to create a statewide system in 1990. James Caillier, state higher education official, proposed creating a single system out of the community colleges and vocational-technical schools around the state. Vo-tech leaders objected because they worried about losing their independence, and four-year college leaders objected because of concerns about losing students. Officials backed off of the comprehensive plan and agreed to a type of pilot plan. The idea of merging vocational and academic curricula was tried on a small scale with the 1992 creation of Elaine P. Nunez Community College (NCC).[946]

Edwards blocked any comprehensive efforts at a statewide system of two-year colleges, though he did follow through with the small pilot plan at NCC. NCC was touted as a model for a statewide community college system. The Board of Regents Feasibility Study for the proposed merger of Elaine P. Nunez Technical Institute[947] and the St. Bernard Parish Community College noted that the merger was an important step in establishing the statewide system and that it "is believed that this merger should be monitored closely to see whether it could serve as a model for other such efforts in various locations in Louisiana." [948]

The period from 1993 to 1996 proved to be an interregnum where the issue of a statewide system of two-year colleges was further studied. In May of 1993, the state Senate passed a resolution authorizing the BOR to create a community college system and report on its progress before the 1994 legislative session. Also, Rep. Tommy Warner, D-Chalmette, sponsored a constitutional amendment in the House of Representatives that helped establish such a system, with the legislation clearing the House Education Committee at the time of the Senate resolution. [949]

The Legislature authorized a process to get feedback on the idea of a statewide system. The state BOR Community College Task Force met with officials representing 44 vo-techs and 6 community colleges with the mandate of giving its suggestions to the Legislature. James Caillier cited the need for such a system because of the expanded opportunities afforded by such a system. The group decided to meet at NCC so that they might get firsthand experience of the results of a merger between a community college and vo-tech school. At the time, NCC had seen great success with a mention that the school's enrollment had nearly doubled since the merger and was "being touted as an example of how that can be done." [950]

The BOR submitted a report on the issue of a community system in March of 1995 as a fulfillment of the 1993 legislative mandate. The report concluded that an "organized statewide system of community colleges is needed, not a series of independent community colleges under numerous boards."[951] The BOR recommended that the community colleges be geographically dispersed, with at least one in each of the eight economic development regions. However, likely aware of the political controversies inherent in such a dramatic overhaul, they "took no firm positions on the governance of a new system."[952] This was typical of the Edwards administration's approach.

In 1996, the ultimately successful attempt at creating a statewide community college system was begun with a study by the Public Affairs Research Council (PARC). LSU economist James Richardson, PARC leader, warned that "'a community college system has the potential to be very useful, but on the other side, it has the potential to be very wasteful.'"[953] At the time, the five existing two-year colleges (plus the proposed Baton Rouge Community College) were divided up among three separate governing boards: the Louisiana State University system, the Southern University System and the University of Louisiana system.[954]

Foster turned his attention to a two-year college system after his attempt to create a superboard for all of higher education failed. The powers of the BOR were bolstered with Acts 151 and 170.[955] His legislative efforts resulted in the passage of two bills that were signed in May 1998. Senate Bill 1 proposed a constitutional amendment to create the Louisiana Community and Technical College System (LCTCS). Senate Bill 2, a 67-page measure, spelled out the details of the implementation. The bills placed the state's vo-tech schools and five two-year colleges under the new governing board, answerable to the BOR.[956]

These bills required a change to the Louisiana Constitution that in turn required a vote of the populace. On October 6, 1998, the constitutional amendment creating the LCTCS was approved for the ballot. In the days leading up to the vote on the constitutional amendment, Harold Callais, Chairman of the BOR, submitted an open letter outlining the official reasoning for the statewide community college system. He wrote that

> the new Louisiana Community and Technical College System would provide a seamless connection between technical colleges, community colleges and universities while empowering the system and schools to respond quickly and effectively to the job needs of our people, business and industry. It will make maximum use of our resources and talents. In recent years, public higher education in Louisiana has been engaged in major reform efforts that will create greater educational and economic opportunities for people of our state.[957]

The measure was then approved by the voters in the November 1998 Congressional election with about two-thirds voting for approval. Governor Foster argued the approval was because of the people's belief that the "state's economy hinges on the ability of those campuses to better educate and train the 80 percent of Louisiana's citizens who do not attend universities."[958]

The LCTCS made its official debut on July 1, 1999, with official oversight of the largest collection of campuses in the state—over 40 technical schools and six community colleges with almost 3,000 employees and a $208 million budget. [959] Harold Suire, president of the watchdog group Council for a Better Louisiana, said that this "'is probably the most critical turnover of power in decades . . . [and Louisiana is] the state that hasn't done a community college system well, and adults have paid the price.'" [960] Wayne Brown, leader of the research effort for the state BOR in developing the community college system, was hired as the first president of the LCTCS.

The creation of the LCTCS streamlined what had been a relatively complex system of governance for community and technical colleges in Louisiana. Three of the oldest community colleges—Bossier Parish Community College, Delgado Community College, and Nunez Community College—had been managed by the Board of Elementary and Secondary Education (BESE) and then the Board of Trustees/ University of Louisiana System. Two other community colleges—River Parishes Community College and South Louisiana Community College—had been managed by the Board of Trustees/ University of Louisiana System. [961] Baton Rouge Community College, mandated by the desegregation Settlement Agreement, was managed by the LSU-Southern University's Joint Management Board, a temporary joint agreement between the LSU and Southern University Boards of Supervisors. [962]

The vocational-technical colleges were also incorporated into a single entity, the Louisiana Technical College (LTC). [963] The vocational-technical schools had been governed by BESE, which renamed the system to the Louisiana Technical College System (LTCS) in 1995. [964] A principal difference was that the LTC was accredited by the Council on Occupational Education (COE) while the community colleges—because they offered academic associate degrees—were accredited by the Southern Association of Colleges and Schools-Commission on Colleges (SACS-COC). [965]

The LCTCS did not encompass all of the public two-year colleges in the state. LSU at Alexandria, LSU at Eunice, and Southern University at Shreveport-Bossier were not included. Most proponents of the LCTCS argued in favor of the inclusion of all two-year colleges. The official reason of Governor Foster's administration was that the three two-year colleges had a special status as feeders of transfer students to their respective four-year institutions. The reasoning was questionable because Delgado Community College transferred over 1,000 students per year and did not earn this status. The likely explanation was that it would have "been a 'poison pill' politically to strip the University systems of their 2-year colleges." [966]

Since its initial configuration, the LCTCS added three two-year colleges. Louisiana Delta Community College was opened in West Monroe. Two vo-tech colleges were approved to award associates degrees, while keeping the technical college status. These hybrids, labeled "technical community colleges," were L. E. Fletcher Technical Community College and Sowela Technical Community College.

The overriding reason given for the establishment of the LCTCS was a concern for the education of workers. This idea was variously called workforce development, career education, workforce training, job training and similar terms. J. Stephen Perry, Governor Foster's chief of staff, was labeled the "point man" for issues of education. He summed up the administration's philosophy when he stated that by 2020, "Louisiana and other states with low college-attendance rates will have had to develop a new work force 'or deal with the social traumas of all these people unprepared for a global economy. This is how you do it—you educate, educate, educate."[967] Supporters contended the LCTCS could develop sorely needed job-training programs to benefit the needs of businesses in the state and was "considered to be the link needed to produce a better-prepared work force and students more capable of tackling a college curriculum." [968] The PARC report concurred with the need for a state-wide system because the "state's emerging emphasis on workforce development requires a coordinated effort to meet occupational education and training needs." [969] The report concluded that a "community and technical college system could play a pivotal role in the state's workforce development efforts."

The LCTCS proponents also relied on the trend of the importance of workforce development nationally. In an analysis of the debate on the LCTCS, a reporter from the *Chronicle of Higher Education* observed that a "growing number of policy makers and business leaders look to occupational education at the community college as a key site for building the work force for the next century." [970] Prominent academic researchers noted that an "emphasis on training to enhance the competitiveness of the state's economy has proved to be a convincing argument in state capitals[971] and that "career education is the only viable core function for most community colleges." [972]

A host of state government officials clearly stated the primary importance of workforce development. State Senator John L. Dardenne, a chief sponsor of the Constitutional amendment to create the LCTCS, said that the "'sole mission of the system would be to advocate for the work-force needs of Louisiana. We have a keen need to adequately train a work force and have jobs created.'" [973] Stephen Perry said that "the plan would provide a smooth transition for the technical and community colleges and would lead to a 'tremendously powerful entity' to spearhead job training." [974] In the organizational stages, the Foster administration indicated that the two-year college system would make "'work-force development its top priority.'" [975] Finally, Harold Callais wrote that the LCTCS "will translate directly into better-paying jobs and more productive lives. Louisiana needs a system that links together all of the state's post-secondary education resources with a long-range strategy to enhance the economic competitiveness and quality of life for all our citizens. The system will do just that." [976]

A corollary of the plan to make workforce development the primary mission of the LCTCS was the conscious decision to allow business people to play a large role. The *Chronicle of Higher Education* article on the LCTCS amendment clearly indicated the role with the subtitle: "State officials hope that giving business leaders more power will improve job training."[977] The article continued with the admonition that the amendment was "aimed at building a work force for the next century, with business leaders given extraordinary influence to guide the effort." [978]

True to the expectations of proponents, the actual organization of the LCTCS policies showed the importance of job-related education. The *Mission* said: "We strive to increase the opportunity for Louisiana's workforce to succeed through skills training programs." [979] In the *Elements of Two-Year Institutional Mission*, the LCTCS listed the primary facets of the mission of the entire system, presumably in order of importance. Of the seven elements, "Economic Development" was first, "Workforce Development" was second, and "Career Skills Development" was fifth.[980]

Another reason cited for the proposed merger was the complex governance structure of public colleges and universities in Louisiana. There were three main management boards, and each one included the full range of schools from two-year colleges up to universities. The BOR served an oversight and coordination role over the three boards. Also, an ongoing expansion of community colleges in the state had no overall plan of coordination. Finally, the community colleges and vocational-technical institutes were both two-year colleges with somewhat related missions, but they had separate governance structures. Proponents argued that the fragmented governance was not the most efficient way of governance for the growing community colleges.

A final major rationale given for the LCTCS creation was the inefficient provision of typical community college functions in Louisiana. Many states used the California Model organization where most of the so-called "community college functions" were delivered in low-cost community colleges versus high cost universities. These functions included the bulk of the freshman and sophomore level education, remedial education, associate degree programs, extension and evening programs, avocational courses, specialized occupational training (e.g., fire and police training), courses at satellite learning centers, and the use of distance learning technologies. In Louisiana, these functions were mainly provided by four-year colleges and universities. Louisiana ranked 38th in enrollment in public two-year colleges, per capita with many of the lower-ranked states being smaller and rural. The argument was made that the LCTCS could relieve the responsibility of some of these functions so that 4-year colleges and universities could concentrate on more specialized functions. [981]

The establishment of the LCTCS was closely related to similar measures in other states due to the consulting efforts of the National Center for Higher Education Management Systems (NCHEMS), a nonprofit education consultancy center in Boulder, Colorado. Aims C. McGuinness, one of the leaders of the small operation— with five consultants and a seven-member research-and-support staff—was a primary consultant on the LCTCS organization. [982] NCHEMS also helped to overhaul the community college governance structure in Kentucky, New Jersey and within the State University of New York system.[983] One of the most famous of the higher-education reform governors, Paul E. Patton of Kentucky, called upon NCHEMS because "'their name always cropped up when it came to higher education.'" [984] In an interesting corollary, Kentucky's two-year college system, the KCTCS, was the most immediate model for the LCTCS. [985] Kentucky also served as a model for the framers of Louisiana's very first constitution. [986]

Illuminating example: Elaine P. Nunez Community College

Before discussing the next phase of Foster's reforms, it is first necessary to look at a brief history of a representative two-year college that became part of the LCTCS. One example, Elaine P. Nunez Community College (NCC), was chosen because it has mirrored many of the reforms of higher education in recent Louisiana history. Its academic precursor was established during the burst of activity in John McKeithen's tenure in the 1960s. Its vocational-technical precursor began in the 1970s when Edwards greatly increased the number of vo-techs. Little changed for either in the 1980s as reform dwindled to almost nothing in the state. Finally, the merger of the two colleges into NCC in 1992 was emblematic of the wave of reform that led to the creation of the LCTCS.

Mirroring the role of the governor on statewide higher education trends, Louisiana State Senate President Sammy Nunez, from Chalmette, took a lead role in the establishment of NCC. He was elected to the state House in 1964 and served in the Senate from 1969 until his defeat in 1995. He was the Senate President from 1983 until his defeat except when he was ousted from 1988-90 by allies of then-Gov. Buddy Roemer. [987] State Representatives Tommy Warner and Ken Odinet, also played a significant role.

NCC was established on July 1, 1992, through a merger of St. Bernard Parish Community College (SBPCC) and Elaine P. Nunez Technical Institute (EPNTI). At its inception, proponents hoped that NCC would experience enrollment growth and serve as a model for a statewide comprehensive community college system.

The first component of the merged NCC was the SBPCC that had as its first year the 1968-69 school year. A resolution of the Louisiana Legislature and the State Board of Education initiated a pilot program for the state of Louisiana in September of 1968 for students wishing to take courses for college credit. A Committee, chaired by Joseph J. Davies, Jr., Superintendent of Schools for St. Bernard Parish, recommended that two years of college be offered at high schools. [988] In the 1968-69 school year, the college began with the name St. Bernard Parish Thirteenth & Fourteenth Grades. [989] Classes were held on the campuses of Chalmette High School and Andrew Jackson High School. By the 1970-71 catalog, the school's name had been changed to the St. Bernard Parish Community College. [990]

The other component, the EPNTI, was originally established in 1973 as the Chalmette Area Vocational-Technical School. It was renamed in 1979 for Mrs. Elaine Potter Nunez, the wife of state Senator Sammy Nunez and "a civic leader and patron of education." A modern facility was dedicated in 1979. [991] The official merging of the two schools to create NCC took place in 1992. [992]

Looking to the Future—2005 and beyond

With the necessary foundational element—a functioning community college system—in place, Foster turned to the next step in going away from the "all-in-one" philosophy. He advocated that admissions standards be raised at four-year colleges and universities with the intent of diverting unprepared students to two-year colleges. Using the approach of institutional differentiation, the two-year colleges would provide developmental education and the first year or two of general education—in a low-cost environment. Upon proving themselves, students would move on to the higher-cost four-year colleges. Ideally, the colleges would deliver the educational services to which they were best suited, and the state would save money.

Policy to Raise Admissions Standards in Fall of 2005

The *Master Plan* clearly defined the rationale for this last plank in Foster's reforms. This policy of raising the admissions standards at many of the colleges and universities in the state in the Fall semester of 2005 will henceforth be abbreviated as the *2005 Policy*. On its face, the *2005 Policy* seemed relatively simple and straightforward. Louisiana's public colleges will be divided into four categories, with different minimum admission requirements for each.[993] The *2005 Policy*, however, represented a marked change in higher education governance philosophy. The long-term approach for Louisiana colleges and universities had been to provide a range of missions—from developmental education to doctorates—in a single institution. Foster's reform measures encouraged institutions to focus on specific missions while leaving other missions to schools believed to be better suited to the task.

State policymakers had identified the previously haphazard development of institutional differentiation, labeled the "all-in-one" approach in earlier chapters, as one of the main reasons for the low performance of higher education in Louisiana. The *Master Plan* stated that one of the fundamental strategies was to establish proper admissions criteria to promote a better "student-to-institution match."[994] With a large number of unprepared students attending four-year colleges and universities, the negative result was seen in more resources devoted to developmental education, higher dropout rates, and low completion rates.[995] The BOR asserted that the differing types of institutions needed to be aligned with the missions they could best serve. *The Master Plan* succinctly argued that the *2005 Policy* was developed "to maximize the probability of student success by linking the expectation of institutions to the aspirations and level of preparedness of entering students."[996]

The *2005 Policy*'s primary intended result, and the main goal of the institutional differentiation, was to move the majority of developmental education offerings from four-year institutions to two-year community and technical colleges. The BOR indicated that two-year institutions were equipped to provide developmental education and related services at a lower cost to the student.[997]

The goals of the *Master Plan*—especially the use of different admissions standards for different types of institutions—were supported by many public organizations. A Public Affairs Research Council (PARC) "White Paper on Higher Education" quite simply stated the problem that "[c]ompared to other southern states, Louisiana enrolls far more of its students in costlier four-year universities than in community and technical colleges." [998] Louisiana enrolled 76% of its students in 4-year universities, while the southern average was 56%. The result of this misallocation was "greater cost, nearly the lowest college graduation rates in the South, a poor match with job opportunities and business needs, and a larger-than-necessary higher education funding deficit."[999] More efficiently matching the needs of students to an appropriate, economical level of instruction will allow higher funding at all levels. [1000] Legislative Fiscal Officer Johnny Rombach suggested "that the problem is not too few tax dollars going to universities but, perhaps, too many students going to expensive four-year institutions instead of to more cost-efficient community colleges."[1001]

In an editorial, *The Advocate* specifically stated support for the California plan. In extolling the virtues of Clark Kerr and the 1960 master plan for higher education in California, the editorial stated that unfortunately, "Louisiana missed the boat, only really embracing the community college concept during the Foster administration. That was a costly 35-year mistake, dating from the adoption of Kerr's master plan." [1002] Specifically addressing the problem of extensive developmental education at the four-year level, the editorial said that in

> California, the middle tier of institutions was limited to mostly producing bachelor's degrees—the job Louisiana's regional colleges seem to find degrading, as they continue to try to add graduate programs at vast expense. For many years this process was almost completely unchecked, although today the Board of Regents exercises a restraining influence.[1003]

The Advocate went further with its analysis, criticizing the "all-in-one" philosophy of then-Governor John McKeithen, when it stated that while

> Kerr was creating effective tiers of 'role, scope and mission' for different types of universities, Louisiana politics was driving toward creating 'universities' in every city that could plausibly promote its junior college, as community colleges were called in the New Deal era. Under the McKeithen administration, the regional colleges were renamed 'universities,' an example of marketing over substance that was thought comic by many people at the time. [1004]

Compared to California, the loose provision of institutional differentiation does not seem to have served the state or its citizens very effectively.

The Council for a Better Louisiana (CABL) agreed that the lack of institutional differentiation was a problem. With fewer students in community colleges compared to the national average,

> not only does it cost the state considerably more to support four-year universities, we have some of the lowest college graduation rates in the nation and South. Many students are simply not ready for university work. In addition, by having a skewed enrollment in four-year colleges, we are not meeting the needs of new and existing employers for high-level skilled people with two-year degrees and specialized certificates. [1005]

CABL further recommended an action that fits with the policy of raising admissions standards when it said that four-year "schools should focus solely on baccalaureate, graduate, research and professional education, depending on the mission of each institution. The emphasis of these institutions must be on helping their students attain the degrees they seek. They should not encumber themselves with adding and maintaining two-year associate degree programs. That is not their mission."[1006]

Brief History of Developmental Education

The linchpin of Foster's reforms is that developmental education will serve as a bridge to universities for the large number of unprepared students in Louisiana. The state-funded TOPS (Tuition Opportunity Program for Students) scholarship and other financial assistance programs have gone a long way to assist college attendance for students prepared for college-level work.[1007] With a four-year college graduation rate of 18.7%, significantly below the national average of 24.4%,[1008] it is the students not prepared for college that will impact the fortunes of the state in the future. Since the primary vehicle of higher education reform in Louisiana is to move the bulk of developmental education from four-year institutions to two-year colleges, it is necessary to examine a brief history of developmental education, as well as to outline its impact on society.

Historian David Arendale found that colleges in the 1800s were faced with a majority of unprepared students because public education in the United States was nonexistent. Many colleges were forced to recruit unprepared students for financial reasons. [1009] For example, the University of Wisconsin in Madison was the site of an important early program of developmental education. Continuing an earlier pattern, in 1865, only 41 of the 331 admitted students were enrolled in college-level courses. The remaining students were enrolled in the academic preparatory academy located in the local high school. Nationally in 1865, approximately 40% of all first-year students were enrolled in some type of developmental courses. This rate was fairly close to the 33% rate recorded in 1991.[1010] Arendale summarized that the "historical record is clear that developmental education and learning assistance programs have been integral and widespread to American higher education since its inception."[1011]

The basic importance of developmental education to society lies in the fact that a four-year college degree has become synonymous with upward mobility in today's society. Logically, a person cannot get to this plateau without first attaining the preparation to enter college. [1012] Also, states and communities need a college-educated population to compete in the global economy. As noted in an earlier chapter, two groups of Americans have not benefited from the gains of the last decades of the twentieth century. Individuals with only a high school education have seen flat real income growth, and individuals who have not completed high school have seen a decrease in real income. On the other hand, individuals with some college education or higher have seen an increase in real income as well as an increasing divergence from the lower-educated. [1013]

Simply stated, a large majority of graduating high school students in Louisiana were not prepared for college-level work. If the four-year colleges and universities accept relatively few students needing developmental classes, then the task of bridging the preparation gap will fall mostly on the state's two-year colleges. It is up to two-year colleges, largely through successful developmental education, to fill the pipelines for four-year institutions. If these universities do their job, then the individuals—and Louisiana—will gain the prosperity afforded by a larger number of university graduates.

Vocational vs. academic higher education

Looking to the higher education landscape in 2005 and beyond, a debate crucial to the future prosperity of Louisiana will have to be decided, probably by a future governor. This often-paradoxical conundrum is how to balance vocational and academic higher education to best serve the interests of the state. As seen in previous chapters, some governors, like John McKeithen, have invested the state's limited resources mostly in "academic" four-year colleges and universities. Others, like Edwin Edwards, have directed funds more to vocational-technical colleges. While no governor would choose exclusively either side, ideally, he or she would devote more resources to the approach that could best benefit the most people. Unfortunately, the choice does not seem clear-cut.

The "vo-tech versus academic" debate is at the heart of two contradictory realities about higher education in Louisiana. First, a clear majority of Louisiana citizens that are eligible to enter college are not prepared to do academic work at a first-year college level. Second, in contemporary society, a bachelor's degree has been commonly associated with being a ticket to a middle class lifestyle. To compound the difficulties, a small percentage of students who enter college unprepared go on to earn a Bachelor's Degree. For example, though statistics are difficult to gather,[1014] the literature indicates that relatively few students who enter a community college go on to graduate from a four-year college or university. One study in the 1980s put the number at 6-10%. [1015]

Educators in Louisiana are thus faced with a decision of emphasis when it comes to higher education reform. With a "vocational" approach, governors might realize that Louisiana has one of the highest high school dropout rates in the country and that a large majority of a graduating high school class will not go on to earn a four-year degree. Barring a turnaround in the effectiveness of public secondary schools in Louisiana, an efficient approach, then, might bolster vocational training opportunities, so that a student might at least have skills that could gain them a job. Perhaps the average vocational student would not be able to gain the significant advantages of being a four-year graduate, but at least it would be better than being a college dropout with no skills and a minimum-wage job. For example, in St. Bernard Parish, 8.9% of people have at least a four-year degree (in comparison to a national average of 24%), so given the cultural factors that go into educational attainment, it would be unrealistic to expect a significant number of college graduates. A governor might choose to direct scarce higher education resources toward vocational higher education and away from academic higher education.

With an "academic" approach, however, another governor might look at the changing occupational outlook and argue that well-paying jobs requiring low-level vocational skills no longer exist in great numbers. In the current situation, if a worker does not have the basic knowledge to read and understand a manual or to adapt to a different position, then he or she will not be able to keep a good job when an industry evolves. With this approach, it would almost amount to educational malpractice to tell a student that basic vocational skills will be valued ten or twenty years into the future with a technologically evolving workplace. Instead, it is better to require at least basic college-level skills—with the hope that at least a good portion will go on to get a four-year degree. The downside is that some marginally prepared students will be left behind.

An interesting wildcard in the debate is a third alternative that is both academic and vocational-technical (in the sense of being preparation for a job). Many students are opting for terminal two-year degrees that prepare them for the workforce but feature an academic—not trades-based—curriculum. Community college nursing schools offer a 2-year LPN (Licensed Practical Nurse) certficate that leads to a well-paying job but is not to the level of the 4-year RN (registered nurse) degree. Other examples include health-related technicians, process technology, and computer certifications. This "third way"—an academic terminal degree—might be where community colleges are headed. However, the unprepared, non-academic student would still be left behind.

The academic versus vo-tech debate is not new—and perhaps a history will aid a future governor in the inevitable decision. The issue was primarily played out in the 1970s movement to form "comprehensive community colleges." The philosophical basis of this movement was the simple question: should academic and vocational-technical programs be housed in the same two-year college.

As discussed earlier, two-year colleges have widely variant missions. One principal mission is "academic"—the equivalent of the first two years of a baccalaureate program intended for transfer. Another important mission is "vocational-technical"—a two-year program intended to terminate with skills allowing a graduate to immediately get a job, generally in a trade. Since the 1970s, nationally, the prevailing philosophy has been to combine these missions into a single institution, the comprehensive community college. The idea was the vo-tech and academic components were complementary enough that the benefits of the whole would exceed the separate parts.

During the 1970s and 1980s, as the nation tended toward comprehensive community colleges, Louisiana took a different approach. A large number of vo-techs provided technical programs, while the "academic" programs (including developmental education) were mostly provided by four-year colleges and universities. Louisiana had very few community colleges. The 1992 merger of a community college and a vo-tech that resulted in Elaine P. Nunez Community College (NCC) was a conscious attempt to try out the comprehensive community college philosophy.

The NCC experience showed the different cultures of the two approaches. At an institutional level, the merger was one of markedly different cultures, governance structures and success levels. As far as mission, the community college part was oriented to more traditional students and preparation for transfer to a four-year college. The vo-tech part was a trades-based school that primarily prepared adults for the workforce, and its students were more likely to be dropouts from traditional education.[1016] The largest split between the academic and technical faculty involved the budget process. Under the pre-merger system, vo-tech instructors were paid based on a 12-month salary, they earned annual leave, they earned vacation time, and they could earn comp time for hours worked over the typical forty-hour week. The "more traditional" academic instructors were nine-month employees and could not be compensated for overtime. NCC moved all instructors to a nine-month calendar.[1017]

A similar vo-tech versus academic split was seen in the debates leading to the formation of the LCTCS. The public conversation over the establishment of the LCTCS left little doubt that the main mission of the LCTCS schools was to prepare students for the workforce with a terminal degree. PARC weighed in that "[p]reparing students to transfer is no longer the primary function of most two-year colleges."[1018] An analysis of the constitutional amendment process revealed that lawmakers "believe that the state's economy hinges on the ability of those campuses to better educate and train the 80 percent of Louisiana's citizens who do not attend universities."[1019] A more recent overview concurred that the "market has a large niche for students with two-year associate degrees but not necessarily four-year baccalaureate degrees."[1020]

An interesting debate revealed the tensions between the dual missions of two-year colleges. A key point of contention in the merger was between the backers of the community colleges and those of the vocational-technical schools. At the heart of the disagreement was the perception that an education designed to prepare students for the workforce is in conflict with a more selective academic education designed to prepare students to transfer to a four-year college. In the proposed LCTCS merger case, the sides were split where "the technical colleges fear[ed] that they will be turned into 'academic' institutions, while community-college advocates s[aw] the 'vo-techs' as a menace to quality education."[1021] The president of the largest community college said that there "'are concerns that we're relegating the community colleges to a vo-tech, trade-school classification.'" [1022]

This split was symbolized by the infighting over the name of the proposed state-wide system. In the negotiations in the Legislature leading to the approval of the eventual constitutional amendment, the original proposal had "Technical" before "Community" in the name of the statewide system. The vocational-technical schools found this to be an important symbolic gesture accompanying their fear that their interests might be subsumed in the new state-wide system. Possibly reflecting this sensitivity, state officials "were quick to correct people if they said 'Community' first."[1023] By the time the bill emerged from the State House of Representatives, community college proponents had been able to rename the system with "Community" preceding "Technical"—a configuration that persisted in the final naming. This change pleased the community college side, obviously, but "it was salt in the wounds of their intended brethren."[1024]

So what does this abstract debate mean to the average student? While no example encompasses the diversity of students and curricula, the symbolic debate comes down to whether a vocational-technical student who wants a welding certificate should be required to pass a college-level algebra class ("College Algebra")—when this might require taking an "extra" year or more of developmental math classes just to have the opportunity. As of 2004, the policy of the LCTCS is that a student is required to pass College Algebra to get a degree from a community college. Based in an "academic" approach, the rationale is that the skills represented by the class (and others, like college-level English) would help the student adapt to a changing workplace.

Critics of this policy take a "vo-tech" approach. They argue that many, if not most, students who want to learn to weld would drop out of college long before passing the class, and these students would be left without either the academic skills or the welding skills. Previously, vo-tech students could take math classes at a less-than-college level that applied specifically to an industry. For example, culinary students might take a math class based around calculations used in cooking. The vo-tech proponents argue that the mathematical skills of College Algebra would likely not be used by a welder. As of 2004, the vo-tech campuses of the LTC do not require the same college-level requirements, so there is an alternative. If the requirements are instituted in the LTC as well, there might not be an alternative for a vo-tech student who cannot reach college-level Math skills.

This history-part of the story of higher education of Louisiana ends with the final days of Mike Foster's governorship. Foster retired from public life in 2004, forbidden by term limits from running for a third term. The final plank of Foster's reforms was scheduled to take effect in the Fall semester of 2005, well after Kathleen Blanco's ascension to the governorship. Only the future—and possibly an epilogue—can say if the intended actions came to fruition.

CHAPTER 9

Conclusion

So ends the history of higher education in Louisiana from its Franco-Spanish origins to the 21st century.

The history was marked by the influence of key universities. From uncertain beginnings, LSU rose to be the most influential public university, gaining favored status both among governmental officials, many of whom counted it as their alma mater, and the general populace, often through a championship football team. Foiled in an early bid to become a public institution, Tulane University carved out a reputation as the premier private university, one of the most prestigious in the Gulf South. Southern University represented a dual, segregated system of higher education and became the largest historically black university in the nation. These developments, along with increasing state-level coordination and over 200,000 students, comprised a picture radically different from the handful of students and primitive conditions of the early Louisiana State Seminary of Learning and Military Academy.

Despite the changes, the history of higher education featured two themes, constant since the beginning. The first was a lack of emphasis on the importance of higher education (as well as education in general) among the populace and leaders. The French and Spanish promoted education much less effectively than the English Thirteen Colonies. When Louisiana joined America in 1803, it was most influenced by the educationally-deficient South. In all eras, including into the 21st century, Louisiana has ranked near the bottom in measures of educational attainment.

The second consistency has been the prevalence of executives with outsized power. The "strong king" tradition of France and Spain was imposed on a captive colony. In the early American period, this cultural trend was manifested in a governor with near-dictatorial powers and a popular aversion to participatory democracy. By the 1930s, Huey Long became known as "America's Dictator." Since that time, governors have played an often dominant role in the development of statewide higher education. Looking to the future, governors will likely continue this primary role—for good or ill—in the development of higher education.

For the benefit of future governors and other decision-makers, there is one story left to be told. But first a question: amid the panoply of governors, governance boards and long-ago events, what is the relevance of higher education to the "average" Louisianan? In a blue-collar state where over 80% do not get a four-year degree, higher education has not occupied a daily role in most people's lives. A personification of this part of the history is the story of Kenny Cooper, a man who did not attend any of the institutions mentioned in the preceding pages, but whose experience was emblematic of Louisiana itself.

Cooper described himself as someone with a high school education that worked hard all of his life. He was born in 1954 and spent most of his life in St. Bernard Parish, a blue-collar area where chemical plants and oil refineries are among the biggest employers. As of 2000, 8.9% of residents there had at least a four-year college degree. His parents both had high school degrees, and Cooper graduated from public Chalmette High School in 1973.

Upon graduation, he applied for an apprenticeship program with the local steamfitters and pipefitters union. The program was so popular that he stayed on the waiting list for over four years. While waiting, he worked as a laborer in a shipyard and oil refinery and also did home construction. Once in the apprenticeship program, he continued to work full-time during the day, and attended class two nights a week for four years. The curriculum was broad-based trades instruction as well as practical training. Apprenticeships have a longer history than formal education, but they are usually not grouped within the general definition of higher education.

This chapter of Cooper's life took place during the "oil boom" prosperity of the 1970s and early 1980s. Petrochemical plants were doing well and more were being constructed. St. Bernard Parish was awash in job opportunities. The plants relied on a large contingent of workers that had skilled training but not a college-level education, including welders, pipefitters, and machinists. These workers ensured that the plant remained operational by directly working on the equipment. Echoing the demand in Cooper's apprenticeship program, the local vocational-technical school could not accommodate the influx of students that wanted to attend. Welders were hired at a good wage before even finishing the two years of the program.

Unions provided a large majority of the workforce at petrochemical plants. Plants applied to the local union halls and were provided trained workers, like Cooper. Union workers were paid a higher hourly wage than comparable non-union positions. In addition, the plants contributed to union-administered health insurance, benefits and pension programs. Even if the workers changed plants, the union insured a good wage and a comfortable retirement—in essence the elements of a comfortable middle-class lifestyle.

After completing the union apprenticeship program, Cooper went to work at a chemical plant. Hired as a pipefitter, he was mechanically gifted and could repair almost all of the systems of the aging plant. While technically working for a subcontractor, not the plant itself, he stayed at the plant for twenty years. After many years as a pipefitter, he rose to management—first as piping superintendent, then as a mechanical planner. In addition to the union-sponsored benefits, he was able to take care of his family with a salary significantly above the national average.

In the two decades Cooper was going to work each day, conditions for workers in Louisiana changed dramatically. Three related trends—all negative—converged. First, the "oil bust" of the mid-1980s changed the nature of the petrochemical industry in Louisiana. No new refineries were built, and operations at existing ones were scaled back. A handful of trades-based maintenance jobs were still available, but not the hundreds of jobs over several years that new construction required. Cooper said that the construction of a single refinery in the 1970s employed hundreds of craftsmen over four years. Also, construction was consciously spaced out so that as one plant was completed, another was just beginning. In addition to the lack of new building, many of the operations were transferred to Texas or other places, costing more jobs.

A second component in the decline was the global economic changes and technological innovations of the late 1980s. At one end, factories utilizing low-skilled workers were moved to low-wage countries. In St. Bernard Parish, Kaiser Aluminum Chalmette Works, the largest employer, moved its operations overseas and with it over 2,000 high-paying industrial jobs. At the other end, the high-skilled tasks were increasingly taken over by computers and automation. At newer refineries, for example, the entire facility could be monitored by a small number of workers staring at computer screens in an air-conditioned control room, and often, the plant could detect a problem itself. An operator trained in computers and process control technology could replace several workers who manually checked valves in the field. Trades-based workers were still needed, just fewer of them.

The final adverse development was Louisiana becoming a "right-to-work" state in 1976. Legally, workers could no longer be required to join a union as a condition of employment. The practical result was a gradual de-unionization of the petrochemical plants. A well-compensated unionized worker was relatively expensive to plant managers. Once it was possible to hire less expensive, non-unionized workers, the plants increasingly did so. Over the twenty years of Cooper's time at the chemical plant, the union presence declined from a substantial majority to just a handful.

Cooper was aware of these changes in an abstract form, of course, but they had little impact on his situation. The new reality did not filter down to his aging plant until about the mid-1990s. He noticed a gradually increasing reliance on computers. Where voicemail had once been exotic, email became the standard method of communication. Where the plant had kept needed parts in stock on location, a computerized just-in-time ordering system using a centralized warehouse greatly diminished this practice.

Cooper saw an increasing automation of plant functions. Before, an operator went out and inspected a valve when a problem occurred. Automated valves became standard and reduced the need for workers. Additionally, small satellite plants essentially ran themselves with no workers present. If a problem occurred, a sensor notified a control room at a neighboring plant and took the needed temporary action until a worker could be dispatched.

Finally, the plant increasingly relied on individuals with college degrees. Cooper worked with a procession of young engineers in their 30s with considerable intelligence and computer experience but little field experience. Much of their job consisted of sitting behind a desk working on a computer.

Cooper was let go in 2004 after twenty years of service. Technically, the plant did not fire him, but simply chose not to rehire the subcontractor for which he worked. In reality, even fellow employees would be hard-pressed to see a difference between Cooper and a worker who had worked directly for the plant. He lost his job primarily—in his view—because of his unwillingness to give up his union membership, his lack of a college degree, his age, and his "old school" mentality.

Probably the main reason was his union membership. By 2004, he was the only union worker on the job. The plant managers asked him to switch to a non-union position. Out of loyalty as well as the maintenance of his pension and benefits, Cooper declined. He also lacked a college degree, and thus the modern technological skills that were increasingly being relied upon. Finally, at 50 years old, his salary and anticipated benefits costs were high, and he could be replaced with a younger worker who would be easier to mold in the new approach put forth by management.

A final reason was his "old school" way of doing things. He found that it was tough to be re-trained in the new system. His old boss had worn workclothes to work and had come up from a mechanic. His new boss wore Dockers and had mousse in his hair. His formative experience was in college, not welding in a 120° storage tank. The old way was for all of the workers to hang out in the coffee room before work and plan out the work for the day. If a problem arose, you found the needed person and talked to them about it. In the new system, the maintenance was planned out on the computer far in advance. The new directives on communications were specific—even phone calls were to be avoided in favor of emails. The old way was to write everything down on a piece of paper. The new way involved no writing at all, with even the yellow post-it notes digitally rendered on a computer screen. Similar changes were taking place at plants all over Louisiana.

Given his skills, contacts and union seniority, Cooper found another job by which he could maintain a comfortable middle-class lifestyle. It was an entry-level job at a position similar to when he started twenty years before. It was not nearly as comfortable or fulfilling, but he felt lucky to have it.

When he was asked about the prospects of a young man following his same career path, Cooper just shook his head. He saw little chance for a high school graduate without college, and even specialty training, to achieve a comfortable middle-class lifestyle. The unions have been essentially shut out of the well-paying industrial jobs. The only way to make a decent wage is to work for a big company, and they have increasingly used subcontractors to avoid paying benefits. In the old days, the sugar refinery, another big St. Bernard Parish employer, only started people in the general labor pool and promoted from within. A hard worker could get the needed training after proving himself and advance through the system. All that changed, and there is little on-the-job training any more, in part because of the influx of skilled workers who are unemployed.

So what of the next Kenny Cooper, an 18-year-old graduating from high school with intentions of work, not college? The math is simple. In 2004, workers 18 and over with an advanced degree earned, on average, $74,602; with a bachelor's degree, $51,206; with a high school diploma, $27,915; and with less than a high school diploma, $18,734.[1025] Associate degree holders, on average, fare little better than those with a high school diploma, earning $3,000 more in 1992 and $700 more in 2000.[1026] Less than $30,000 a year will likely not bring the comfortable middle-class lifestyle that the previous generation of refinery workers enjoyed. The goal should clearly be a university education.

Kenny Cooper's story, played out among thousands of non-college-educated individuals, has affected society in Louisiana (and the nation). A new generation of workers has a difficult prognosis. With just a trades-based education (without an academic component), the pool of potential high-paying jobs is much smaller than before. The competition for the dwindling number of jobs is often displaced older workers, like Cooper, who have considerable experience and skills. Union membership has also declined as more industries seek to pay lower, non-union wages to semi-skilled workers. Finally, the enrollment in the trades-based college programs have declined in line with the decreased job opportunities. Some of the vo-tech programs that had to turn people away in the 1970s have either closed or are facing closure due to lack of demand.

The goal of this next generation of workers should be the goal of state leaders, especially the governor. Increasing the number of Louisianans with the knowledge and skills represented by a four-year degree is the single best way to break the cycle of low education and poverty that has plagued the state since its inception. It is a long-term solution, but if begun now, my daughter will grow up to live in a prosperous state that not only offers more higher-educational opportunities but also more jobs upon her graduation.

APPENDIX

"Character" events of public four-year colleges & universities in Louisiana

The first column indicates official name changes with the year of occurrence. The next three columns indicate the typical course of study offered—a two-year degree (or less), a four-year degree and a university degree—and the date authorization was granted. The final column lists the date the institutions began offering graduate degrees.

Higher Education Institution (Date of Name Change) with previous names	2-year or less	4-year	University	Grad. Degrees
Grambling State Univ. (1974) Grambling College of Louisiana (1949) Louisiana Negro Normal and Industrial Institute (1928) Lincoln Parish Training School (1918) North Louisiana Industrial & Agricultural Institute (1905) Colored Industrial & Agricultural Institute of Lincoln Parish or Colored Industrial and Agricultural School (1901)	1901	1940	1974	1974
Louisiana State University and Agricultural and Mechanical College (1877) Louisiana Agricultural and Mechanical College (1874) Louisiana State University (1870) Louisiana State Seminary of Learning and Military Academy at Pineville (1860) Louisiana State Seminary of Learning and Military Academy (1860) State Seminary of Learning (1853) Louisiana State Seminary of Learning at Pineville (1853)	1853	1870	1870	1905
Louisiana Tech University (1970) Louisiana Polytechnic Institute (1921) Industrial Institute & College of Louisiana (1894)	1894	1921	1970	1956
LSU at Alexandria (1959)	1959	2001		
LSU-Shreveport (1964)	1964	1972		
McNeese State Univ. (1970) McNeese State College (1950) John McNeese Junior College (1940) Lake Charles Junior College, div. of LSU (1939)	1939	1950	1970	1960
Nicholls State University (1970) Francis T. Nicholls State College (1956) Francis T. Nicholls Junior College (of LSU) (1948)	1948	1956	1970	1965
Northwestern State Univ. of Louisiana (1970) Northwestern State College of Louisiana (1944) Louisiana State Normal College (1921) Louisiana State Normal School (1884)	1884	1918	1970	1954
Southeastern Louisiana Univ. (1970) Southeastern Louisiana College (1928) Hammond Junior College (1925)	1925	1937	1970	1960

Southern Univ. and A & M College (1891) Southern University (1880)	1880	1891	1891	n/a
Southern University at New Orleans (1956)			1956	n/a
Univ of Louisiana—Lafayette (1999) Univ. of Southwestern Louisiana (1960) Southwestern La. Inst. of Liberal & Technical Learning (1921) Southwestern Louisiana Industrial Institute (1898)	1898	1921	1960	1956
Univ. of Louisiana at Monroe (1999) Northeast Louisiana Univ. (1970) Northeast Louisiana State College (1950) Northeast Junior College of LSU (1939) . . . branch of LSU (1934) Ouachita Parish Junior College (1931)	1931	1950	1970	1961
University of New Orleans (1974) LSU—New Orleans (1956)			1956	1965

BIBLIOGRAPHY

Advocate, The. "BRCC to offer more aid." Downloaded from *http://www.theadvocate. com/stories/121102/new_aid001.shtml* on 12/19/2002.

_____ . "Louisiana lost way in policy." Downloaded from *http://www.2theadvocate. com/stories/120403/opi_edi001.shtml* on 12/4/2003.

Alexis, Rochelle Nash. *A Description and Analysis of the Perceived Impact of the Academic Governance Structure of Higher Education in the State of Louisiana After the Adoption of the Constitution of 1974.* Ph.D. Dissertation, University of New Orleans, 1985. Located at UNO Library, Louisiana Collection.

Anderson, Ed. "Foster quietly signs community college bill." *New Orleans Times-Picayune,* 8 May 1998, A3.

_____ . "Foster: Set up 1 board for colleges; Push connected to money plans." *New Orleans Times-Picayune,* 10 February 1996.

_____ . "Tulane scholarships survive," *New Orleans Times-Picayune,* 30 May 1996.

Associated Press. "Long Still Seeks New L.S.U. Coach." *New York Times,* 20 December 1934.

_____ . "Long Usurps Rule At State Capital." *New York Times,* 20 December 1934.

_____ . "Nola.com Newsflash—Louisiana Editorial Roundup," 14 May 2003.

Bacon-Blood, Littice. "Community College System to Debut; Single Board Touted As Way To Improve La. Job Training." *New Orleans Times-Picayune,* 1 July 1999, A1.

Bailey, Thomas R., and Irina E. Averianova. *Multiple Missions of Community Colleges: Conflicting or Complementary?* New York: Community College Research Center, 1998.

Bergeron, Jr., Arthur W. "John J. McKeithen." In *The Louisiana Governors: From Iberville to Edwards,* edited by Joseph G. Dawson III. Baton Rouge, Louisiana: Louisiana State University Press, 1990.

Blocker, Clyde E., Robert H. Plummer, and Richard C. Richardson, Jr. *The Two-Year College: A Social Synthesis.* Englewood Cliffs, NJ: Prentice-Hall, Inc., 1965.

Breneman, David W. and Susan C. Nelson. *Financing Community Colleges: An Economic Perspective.* Washington, D. C.: Brookings Institution, 1981.

Brint, Steven and Jerome Karabel, *The Diverted Dream: Community Colleges and the Promise of Educational Opportunity in America, 1900-1985.* New York: Oxford University Press, 1989.

Cage, Mary Crystal. "Academics Protest Governor's Choice to head La. University." *The Chronicle of Higher Education,* 16 January 1991. Downloaded from *http:// chronicle.com* on 4/9/2004.

_____ . "College Leaders Pleased With Outcome of La. Governor's Race." *The Chronicle of Higher Education*, 27 November 1991. Downloaded from *http://chronicle.com* on 4/9/2004.

_____ . "Gubernatorial Contest Poses Distinct Choices for Future of Higher Education in Louisiana." *The Chronicle of Higher Education*, 16 October 1991. Downloaded from *http://chronicle.com* on 4/9/2004.

_____ . "Higher-Education Probes by Crusty Louisiana Watchdog Bring Headlines and Headaches." *The Chronicle of Higher Education*, 18 October 1989. Downloaded from *http://chronicle.com* on 4/9/2004.

_____ . "Louisiana's College Officials Fear the Consequences if Ex-Leader of Ku Klux Klan Becomes Governor." *The Chronicle of Higher Education*, 6 November 1991. Downloaded from *http://chronicle.com* on 4/9/2004.

_____ . "Reform Plan Stymied: Governor's Effort to Simplify Louisiana's Higher-Education System Deepens the Bitter Divisions Created by Years of Segregation and Political Turf Wars." *The Chronicle of Higher Education*, 18 October 1989, A29-31.

_____ . "Southern Voters Defeat 2 Pro-Education Governors." *The Chronicle of Higher Education,* 20 November 1991. Downloaded from *http://chronicle.com* on 4/9/2004.

_____ . "Supreme Court Says It Lacks Jurisdiction in La. Desegregation Dispute." *The Chronicle of Higher Education,* 17 January 1990. Downloaded from *http://chronicle.com* on 4/9/2004.

Callais, Harold. "Regents to Voters: OK Community College Plan." *New Orleans Times-Picayune*, 25 September 1998, B6.

Callan, Patrick M. "Reframing Access and Opportunity: Problematic State and Federal Higher Education Policy in the 1990s." In *The States and Public Higher Education Policy: Affordability, Access, and Accountability*, edited by Donald Heller, 83-99. Baltimore, Maryland: The John Hopkins University Press, 2001.

_____ . "Measuring Up 2002: Introduction." *National Center for Public Policy and Higher Education.* Downloaded from *http://measuringup.highereducation.org/2002/articles/introduction.htm* on 11/15/2003.

Carleton, Mark T. "Newton Crain Blanchard." In *The Louisiana Governors: From Iberville to Edwards*, edited by Joseph G. Dawson III. Baton Rouge, Louisiana: Louisiana State University Press, 1990.

_____ . "Richard Webster Leche." In *The Louisiana Governors: From Iberville to Edwards*, edited by Joseph G. Dawson III. Baton Rouge, Louisiana: Louisiana State University Press, 1990.

_____ . "The Louisiana Constitution of 1974." In *Louisiana Politics: Festival in a Labyrinth,* edited by James Bolner. Baton Rouge, Louisiana: Louisiana State University Press, 1982.

_____ . "William Wright Heard." In *The Louisiana Governors: From Iberville to Edwards*, edited by Joseph G. Dawson III. Baton Rouge, Louisiana: Louisiana State University Press, 1990.

Carter, Hodding. "Huey Long: American Dictator." In *The Louisiana Purchase Bicentennial Series in Louisiana History, Volume VIII, The Age of the Longs: Louisiana 1928-1960,* edited by Edward F. Haas. Lafayette, Louisiana: Center for Louisiana Studies, 2001.

Cash, W. J. *The Mind of the South.* New York: Vintage Books, 1991—reprint of 1941.

Cassimere, Jr., Raphael. "Crisis of Public Higher Education in Louisiana." In *The Louisiana Purchase Bicentennial Series in Louisiana History, Volume XVIII, Education in Louisiana,* edited by Michael G. Wade. Lafayette, Louisiana: Center for Louisiana Studies, 1999.

Chronicle of Higher Education, The. "State Notes: Louisiana's Gov. Said to Interfere in President Search." *The Chronicle of Higher Education,* 14 November 1990. Downloaded from *http://chronicle.com* on 4/9/2004.

_____ . "Ways & Means: Louisiana Voters Approve New 2-Year-College System." *The Chronicle of Higher Education,* 16 October 1998. Downloaded from *http://chronicle.com* on 4/9/2004.

_____ . "Ways and Means: 27-Year-Old Nominee to Lead U. of Louisiana System Lands on Fast Track." *The Chronicle of Higher Education,* 30 April 1999. Downloaded from *http://chronicle.com* on 4/9/2004.

Clark, Donna. Vice Chancellor for Student Affairs at Nunez Community College. Interview on June 27, 2002.

Clay, Floyd M. "Jimmie Davis." In *The Louisiana Governors: From Iberville to Edwards,* edited by Joseph G. Dawson III. Baton Rouge, Louisiana: Louisiana State University Press, 1990.

Cline, Rodney. *Pioneer Leaders and Early Institutions in Louisiana Education.* Baton Rouge: Claitor's Publishing Division, 1969.

Comminey, Shawn C. *A History of Straight College, 1869-1935.* Ph.D. Dissertation for Florida State University, 2003.

Council for a Better Louisiana. *Community and Technical Colleges.* Downloaded from *http://cabl.org*—Education Issues—> Community and Technical Colleges on 9/14/2003.

Crouere, Jeff. "Louisiana Double Standard." Downloaded from http://www.Bayou Buzz.com on 1/ 20/2004.

Degel, Carl H. *Creation of the Louisiana Coordinating Counicl for Higher Education: Perspectives in Public Organizational Decision-making.* Masters Thesis for Tulane Graduate School, May 28, 1971.

Delahaye, Alfred N. *Nicholls State University: The Elkins-Galliano Years, 1948-1983.* Thibodaux, Louisiana: Nicholls State University Foundation, 1999.

Dethloff, Henry C. "Huey P. Long." In *The Louisiana Governors: From Iberville to Edwards,* edited by Joseph G. Dawson III. Baton Rouge, Louisiana: Louisiana State University Press, 1990.

Diener, Thomas. *Growth of an American Invention: A Documentary History of the Junior and Community College Movement.* New York: Greenwood Press, 1986.

Douglass, John Aubrey. *The California Idea and American Higher Education: 1850 to the 1960 Master Plan.* Stanford, California: Stanford University Press, 2000.

Duffy, John. *The Tulane University Medical Center.* Baton Rouge, Louisiana: Louisiana State University Press, 1984.

Dyer, John P. *Tulane: The Biography of a University.* New York: Harper & Row, Publishers, 1966.

Dyer, Scott. "Community college system creation studied by group." *The Advocate,* 11 March 1996.

Eaton, Judith S. *Colleges of Choice: The Enabling Impact of the Community College.* New York: American Council of Education and Macmillan Publishing Company, 1988.

Eells, Walter Crosby. *The Junior College.* Boston: Houghton Mifflin Company, 1931.

Fagan, Amy. "Vitter plans to carve own path." *The Washington Times,* December 28, 2004.

Fairclough, Adam. *Race & Democracy: The Civil Rights Struggle in Louisiana, 1915-1972.* Athens, Georgia: the University of Georgia Press, 1995.

Ferguson, Hayes. "First Grads Leave Nunez: College Being Used As Model." *New Orleans Times-Picayune,* 20 May 1993, B1.

Field, Betty M. "Alvin Olin King." In *The Louisiana Governors: From Iberville to Edwards,* edited by Joseph G. Dawson III. Baton Rouge, Louisiana: Louisiana State University Press, 1990.

_____. "James A. Noe." In *The Louisiana Governors: From Iberville to Edwards,* edited by Joseph G. Dawson III. Baton Rouge, Louisiana: Louisiana State University Press, 1990.

_____. "Oscar K. Allen." In *The Louisiana Governors: From Iberville to Edwards,* edited by Joseph G. Dawson III. Baton Rouge, Louisiana: Louisiana State University Press, 1990.

_____. "The Louisiana Scandals." In *The Louisiana Purchase Bicentennial Series in Louisiana History, Volume VIII, The Age of the Longs: Louisiana 1928-1960,* edited by Edward F. Haas. Lafayette, Louisiana: Center for Louisiana Studies, 2001.

Fischer, David Hackett. *Albion's Seed.* Oxford: Oxford University Press, 1991.

Fleming, Walter L. *Louisiana State University 1860-1896.* Baton Rouge: Louisiana State University Press, 1936.

Frink, Chris. "Gov. Mike Foster's legacy." *The Advocate,* 28 December 2003. Downloaded from 2theadvocate.com on 3/18/2004.

Gilley, J. Wade. "Governors versus College Presidents: Who Leads?" In *ASHE Reader: Public Policy and Higher Education,* edited by Lester F. Goodchild, Cheryl D. Lovell, Edward R. Hines, and Judith I. Gill. Ginn Press, 1997.

Gimon, Jack. "Delgado School To Teach Trades Now in Operation." *New Orleans Times-Picayune,* 4 September 1921, 1.

Glenn, David. "Education Researchers Use Survey Data to Discern Trends and Differences Among Community-College Students." *The Chronicle of Higher Education,* 12 April

2005. Downloaded from http://chronicle.com/free/2005/04/2005041202n.htm on 4/20/2005.

Goodwin, Gregory Lang. "The Historical Development of the Community-Junior College Ideology: An Analysis and Interpretation of the Writings of Selected Community-Junior College National Leaders from 1890 to 1970." Ph.D. diss., University of Illinois at Urbana-Champaign, 1971.

Gordon, Howard R. D. *The History and Growth of Vocational Education in America.* Needham Heights, Massachusetts: Allyn & Bacon, 1999.

Hardy, Jr., Florent. *A Brief History of the University of Southwestern Louisiana: 1900 to 1960.* Baton Rouge: Claitor's Publishing Division, 1973.

Harris, Ronald. *We Hail Thee Now Southeastern: Remembering the First Seventy-Five Years of Southeastern Louisiana University.* Hammond, Louisiana: Southeastern Development Foundation, 2001.

Healy, Patrick. "Black Educators in Louisiana Unhappy With Pace of Desegregation." *The Chronicle of Higher Education*, 30 June 1995. Downloaded from *http:// chronicle.com* on 4/9/2004.

_____ . "Legislator-Awarded Scholarships Come Under Attack in 3 States." *The Chronicle of Higher Education,* 5 April 1996. Downloaded from *http://chronicle.com* on 4/9/2004.

_____ . "Louisiana Governor's Chief of Staff . . ." *The Chronicle of Higher Education*, 1 May 1998.

_____ . "Louisiana NAACP May Challenge State's Desegregation Plan." *The Chronicle of Higher Education,* 23 November 1994. Downloaded from *http:// chronicle.com* on 4/9/2004.

_____ . "Louisiana Plans to Meld 50 Campuses Into a Coherent 2-Year College System." *The Chronicle of Higher Education*, 1 May 1998, A41.

_____ . "Louisiana's Governor-Elect Promises to Support Colleges." *The Chronicle of Higher Education*, 1 December 1995. Downloaded from *http://chronicle.com* on 4/9/2004.

_____ . "Plan for Public-College 'Superboard' Irks Louisiana Educators." *The Chronicle of Higher Education,* 1 March 1996. Downloaded from *http:// chronicle.com* on 4/9/2004.

_____ . "Proposal to Merge Louisiana Colleges Worries Black Colleges." *The Chronicle of Higher Education,* 2 February 1996. Downloaded from *http:// chronicle.com* on 4/9/2004.

Hebel, Sara. "Desegregation Pacts Set in Maryland, Tennessee, and Louisiana." *The Chronicle of Higher Education*, 5 January 2001. Downloaded from *http://chronicle. com* on 4/9/2004.

_____ . "Segregation's Legacy Still Troubles Campuses." *The Chronicle of Higher Education,* 14 May 2004. Downloaded from *http://chronicle.com* on 5/10/2004.

Hebert, Jr., Adam Otis. "History of Education in Colonial Louisiana." In *The Louisiana Purchase Bicentennial Series in Louisiana History, Volume XVIII, Education in*

Louisiana, edited by Michael G. Wade. Lafayette, Louisiana: Center for Louisiana Studies, 1999.

Hill, John. "From powerhouse to prisoner: Former La. governor prepares to serve jail time." *Louisiana Gannett News*, 20 October 2002. Downloaded from *www.shreveporttimes.com* on 3/18/2004.

Hoffmeyer, Jr., Oscar. *Louisiana College 75 years: A Pictorial History.* Pineville, Louisiana: Louisiana College, 1981.

Honan, William H. "J. J. McKeithen, 81, Governor of Louisiana, 1964 to 1972." *New York Times*, June 5, 1999.

Jaschik, Scott. "Back to the Drawing Board in Louisiana." *The Chronicle of Higher Education*, 5 January 1994. Downloaded from *http://chronicle.com* on 4/9/2004.

_____ . "Overhaul to End Segregation Ordered in Louisiana." *The Chronicle of Higher Education*, 6 January 1993. Downloaded from *http://chronicle.com* on 4/9/2004.

_____ . "U. S. Judge Reverses Order to Reorganize Higher Education." *The Chronicle of Higher Education*, 7 November 1990. Downloaded from *http:// chronicle.com* on 4/9/2004.

Jeansonne, Glen. "Sam Houston Jones and the Revolution of 1940." In *The Louisiana Purchase Bicentennial Series in Louisiana History, Volume VIII, The Age of the Longs: Louisiana 1928-1960*, edited by Edward F. Haas. Lafayette, Louisiana: Center for Louisiana Studies, 2001.

Johnson, Larry. "Politics, Markets, and Ideology: The Transformation of a Technical College into a Community College." Ph.D. diss., University of Utah, May 2000.

Kane, Harnett T. *Louisiana Hayride: The American Rehearsal for Dictatorship 1928-1940.* Gretna, Louisiana: Pelican Publishing Company, 1971.

Knesel, John A. and Holly B. Casey. *"I think you can, and I believe you will:" selected writings of C. C. Colvert, 1932-1943.* Monroe, Louisiana: ULM Friends of the Library, 2003.

Kurtz, Michael L. "Robert F. Kennon." In *The Louisiana Governors: From Iberville to Edwards*, edited by Joseph G. Dawson III. Baton Rouge, Louisiana: Louisiana State University Press, 1990.

Kurtz, Michael L. and Morgan D. Peoples, *Earl K. Long: The Saga of Uncle Earl and Louisiana Politics.* Baton Rouge: Louisiana State University Press, 1990.

Landry, David M. and Joseph B. Parker. "The Louisiana Political Culture." In *Louisiana Politics: Festival in a Labyrinth*, edited by James Bolner, Chapter 1, 1-13. Baton Rouge, Louisiana: Louisiana State University Press.

Laplante, John. "Higher education integration a costly failure." *The Advocate*, 26 July 2004. Downloaded from *http://www.2theadvocate.com* on 7/26/2004.

LeBreton, Marietta M. *Northwestern State University of Louisiana 1884-1984: A History.* Natchitoches, Louisiana: Northwestern State University Press, 1985.

Leslie, Jr., J. Paul. "Earl K. Long." In *The Louisiana Governors: From Iberville to Edwards*, edited by Joseph G. Dawson III. Baton Rouge, Louisiana: Louisiana State University Press, 1990.

Lewis, Ted. "O'Keefe eager to take in sports." *New Orleans Times-Picayune*, 4 June 2005, D3.

Library of Congress. "Report to the President on the Economic Conditions of the South." July 25, 1938 (Library of Congress Document) [cited in James Webb, *Born Fighting: How the Scots-Irish Shaped America*. New York: Broadway Books, 2004].

Louisiana Association of Independent Colleges and Universities website. Downloaded from *www.laicu.org* on 1/4/2005.

Louisiana Board of Regents. *Board of Regents—The 2000 Accountability Report.*

_____ . *Board of Regents' Feasibility Study: Proposed Merging of St. Bernard Parish Community College with the Elaine P. Nunez Vocational-Technical Institute Prepared in Response to Senate Concurrent Resolution Number 50 of the 1992 Regular Session of the Louisiana Legislature—Staff Draft—May 1992.*

_____ . *Master Plan for Public Postsecondary Education: 2001.*

Louisiana Community and Technical College System. *LCTCS Mission.* Downloaded from www.lctcs.net/about/mission.htm.

_____ . *LCTCS Policy #I.1.003—Title: Elements of Two-Year Institutional Mission.* Downloaded from www.lctcs.net.

Louisiana Economic Development Council. *Louisiana: Vision 2020-2003 Update: Master Plan for Economic Development.* Downloaded from *http://Vision2020/louisiana.gov/.*

Louisiana State Legislature. *State of Louisiana Acts of the Legislature Volume I—Regular Session 1992.*

Louisiana State University at Eunice. *Establishment of LSU at Eunice.* Downloaded from *http://www.lsue.edu/about.html* on 11/8/2003.

Louisiana Technical College. *History of LTC.* Downloaded from *http://www.theltc.net/ltc_history.htm* on 6/14/2004.

Loyola University. "The Story of Loyola University." *1997-99 Undergraduate Bulletin* (New Orleans: Loyola University).

Maginnis, John. "Blanco built agenda along the way." *New Orleans Times-Picayune*, 23 June 2004, B7.

_____ . Business Report.com, 17 March 2003.

Mangan, Katherine S. "La. Governor Threatens to End Tax Breaks for Tulane U. in Dispute Over Law Clinic." *The Chronicle of Higher Education,* 5 September 1997. Downloaded from *http://chronicle.com* on 4/9/2004.

Maxcy, Spencer J., and Doreen O. Maxcy. "Educational Reform in Louisiana." *International Journal of Educational Reform,* Volume 2, No. 3, July 1993, 236-241.

McBride, Mary G. "The Establishment of Tulane University." In *The Louisiana Purchase Bicentennial Series in Louisiana History, Volume XVIII, Education in Louisiana,* edited by Michael G. Wade. Lafayette, Louisiana: Center for Louisiana Studies, 1999.

McKeithen, John J. Interview by Jack Fiser. Located at LSU Libraries Special Collections (call number L4700.0042), 1982.

McKeithen, John J. Interview by Mark Carleton. Located at LSU Libraries Special Collections (call number L4700.0334), 1993.

Mercer, Joye. "Judge Refuses to Delay Louisiana Desegregation Order. *The Chronicle of Higher Education*, 3 March 1993. Downloaded from *http://chronicle.com* on 4/9/2004.

_____ . "La. Board Proposes Higher-Education Desgregation Plan." *The Chronicle of Higher Education*, 16 December 1992. Downloaded from *http://chronicle.com* on 4/9/2004.

_____ . "Louisiana Desegregation Trial is Delayed Until March." *The Chronicle of Higher Education*, 3 August 1994. Downloaded from *http://chronicle.com* on 4/9/2004.

_____ . "Order for La. 'Superboard' Blocked by Appeals Court." *The Chronicle of Higher Education*. 17 March 1993. Downloaded from *http://chronicle.com* on 4/9/2004.

Morrison, Betty L. *A History of Our Lady of Holy Cross College, New Orleans, Louisiana*. Gretna, Louisiana: Her Publishing Co., Inc., 1977.

Nevin, Jr., R. Frantz. "The Contributions of Booker T. Washington and W. E. B. DuBois in the Development of Vocational Education." *Journal of Industrial Teacher Education*, Vol. 34, No 4, 1996. Downloaded from *http://scholar.lib.vt.edu/ejournals/JITE/v34n4/html/frantz.html*.

New Orleans Baptist Theological Seminary website. Downloaded from *http://www.nobts.edu/About.html on 1/4/2005*.

Noble, Stuart Grayson. "Governor Claiborne and the Public School System of the Territorial Government of Louisiana." In *The Louisiana Purchase Bicentennial Series in Louisiana History, Volume XVIII, Education in Louisiana*, edited by Michael G. Wade. Lafayette, Louisiana: Center for Louisiana Studies, 1999.

Owen, Mary. "A Desegregation Success Story in the Making in Louisiana." *The Chronicle of Higher Education*, 14 April 1998. Downloaded from *http://chronicle.com* on 4/9/2004.

Owen, Russell. "Huey Long Gives His View of Dictators." *New York Times*, 10 February 1935, SM3.

Parker, Joseph B. "David Treen." In *The Louisiana Governors: From Iberville to Edwards*, edited by Joseph G. Dawson III. Baton Rouge, Louisiana: Louisiana State University Press, 1990.

_____ . "Edwin Edwards." In *The Louisiana Governors: From Iberville to Edwards*, edited by Joseph G. Dawson III. Baton Rouge, Louisiana: Louisiana State University Press, 1990.

Patureau, Stephen Irwin. *A History of the Isaac Delgado Central Trades School*. Masters Thesis, Tulane University, July 6, 1939. Located in Tulane University Howard-Tilton Memorial Library.

Pearce, Ruby B., Sallie Robinson, and Helen Graham, eds. *Alma Mater: 1895-1945: A Memorial History of Louisiana Polytechnic Institute*. Ruston, La.: Executive Board of the Alumni Association of the Louisiana Polytechnic Institute, 1945.

Peoples, Morgan D. "Earl Kemp Long: The Man from Pea Patch Farm." In *The Louisiana Purchase Bicentennial Series in Louisiana History, Volume VIII, The Age of the Longs: Louisiana 1928-1960*, edited by Edward F. Haas. Lafayette, Louisiana: Center for Louisiana Studies, 2001.

Pinsel, Jerry. "A Brief Historic Profile of the Louisiana Higher Education Community: An Unfinished Journey" (Unpublished Draft), 2003.

_____ . Vice President for Academic and Student Affairs of the Louisiana Community and Technical College System. Informal correspondence, 2004.

Public Affairs Research Council of La., Inc. *The Community College Question: Summary Report*, August 1997.

_____ . *White Paper on Higher Education* (Issue 1, April 2003).

_____ . *PAR 1998 Guide to the Constitutional Amendments,* August 1998.

_____ . *PAR Analysis: Meeting Louisiana's Need For Vocational-Technical Education: A Summary,* Number 184, 1973.

_____ . *PAR Analysis: Vo-tech—In Search of A System,* Number 254, December 1981.

Ravitch, Diane. *Left Back: A Century of Battles Over School Reform*. New York: Simon & Schuster, 2000.

Reilly, Shannon, and Robert W. Ahrens. "USA Today Snapshots: Paychecks increase with education." *USA Today*, 22 April 2005, 1A.

Renwick, Ed. "The Governor." In *Louisiana Politics: Festival in a Labyrinth*, edited by James Bolner, Chapter 4, 75-88. Baton Rouge, Louisiana: Louisiana State University Press.

Richardson, Joe M. "Edgar B. Stern: A White New Orleans Philanthropist Helps Build a Black University." *The Journal of Negro History*, Vol. 82, No. 3 (Summer 1997), 328-342. Downloaded from *www.jstor.org* on 4/10/2005.

Schmidt, Peter. "'Report Card' Spurs Calls for Change in Academe." *The Chronicle of Higher Education*, 24 September 2004.

_____ . "A Small Team of Consultants With Large Sway in Higher Education." *The Chronicle of Higher Education*, 29 September 2000. Downloaded from *http://chronicle.com* on 4/9/2004.

Schott, Matthew J. "John M. Parker." In *The Louisiana Governors: From Iberville to Edwards*, edited by Joseph G. Dawson III. Baton Rouge, Louisiana: Louisiana State University Press, 1990.

Schumacher, Edward Daniel. *The Struggle Against Adult Functional Illiteracy in Louisiana: A Historical Analysis*. Sulphur, Louisiana: Maplewood Books, 1973.

Selingo, Jeffrey. "Louisiana Judge Blocks Law Expanding Authority of Board of Regents." *The Chronicle of Higher Education*, 16 January 1998. Downloaded from *http://chronicle.com* on 4/9/2004.

Southern University at Shreveport. *Historical Sketch of Southern University at Shreveport.* Downloaded from *http://www.susla.edu/html/catalog/general/history.htm* on 11/8/2003.

Southern University website. "Historical Statement." Downloaded on 11/8/2003.

Southwest Educational Development Laboratory. Downloaded from *www.sedl.org/pubs/pic01/priority.html* on 11/13/2003.

St. Bernard Parish Community College. *Catalog for St. Bernard Parish Community College, 1970-71 School Session.*

_____ . *Catalog for St. Bernard Parish Thirteenth and Fourteenth Grades, 1968-69 School Session.*

Stine, Dennis. *A Vision of Louisiana's Community and Technical College System.* March 1999. Downloaded from *http://cabl.org*—Briefings—> Community and Technical College System on 9/14/2003.

Suarez, Raleigh A. "Chronicle of a Failure: Public Education in Antebellum Louisiana." In *The Louisiana Purchase Bicentennial Series in Louisiana History, Volume XVIII, Education in Louisiana,* edited by Michael G. Wade. Lafayette, Louisiana: Center for Louisiana Studies, 1999.

Taylor, Joe Gray. *Louisiana Reconstructed: 1863-1877.* Baton Rouge: Louisiana State University Press, 1974.

_____ . *McNeese State University, 1939-1987: A Chronicle.* McNeese State University, 1990.

Thelin, John R. *A History of American Higher Education.* Baltimore, Maryland: Johns Hopkins University Press, 2004.

Turni, Karen. "College Merger Plan Studied." *New Orleans Times-Picayune,* 19 November 1994, B1.

U. S. Census Bureau. *Educational Attainment of the Population 25 Years and Over for the United States, Regions, and States, and for Puerto Rico: 1990 and 2000.* Downloaded from *www.census.gov/prod/cen2000/doc/st3.pdf.*

University of Louisiana at Lafayette. *100 Years: The University of Louisiana at Lafayette: 1900-2000.* Lafayette, Louisiana: The University of Louisiana at Lafayette Office of Public Relations and News Services, 1999.

USA Today. "Western states yield high graduation rates." 15 December 2003, 6D.

Vaughan, George B. *The Community College Story.* Washington, D. C.: Community College Press, 2000.

Vincent, Charles. *A Centennial History of Southern University and A&M College, 1880-1980.* Charles Vincent, 1981.

Vyhnanek, Louis. "Henry L. Fuqua." In *The Louisiana Governors: From Iberville to Edwards,* edited by Joseph G. Dawson III. Baton Rouge, Louisiana: Louisiana State University Press, 1990.

_____ . "J. Y. Sanders." In *The Louisiana Governors: From Iberville to Edwards,* edited by Joseph G. Dawson III. Baton Rouge, Louisiana: Louisiana State University Press, 1990.

Walker, George Thomas. *The Building of a University.* Dallas, Texas: Taylor Publishing Company, 1991.

Wall, Bennett H., ed. *Louisiana: A History, 3rd Edition.* Harlan Davidson, 1997.

Warner, Coleman. "TOPS ups retention, test scores: But lawmakers say many miss benefits." *New Orleans Times-Picayune,* 17 November 2004, A1.

Washington, Booker T. "The Atlanta Exposition Address." *Up from Slavery: An Autobiography.* 1901. Downloaded from http://www.bartleby.com/1004/14.html.

Weiss, Joanna. "Nunez Kicks Off Campaign For Re-Election At College." *New Orleans Times-Picayune,* 2 August 1995, B3.

Whitfield, Tonya. "Louisiana Official Stopped From Investigating Colleges." *The Chronicle of Higher Education,* 2 September 1992. Downloaded from *http://chronicle.com* on 4/9/2004.

Wilkerson, Marcus M. *Thomas Duckett Boyd: The Story of a Southern Educator.* Baton Rouge: Louisiana State University Press, 1935.

Will, George F. "Echoes of the GI Bill." *Newsweek,* 27 October 1997.

ENDNOTES

1   Peter Schmidt. "'Report Card' Spurs Calls for Change in Academe," *The Chronicle of Higher Education*, 24 September 2004.

2   Technically, O'Reilly did not hold the title of governor—this was Luis de Unzaga. O'Reilly was clearly in charge during his stay in Louisiana—from August 1769 to March 1770. O'Reilly re-established Spain's control over the colony after the Insurrection of 1768. (textbook 59-62).

3   Bennett H. Wall, ed., *Louisiana: A History, 3rd Edition* (Harlan Davidson, 1997), 18-20.

4   A more technically correct name is Great Britain.

5   John R. Thelin, *A History of American Higher Education* (Baltimore, Maryland: Johns Hopkins University Press, 2004), 1.

6   Bennett H. Wall, ed., *Louisiana: A History, 3rd Edition* (Harlan Davidson, 1997), 37.

7   Rodney Cline, *Pioneer Leaders and Early Institutions in Louisiana Education* (Baton Rouge: Claitor's Publishing Division, 1969), viii.

8   Adam Otis Hebert, Jr., "History of Education in Colonial Louisiana," In *The Louisiana Purchase Bicentennial Series in Louisiana History, Volume XVIII, Education in Louisiana*, edited by Michael G. Wade (Lafayette, Louisiana: Center for Louisiana Studies, 1999), 17.

9   Ibid, 26.

10   Walter L. Fleming, *Louisiana State University 1860-1896* (Baton Rouge: Louisiana State University Press, 1936), 6.

11   Adam Otis Hebert, Jr., "History of Education in Colonial Louisiana," In *The Louisiana Purchase Bicentennial Series in Louisiana History, Volume XVIII, Education in Louisiana*, edited by Michael G. Wade (Lafayette, Louisiana: Center for Louisiana Studies, 1999), 26.

12   Ibid, 9.

13   Rodney Cline, *Pioneer Leaders and Early Institutions in Louisiana Education* (Baton Rouge: Claitor's Publishing Division, 1969), viii.

14   Bennett H. Wall, ed., *Louisiana: A History, 3rd Edition* (Harlan Davidson, 1997), 59-60.

15   Ibid, 70.

16   Adam Otis Hebert, Jr., "History of Education in Colonial Louisiana," In *The Louisiana Purchase Bicentennial Series in Louisiana History, Volume XVIII, Education in Louisiana*, edited by Michael G. Wade (Lafayette, Louisiana: Center for Louisiana Studies, 1999), 31-3.

17   Bennett H. Wall, ed., *Louisiana: A History, 3rd Edition* (Harlan Davidson, 1997), 75-6.

18   Adam Otis Hebert, Jr., "History of Education in Colonial Louisiana," In *The Louisiana Purchase Bicentennial Series in Louisiana History, Volume XVIII, Education in Louisiana*, edited by Michael G. Wade (Lafayette, Louisiana: Center for Louisiana Studies, 1999), 33.

19   David Hackett Fischer, *Albion's Seed* (Oxford: Oxford University Press, 1991), 854-5. [cited in James Webb, *Born Fighting: How the Scots-Irish Shaped America* (New York: Broadway Books, 2004), 216].

20   "Thorough" in this context is another name for the period of Reconstruction in the South.

21   W. J. Cash, *The Mind of the South* (New York: Vintage Books, 1991—reprint of 1941), 131.

22   Library of Congress, "Report to the President on the Economic Conditions of the South" July 25, 1938 (Library of Congress Document), 1-2. [cited in James Webb, *Born Fighting: How the Scots-Irish Shaped America* (New York: Broadway Books, 2004), 268].

23   Ibid.

24   The exact definition of the term "creole" is a hotly contested topic. Here is it used to describe Louisianans of French and Spanish ancestries.

25   Bennett H. Wall, ed., *Louisiana: A History, 3rd Edition* (Harlan Davidson, 1997), 91.

26   Ibid.

27   Walter L. Fleming, *Louisiana State University 1860-1896* (Baton Rouge: Louisiana State University Press, 1936), 232.

28   Bennett H. Wall, ed., *Louisiana: A History, 3rd Edition* (Harlan Davidson, 1997), 91.

29   Edward Daniel Schumacher, *The Struggle Against Adult Functional Illiteracy in Louisiana: A Historical Analysis* (Sulphur, Louisiana: Maplewood Books, 1973), 6.

30   Bennett H. Wall, ed., *Louisiana: A History, 3rd Edition* (Harlan Davidson, 1997), 93-4.

31   Ibid, 93.

32   Ibid, 104.

33   Ibid, 90-1.

34   Ibid, 114.

35   Ibid, 108-109.

36   Stuart Grayson Noble, "Governor Claiborne and the Public School System of the Territorial Government of Louisiana," In *The Louisiana Purchase Bicentennial Series in Louisiana History, Volume XVIII, Education in Louisiana*, edited by Michael G. Wade (Lafayette, Louisiana: Center for Louisiana Studies, 1999), 52.

37   Ibid, 51-2)

38   Bennett H. Wall, ed., *Louisiana: A History, 3rd Edition* (Harlan Davidson, 1997), 100-101.

39   Stuart Grayson Noble, "Governor Claiborne and the Public School System of the Territorial Government of Louisiana," In *The Louisiana Purchase Bicentennial Series in Louisiana History, Volume XVIII, Education in Louisiana*, edited by Michael G. Wade (Lafayette, Louisiana: Center for Louisiana Studies, 1999), 51.

40   Raleigh A. Suarez, "Chronicle of a Failure: Public Education in Antebellum Louisiana," In *The Louisiana Purchase Bicentennial Series in Louisiana History, Volume XVIII, Education in Louisiana*, edited by Michael G. Wade (Lafayette, Louisiana: Center for Louisiana Studies, 1999), 67.

41   Bennett H. Wall, ed., *Louisiana: A History, 3rd Edition* (Harlan Davidson, 1997), 100-101

42   Raphael Cassimere, Jr., "Crisis of Public Higher Education in Louisiana," In *The Louisiana Purchase Bicentennial Series in Louisiana History, Volume XVIII, Education in Louisiana*, edited by Michael G. Wade (Lafayette, Louisiana: Center for Louisiana Studies, 1999), 544.

43   Rodney Cline, *Pioneer Leaders and Early Institutions in Louisiana Education* (Baton Rouge: Claitor's Publishing Division, 1969), 248.

44   Ibid, 318-21.

45   Ibid, 321.

[46]   Ibid, 248.

[47]   Centenary College of Louisiana website. "About Centenary College." *http://www.centenary.edu/about*. Downloaded 11/9/2003.

[48]   Rodney Cline, *Pioneer Leaders and Early Institutions in Louisiana Education* (Baton Rouge: Claitor's Publishing Division, 1969), 321.

[49]   Ibid, 249-251.

[50]   Ibid.

[51]   Ibid, 254.

[52]   Ibid.

[53]   Ibid, 329-30.

[54]   John P. Dyer, *Tulane: The Biography of a University* (New York: Harper & Row, Publishers, 1966), 19.

[55]   Rodney Cline, *Pioneer Leaders and Early Institutions in Louisiana Education* (Baton Rouge: Claitor's Publishing Division, 1969), 329-30.

[56]   John Duffy, *The Tulane University Medical Center* (Baton Rouge, Louisiana: Louisiana State University Press, 1984), 2.

[57]   Ibid.

[58]   Rodney Cline, *Pioneer Leaders and Early Institutions in Louisiana Education* (Baton Rouge: Claitor's Publishing Division, 1969), 330.

[59]   John Duffy, *The Tulane University Medical Center* (Baton Rouge, Louisiana: Louisiana State University Press, 1984), 35.

[60]   Ibid.

[61]   Ibid, 2.

[62]   Ibid, 39.

[63]   Ibid,37-8.

[64]   Ibid, 68-70.

[65]   Ibid, 38.

[66]   Ibid.

[67]   Ibid.

[68]   Walter L. Fleming, *Louisiana State University 1860-1896* (Baton Rouge: Louisiana State University Press, 1936), 14-5.

[69]   Ibid, 18.

[70]   John P. Dyer, *Tulane: The Biography of a University* (New York: Harper & Row, Publishers, 1966), 21f.

[71]   Ibid, 21-2.

[72]   Walter L. Fleming, *Louisiana State University 1860-1896* (Baton Rouge: Louisiana State University Press, 1936), 18-9.

[73]   John P. Dyer, *Tulane: The Biography of a University* (New York: Harper & Row, Publishers, 1966), 22.

[74]   Ibid, 24.

[75]   Ibid, 25.

[76]   Ibid, 26.

77   Ibid, 28.

78   Ibid, 29.

79   Joe Gray Taylor, Louisiana Reconstructed: 1863-1877 (Baton Rouge: Louisiana State University Press, 1974), 474.

80   Walter L. Fleming, *Louisiana State University 1860-1896* (Baton Rouge: Louisiana State University Press, 1936), 328.

81   John P. Dyer, *Tulane: The Biography of a University* (New York: Harper & Row, Publishers, 1966), 36.

82   Ibid, 37.

83   Walter L. Fleming, *Louisiana State University 1860-1896* (Baton Rouge: Louisiana State University Press, 1936), 18-20.

84   Ibid, 21.

85   Ibid, 23-4.

86   Ibid, 25.

87   Ibid, 24.

88   Ibid, 29.

89   Ibid, 33.

90   Ibid, 34.

91   Ibid, 28.

92   J. Fair Hardin, "The Early History of the Louisiana State University," In *The Louisiana Purchase Bicentennial Series in Louisiana History, Volume XVIII, Education in Louisiana*, edited by Michael G. Wade (Lafayette, Louisiana: Center for Louisiana Studies, 1999), 125.

93   Ibid.

94   Walter L. Fleming, *Louisiana State University 1860-1896* (Baton Rouge: Louisiana State University Press, 1936), 31.

95   Ibid, 45-7.

96   Ibid, 76.

97   Ibid, 98.

98   Ibid, 100-101.

99   J. Fair Hardin, "The Early History of the Louisiana State University," In *The Louisiana Purchase Bicentennial Series in Louisiana History, Volume XVIII, Education in Louisiana*, edited by Michael G. Wade (Lafayette, Louisiana: Center for Louisiana Studies, 1999), 129, 133.

100   Walter L. Fleming, *Louisiana State University 1860-1896* (Baton Rouge: Louisiana State University Press, 1936), 121.

101   Ibid.

102   Ibid, 105-6.

103   J. Fair Hardin, "The Early History of the Louisiana State University," In *The Louisiana Purchase Bicentennial Series in Louisiana History, Volume XVIII, Education in Louisiana*, edited by Michael G. Wade (Lafayette, Louisiana: Center for Louisiana Studies, 1999), 133.

104   Bennett H. Wall, ed., *Louisiana: A History, 3rd Edition* (Harlan Davidson, 1997), 205

[105]   Joe Gray Taylor, *Louisiana Reconstructed: 1863-1877* (Baton Rouge: Louisiana State University Press, 1974), 474-5.

[106]   Marcus M. Wilkerson, *Thomas Duckett Boyd: The Story of a Southern Educator* (Baton Rouge: Louisiana State University Press, 1935), 38.

[107]   Joe Gray Taylor, *Louisiana Reconstructed: 1863-1877* (Baton Rouge: Louisiana State University Press, 1974), 476.

[108]   Marcus M. Wilkerson, *Thomas Duckett Boyd: The Story of a Southern Educator* (Baton Rouge: Louisiana State University Press, 1935), 27.

[109]   Walter L. Fleming, *Louisiana State University 1860-1896* (Baton Rouge: Louisiana State University Press, 1936), 252-3.

[110]   Marcus M. Wilkerson, *Thomas Duckett Boyd: The Story of a Southern Educator* (Baton Rouge: Louisiana State University Press, 1935), 31.

[111]   Joe Gray Taylor, *Louisiana Reconstructed: 1863-1877* (Baton Rouge: Louisiana State University Press, 1974), 474-5.

[112]   Marcus M. Wilkerson, *Thomas Duckett Boyd: The Story of a Southern Educator* (Baton Rouge: Louisiana State University Press, 1935), 22.

[113]   Marcus M. Wilkerson, *Thomas Duckett Boyd: The Story of a Southern Educator* (Baton Rouge: Louisiana State University Press, 1935), 22; Walter L. Fleming, *Louisiana State University 1860-1896* (Baton Rouge: Louisiana State University Press, 1936), 180.

[114]   Walter L. Fleming, *Louisiana State University 1860-1896* (Baton Rouge: Louisiana State University Press, 1936), 180.

[115]   Ibid, 185.

[116]   Marcus M. Wilkerson, *Thomas Duckett Boyd: The Story of a Southern Educator* (Baton Rouge: Louisiana State University Press, 1935), 23.

[117]   Ibid, 27.

[118]   Ibid, 28.

[119]   Walter L. Fleming, *Louisiana State University 1860-1896* (Baton Rouge: Louisiana State University Press, 1936), 184.

[120]   Ibid, 187.

[121]   Ibid, 163.

[122]   Ibid, 193.

[123]   J. Fair Hardin, "The Early History of the Louisiana State University," In *The Louisiana Purchase Bicentennial Series in Louisiana History, Volume XVIII, Education in Louisiana*, edited by Michael G. Wade (Lafayette, Louisiana: Center for Louisiana Studies, 1999), 133.

[124]   Walter L. Fleming, *Louisiana State University 1860-1896* (Baton Rouge: Louisiana State University Press, 1936), 200.

[125]   Ibid, 200.

[126]   Ibid, 268.

[127]   Ibid, 270.

[128]   Ibid, 147-8.

[129]   Ibid, 268.

[130] Ibid, 278.

[131] John P. Dyer, *Tulane: The Biography of a University* (New York: Harper & Row, Publishers, 1966), 33.

[132] Ibid, 33.

[133] Walter L. Fleming, *Louisiana State University 1860-1896* (Baton Rouge: Louisiana State University Press, 1936), 279.

[134] Ibid, 278-9.

[135] Ibid, 281.

[136] Ibid.

[137] Ibid, 282.

[138] Joe Gray Taylor, *Louisiana Reconstructed: 1863-1877* (Baton Rouge: Louisiana State University Press, 1974), 475-6.

[139] Walter L. Fleming, *Louisiana State University 1860-1896* (Baton Rouge: Louisiana State University Press, 1936), 283.

[140] John P. Dyer, *Tulane: The Biography of a University* (New York: Harper & Row, Publishers, 1966), 34.

[141] Walter L. Fleming, *Louisiana State University 1860-1896* (Baton Rouge: Louisiana State University Press, 1936), 284.

[142] Ibid, 283.

[143] Ibid.

[144] Walter L. Fleming, *Louisiana State University 1860-1896* (Baton Rouge: Louisiana State University Press, 1936), 287.

[145] Ibid.

[146] John P. Dyer, *Tulane: The Biography of a University* (New York: Harper & Row, Publishers, 1966), 34.

[147] Joe Gray Taylor, *Louisiana Reconstructed: 1863-1877* (Baton Rouge: Louisiana State University Press, 1974), 475-6.

[148] Walter L. Fleming, *Louisiana State University 1860-1896* (Baton Rouge: Louisiana State University Press, 1936), 289.

[149] Bennett H. Wall, ed., *Louisiana: A History, 3rd Edition* (Harlan Davidson, 1997), 195-6

[150] Ibid.

[151] Sometimes also known as "Bourbon Redeemers" (as the South was "redeemed" from the alleged misrule of the Reconstruction governments) or "Bourbon Oligarchs."

[152] Ibid, 205

[153] Ibid, 215

[154] Mark T. Carleton, "William Wright Heard," In *The Louisiana Governors: From Iberville to Edwards*, edited by Joseph G. Dawson III (Baton Rouge, Louisiana: Louisiana State University Press, 1990), 197.

[155] Marcus M. Wilkerson, *Thomas Duckett Boyd: The Story of a Southern Educator* (Baton Rouge: Louisiana State University Press, 1935), 97.

[156] Bennett H. Wall, ed., *Louisiana: A History, 3rd Edition* (Harlan Davidson, 1997), 215, 223

[157]   Mark T. Carleton, "Newton Crain Blanchard," In *The Louisiana Governors: From Iberville to Edwards*, edited by Joseph G. Dawson III (Baton Rouge, Louisiana: Louisiana State University Press, 1990), 202.

[158]   Louis Vyhnanek, "J. Y. Sanders," In *The Louisiana Governors: From Iberville to Edwards*, edited by Joseph G. Dawson III (Baton Rouge, Louisiana: Louisiana State University Press, 1990).

[159]   Walter L. Fleming, *Louisiana State University 1860-1896* (Baton Rouge: Louisiana State University Press, 1936), 290.

[160]   Ibid, 291.

[161]   Ibid, 293.

[162]   Ibid, 295-6.

[163]   Ibid.

[164]   Ibid, 296.

[165]   Ibid, 298.

[166]   J. Fair Hardin, "The Early History of the Louisiana State University," In *The Louisiana Purchase Bicentennial Series in Louisiana History, Volume XVIII, Education in Louisiana*, edited by Michael G. Wade (Lafayette, Louisiana: Center for Louisiana Studies, 1999), 133.

[167]   Walter L. Fleming, *Louisiana State University 1860-1896* (Baton Rouge: Louisiana State University Press, 1936), 292.

[168]   Ibid, 298.

[169]   Ibid, 312.

[170]   Ibid, 308.

[171]   Marcus M. Wilkerson, *Thomas Duckett Boyd: The Story of a Southern Educator* (Baton Rouge: Louisiana State University Press, 1935), 61.

[172]   Walter L. Fleming, *Louisiana State University 1860-1896* (Baton Rouge: Louisiana State University Press, 1936), 328.

[173]   John P. Dyer, *Tulane: The Biography of a University* (New York: Harper & Row, Publishers, 1966), 34.

[174]   Ibid, 35.

[175]   J. Fair Hardin, "The Early History of the Louisiana State University," In *The Louisiana Purchase Bicentennial Series in Louisiana History, Volume XVIII, Education in Louisiana*, edited by Michael G. Wade (Lafayette, Louisiana: Center for Louisiana Studies, 1999), 134.

[176]   Walter L. Fleming, *Louisiana State University 1860-1896* (Baton Rouge: Louisiana State University Press, 1936), 431.

[177]   Ibid.

[178]   Marcus M. Wilkerson, *Thomas Duckett Boyd: The Story of a Southern Educator* (Baton Rouge: Louisiana State University Press, 1935), 84.

[179]   Walter L. Fleming, *Louisiana State University 1860-1896* (Baton Rouge: Louisiana State University Press, 1936), 433-4.

[180]   Ibid, 437.

[181]   1718-1720: Mississippi Company granted to Sieur Diron d'Artagnette

182 Ibid, 436.

183 Ibid, 436-9.

184 Ibid, 431.

185 Ibid, 465.

186 Ibid, 434.

187 Ibid, 443.

188 Marcus M. Wilkerson, *Thomas Duckett Boyd: The Story of a Southern Educator* (Baton Rouge: Louisiana State University Press, 1935), 71.

189 Walter L. Fleming, *Louisiana State University 1860-1896* (Baton Rouge: Louisiana State University Press, 1936), 331.

190 Marcus M. Wilkerson, *Thomas Duckett Boyd: The Story of a Southern Educator* (Baton Rouge: Louisiana State University Press, 1935), 72.

191 Ibid, 74.

192 Amy Fagan, "Vitter plans to carve own path," *The Washington Times*, December 28, 2004. Downloaded from *www.washingtontimes.com* on 1/5/2005.

193 Ibid.

194 John P. Dyer, *Tulane: The Biography of a University* (New York: Harper & Row, Publishers, 1966), 6.

195 No author, "Paul Tulane's Plans: What he hopes to accomplish by his large gift to Louisiana," *New York Times*, December 31, 1883.

196 Mary G. McBride, "The Establishment of Tulane University," In *The Louisiana Purchase Bicentennial Series in Louisiana History, Volume XVIII, Education in Louisiana*, edited by Michael G. Wade (Lafayette, Louisiana: Center for Louisiana Studies, 1999), 446, 450.

197 The term "Tulane Educational Fund" was used by the charter and official documents of the University. Act No. 43 of 1884 uses "Tulane Education Fund." Early minutes of the Board of Administrators use both.

198 John P. Dyer, *Tulane: The Biography of a University* (New York: Harper & Row, Publishers, 1966), 13f.

199 Ibid, 11.

200 Mary G. McBride, "The Establishment of Tulane University," In *The Louisiana Purchase Bicentennial Series in Louisiana History, Volume XVIII, Education in Louisiana*, edited by Michael G. Wade (Lafayette, Louisiana: Center for Louisiana Studies, 1999), 451.

201 John P. Dyer, *Tulane: The Biography of a University* (New York: Harper & Row, Publishers, 1966), 14.

202 Ibid, 15.

203 Ibid.

204 Ibid, 12.

205 Ibid, 38.

206 Ibid, 13.

207 Mary G. McBride, "The Establishment of Tulane University," In *The Louisiana Purchase Bicentennial Series in Louisiana History, Volume XVIII, Education in Louisiana*, edited by Michael G. Wade (Lafayette, Louisiana: Center for Louisiana Studies, 1999), 450.

[208] John P. Dyer, *Tulane: The Biography of a University* (New York: Harper & Row, Publishers, 1966), 82.

[209] The son of famed Confederate general Albert Sidney Johnston.

[210] Ibid, 39.

[211] Ibid, 41.

[212] Mary G. McBride, "The Establishment of Tulane University," In *The Louisiana Purchase Bicentennial Series in Louisiana History, Volume XVIII, Education in Louisiana*, edited by Michael G. Wade (Lafayette, Louisiana: Center for Louisiana Studies, 1999), 450.

[213] John P. Dyer, *Tulane: The Biography of a University* (New York: Harper & Row, Publishers, 1966), 46.

[214] Ibid.

[215] Ibid.

[216] Ibid.

[217] Patrick Healy, "Legislator-Awarded Scholarships Come Under Attack in 3 States," *The Chronicle of Higher Education*, 5 April 1996. Downloaded from *http://chronicle.com* on 4/9/2004.

[218] John P. Dyer, *Tulane: The Biography of a University* (New York: Harper & Row, Publishers, 1966), 310.

[219] Ed Anderson, "Tulane scholarships survive," *New Orleans Times-Picayune*, 30 May 1996.

[220] For more details, see "The Louisiana Decision (Part 3)" at www.tulanelink.com/tulanelink/decision_03d.htm

[221] Bennett H. Wall, ed., *Louisiana: A History, 3rd Edition* (Harlan Davidson, 1997), 147.

[222] Joe Gray Taylor, *Louisiana Reconstructed: 1863-1877* (Baton Rouge: Louisiana State University Press, 1974), 479

[223] "turn of the century"

[224] Mildred B. G. Gallot, A History of Grambling State University (Lanham, MD: University Press of America, Inc., 1985), xii.

[225] R. Frantz Nevin, Jr., "The Contributions of Booker T. Washington and W. E. B. DuBois in the Development of Vocational Education," *Journal of Industrial Teacher Education*, Volume 34, Number 4, 1996. (Downloaded from *http://scholar.lib.vt.edu/ejournals/JITE/v34n4/html/frantz.html*)

[226] Howard R. D. Gordon, *The History and Growth of Vocational Education in America*, (Needham Heights, Massachusetts: Allyn & Bacon, 1999).

[227] Booker T. Washington, "The Atlanta Exposition Address," *Up from Slavery: An Autobiography* (1901). (Downloaded from http://www.bartleby.com/1004/14.html)

[228] Joe Gray Taylor, *Louisiana Reconstructed: 1863-1877* (Baton Rouge: Louisiana State University Press, 1974), 478-9.

[229] Charles Vincent, *A Centennial History of Southern University and A&M College, 1880-1980* (Charles Vincent, 1981), xi.

[230] Ibid, 4.

[231] Ibid.

[232] Ibid, 6.

233   Ibid, 8.

234   Ibid, 14.

235   Ibid, xii.

236   Ibid, 273.

237   Joe Gray Taylor, *Louisiana Reconstructed: 1863-1877* (Baton Rouge: Louisiana State University Press, 1974), 477.

238   Charles Vincent, *A Centennial History of Southern University and A&M College, 1880-1980* (Charles Vincent, 1981), 31.

239   Ibid, 16.

240   Ibid, 30.

241   Joe Gray Taylor, *Louisiana Reconstructed: 1863-1877* (Baton Rouge: Louisiana State University Press, 1974), 478-9.

242   Charles Vincent, *A Centennial History of Southern University and A&M College, 1880-1980* (Charles Vincent, 1981), 9.

243   Some sources call it Straight College.

244   Now the United Church of Christ

245   Shawn C. Comminey, *A History of Straight College, 1869-1935* (Ph.D. Diss., Florida State University, 2003).

246   Ernest J. Middleton, History of the Louisiana Education Association (Washington, DC: National Education Association, 1984), 33.

247   Ibid.

248   Ibid, 34.

249   Ibid, 33.

250   Charles Vincent, *A Centennial History of Southern University and A&M College, 1880-1980* (Charles Vincent, 1981), xii.

251   Ernest J. Middleton, History of the Louisiana Education Association (Washington, DC: National Education Association, 1984), 33-4.

252   Joe M. Richardson, "Edgar B. Stern: A White New Orleans Philanthropist Helps Build a Black University," *The Journal of Negro History,* Vol. 82, No. 3 (Summer, 1997), 328-342 (Downloaded from *www.jstor.org* on April 10, 2005), 330.

253   Ibid.

254   Bennett H. Wall, ed., *Louisiana: A History, 3rd Edition* (Harlan Davidson, 1997), 224-5

255   Ibid

256   Ibid, 230

257   Ibid, 233.

258   Ibid.

259   John R. Thelin, *A History of American Higher Education* (Baltimore, Maryland: Johns Hopkins University Press, 2004).

260   Marcus M. Wilkerson, *Thomas Duckett Boyd: The Story of a Southern Educator* (Baton Rouge: Louisiana State University Press, 1935), 16.

261   Ibid, 7.

262   Ibid, 51.

[263] Ibid, 88.

[264] Ibid, 51.

[265] Ibid, 303.

[266] Ibid, 214, 216.

[267] Walter L. Fleming, *Louisiana State University 1860-1896* (Baton Rouge: Louisiana State University Press, 1936), 233.

[268] Marcus M. Wilkerson, *Thomas Duckett Boyd: The Story of a Southern Educator* (Baton Rouge: Louisiana State University Press, 1935), 295.

[269] Ibid, 296.

[270] Ibid, 133.

[271] Ibid, 113.

[272] Ibid, 130.

[273] Ibid, 113.

[274] Ibid, 163.

[275] Ibid, 323.

[276] Ibid, 208.

[277] Matthew J. Schott, "John M. Parker," In *The Louisiana Governors: From Iberville to Edwards*, edited by Joseph G. Dawson III (Baton Rouge, Louisiana: Louisiana State University Press, 1990), 218.

[278] Marcus M. Wilkerson, *Thomas Duckett Boyd: The Story of a Southern Educator* (Baton Rouge: Louisiana State University Press, 1935), 315.

[279] Ibid, 333.

[280] Ibid, 316-7.

[281] Ibid, 333.

[282] Louis Vyhnanek, "Henry L. Fuqua," In *The Louisiana Governors: From Iberville to Edwards*, edited by Joseph G. Dawson III (Baton Rouge, Louisiana: Louisiana State University Press, 1990), 222.

[283] Marcus M. Wilkerson, *Thomas Duckett Boyd: The Story of a Southern Educator* (Baton Rouge: Louisiana State University Press, 1935), 225.

[284] Ibid, 239.

[285] Ibid, 240, 245.

[286] Ibid, 244-5.

[287] John P. Dyer, *Tulane: The Biography of a University* (New York: Harper & Row, Publishers, 1966), 123.

[288] Marcus M. Wilkerson, *Thomas Duckett Boyd: The Story of a Southern Educator* (Baton Rouge: Louisiana State University Press, 1935), 252.

[289] John P. Dyer, *Tulane: The Biography of a University* (New York: Harper & Row, Publishers, 1966), 60.

[290] Ibid, 105.

[291] Ibid, 121.

[292] Ibid, 120.

[293] Ibid, 121.

[294] Marcus M. Wilkerson, *Thomas Duckett Boyd: The Story of a Southern Educator* (Baton Rouge: Louisiana State University Press, 1935), 243.

[295] Ibid, 254.

[296] Ibid, 260-1.

[297] Ibid.

[298] Ibid, 262.

[299] John P. Dyer, *Tulane: The Biography of a University* (New York: Harper & Row, Publishers, 1966), 64.

[300] Ibid, 65.

[301] Ibid, 66f.

[302] Ibid, 74.

[303] Ibid, 81-2.

[304] Ibid, 74.

[305] Ibid, 73.

[306] Marietta M. LeBreton, *Northwestern State University of Louisiana 1884-1984: A History* (Natchitoches, Louisiana: Northwestern State University Press, 1985), 13.

[307] Ibid, xiii.

[308] Ibid, xiv.

[309] Ibid, 6.

[310] Ibid, 6.

[311] Ibid, 9.

[312] Ibid, 10.

[313] Ibid, 1.

[314] Ibid, 17.

[315] Ibid.

[316] Ibid, 18.

[317] Ibid.

[318] Marcus M. Wilkerson, *Thomas Duckett Boyd: The Story of a Southern Educator* (Baton Rouge: Louisiana State University Press, 1935), 95.

[319] Marietta M. LeBreton, *Northwestern State University of Louisiana 1884-1984: A History* (Natchitoches, Louisiana: Northwestern State University Press, 1985), 27.

[320] Ibid, 31.

[321] Ibid, 32.

[322] Ibid, 36.

[323] Ibid, 46.

[324] Ibid, 37.

[325] Ibid, 43.

[326] Ibid, 55.

[327] Ibid, 43.

[328] Ibid, 150.

[329] Ibid, 151.

[330] Ibid, 58.

[331] Ibid, 59.

[332] Ibid.

[333] Ibid, 61.

[334] Ibid, 65.

[335] Not modern Southern University at New Orleans, but the predecessor to Southern University in Baton Rouge.

[336] Ibid, 88.

[337] Ibid, 99.

[338] Ibid, 92.

[339] Ibid, 99.

[340] Ibid, 96.

[341] Florent Hardy, Jr., *A Brief History of the University of Southwestern Louisiana: 1900 to 1960* (Baton Rouge: Claitor's Publishing Division, 1973), 30.

[342] Ibid.

[343] Marietta M. LeBreton, *Northwestern State University of Louisiana 1884-1984: A History* (Natchitoches, Louisiana: Northwestern State University Press, 1985), 89.

[344] Ibid, 101.

[345] Ibid, 129.

[346] Ruby B. Pearce, Sallie Robinson, and Helen Graham, eds., *Alma Mater: 1895-1945: A Memorial History of Louisiana Polytechnic Institute* (Ruston, La.: Executive Board of the Alumni Association of the Louisiana Polytechnic Institute, 1945), 8.

[347] Ibid, 9-10.

[348] Ibid, 11.

[349] Florent Hardy, Jr., *A Brief History of the University of Southwestern Louisiana: 1900 to 1960* (Baton Rouge: Claitor's Publishing Division, 1973), 1.

[350] University of Louisiana at Lafayette, *100 Years: The University of Louisiana at Lafayette: 1900-2000* (Lafayette, Louisiana: The University of Louisiana at Lafayette Office of Public Relations and News Services, 1999), 10.

[351] Florent Hardy, Jr., *A Brief History of the University of Southwestern Louisiana: 1900 to 1960* (Baton Rouge: Claitor's Publishing Division, 1973), 3.

[352] Ibid, 4.

[353] University of Louisiana at Lafayette, *100 Years: The University of Louisiana at Lafayette: 1900-2000* (Lafayette, Louisiana: The University of Louisiana at Lafayette Office of Public Relations and News Services, 1999), 9, 11.

[354] Florent Hardy, Jr., *A Brief History of the University of Southwestern Louisiana: 1900 to 1960* (Baton Rouge: Claitor's Publishing Division, 1973), 27.

[355] Ibid, 13.

[356] University of Louisiana at Lafayette, *100 Years: The University of Louisiana at Lafayette: 1900-2000* (Lafayette, Louisiana: The University of Louisiana at Lafayette Office of Public Relations and News Services, 1999), 11.

[357] Ibid, 12.

[358] Ibid, 25.

359   Ibid, 30.

360   Ibid, 110.

361   Stephen Irwin Patureau, *A History of the Isaac Delgado Central Trades School* (Unpublished Masters Thesis, Tulane University Howard-Tilton Memorial Library, July 6, 1939), 1.

362   Ibid.

363   Jack Gimon, "Delgado School To Teach Trades Now in Operation," *New Orleans Times-Picayune*, 4 September 1921, 1.

364   Ibid.

365   Stephen Irwin Patureau, *A History of the Isaac Delgado Central Trades School* (Unpublished Masters Thesis, Tulane University Howard-Tilton Memorial Library, July 6, 1939), 79.

366   Ibid, 74.

367   Raphael Cassimere, Jr., "Crisis of Public Higher Education in Louisiana," In *The Louisiana Purchase Bicentennial Series in Louisiana History, Volume XVIII, Education in Louisiana*, edited by Michael G. Wade (Lafayette, Louisiana: Center for Louisiana Studies, 1999), 545-6.

368   Ibid, 548.

369   Doris Dorcas Carter, "Charles P. Adams and Grambling State University: The Formative Years (1901-1928)," In *The Louisiana Purchase Bicentennial Series in Louisiana History, Volume XVIII, Education in Louisiana*, edited by Michael G. Wade (Lafayette, Louisiana: Center for Louisiana Studies, 1999), 456.

370   Mildred B. G. Gallot, A History of Grambling State University (Lanham, MD: University Press of America, Inc., 1985), xiv.

371   Ibid, 5-7.

372   Ibid, 6-7.

373   Ibid, xiv.

374   Doris Dorcas Carter, "Charles P. Adams and Grambling State University: The Formative Years (1901-1928)," In *The Louisiana Purchase Bicentennial Series in Louisiana History, Volume XVIII, Education in Louisiana*, edited by Michael G. Wade (Lafayette, Louisiana: Center for Louisiana Studies, 1999), 456.

375   Mildred B. G. Gallot, A History of Grambling State University (Lanham, MD: University Press of America, Inc., 1985), 15.

376   Ibid, 8.

377   Ibid, 12.

378   Doris Dorcas Carter, "Charles P. Adams and Grambling State University: The Formative Years (1901-1928)," In *The Louisiana Purchase Bicentennial Series in Louisiana History, Volume XVIII, Education in Louisiana*, edited by Michael G. Wade (Lafayette, Louisiana: Center for Louisiana Studies, 1999), 459.

379   Sometimes referred to as the "North Louisiana Agricultural and Industrial School"

380   Sometimes referred to as the "North Louisiana Agricultural and Industrial School": "Institute" (see Doris Carter, 460) / "School" (see Mildred B. G. Gallot, 17, 18)

381   Mildred B. G. Gallot, A History of Grambling State University (Lanham, MD: University Press of America, Inc., 1985), 42.

[382] Ibid, 18.

[383] Ibid, 94

[384] Ibid, 17, 18.

[385] Ibid.

[386] Ibid, 22.

[387] Ibid, 19.

[388] Ibid, 23.

[389] Charles Vincent, *A Centennial History of Southern University and A&M College, 1880-1980* (Charles Vincent, 1981), 57.

[390] Southern University website, "Historical Statement". Downloaded on 11/8/2003.

[391] Valera Theresa Francis, "Pride and Paradox: The History and Development of Southern University at New Orleans, 1954-1975" (Ph.D. diss., University of New Orleans, 2004), 3.

[392] Charles Vincent, *A Centennial History of Southern University and A&M College, 1880-1980* (Charles Vincent, 1981), 66.

[393] Ibid, 69.

[394] Ibid, 64.

[395] Ibid, 65.

[396] Ibid, 63.

[397] Ibid, 73.

[398] Ibid, 76.

[399] Ibid, 78.

[400] Ibid, 79.

[401] Ibid, 82.

[402] Ibid, 98.

[403] Ibid, 146.

[404] Ibid, 148.

[405] Loyola University, "The Story of Loyola University," *1997-99 Undergraduate Bulletin* (New Orleans: Loyola University), 423-6.

[406] Ibid.

[407] Betty L. Morrison, A History of Our Lady of Holy Cross College, New Orleans, Louisiana (Gretna, Louisiana: Her Publishing Co., Inc., 1977), 30, 33.

[408] Ibid, 38.

[409] Louisiana Association of Independent Colleges and Universities website. (Downloaded from *www.laicu.org* on 1/4/2005)

[410] Xavier University of Louisiana website.

[411] Louisiana Association of Independent Colleges and Universities website. (Downloaded from *www.laicu.org* on 1/4/2005)

[412] Oscar Hoffmeyer, Jr., *Louisiana College 75 years: A Pictorial History* (Pineville, Louisiana: Louisiana College, 1981), 2.

[413] Ibid, 9.

[414] Ibid, 24.

[415] Ibid, 44.

416   New Orleans Baptist Theological Seminary website. (Downloaded from *http://www.nobts. edu/About.html* on 1/4/2005)

417   John P. Dyer, *Tulane: The Biography of a University* (New York: Harper & Row, Publishers, 1966), 95.

418   Ibid, 53.

419   Ibid, 53f.

420   Ibid, 52.

421   Marcus M. Wilkerson, *Thomas Duckett Boyd: The Story of a Southern Educator* (Baton Rouge: Louisiana State University Press, 1935), 246-7.

422   Ibid, 247.

423   Ibid, 285.

424   Ibid, 273.

425   Ibid, 283.

426   Ibid, 271.

427   Ibid, 270.

428   Marietta M. LeBreton, *Northwestern State University of Louisiana 1884-1984: A History* (Natchitoches, Louisiana: Northwestern State University Press, 1985), 73-4.

429   John P. Dyer, *Tulane: The Biography of a University* (New York: Harper & Row, Publishers, 1966), 167.

430   Ted Lewis, "O'Keefe eager to take in sports," *New Orleans Times-Picayune*, 4 June 2005, D3.

431   Ibid.

432   John P. Dyer, *Tulane: The Biography of a University* (New York: Harper & Row, Publishers, 1966), 165-6.

433   Marcus M. Wilkerson, *Thomas Duckett Boyd: The Story of a Southern Educator* (Baton Rouge: Louisiana State University Press, 1935), 267-8.

434   John P. Dyer, *Tulane: The Biography of a University* (New York: Harper & Row, Publishers, 1966), 233f.

435   Ibid, 203.

436   Ibid, 232.

437   Ibid, 292.

438   University of Louisiana at Lafayette, *100 Years: The University of Louisiana at Lafayette: 1900-2000* (Lafayette, Louisiana: The University of Louisiana at Lafayette Office of Public Relations and News Services, 1999), 37.

439   Ibid, 48.

440   Florent Hardy, Jr., *A Brief History of the University of Southwestern Louisiana: 1900 to 1960* (Baton Rouge: Claitor's Publishing Division, 1973), 83.

441   Ibid, 85.

442   Ibid, 86.

443   Ibid, 93.

444   Betty M. Field, "Oscar K. Allen," In *The Louisiana Governors: From Iberville to Edwards*, edited by Joseph G. Dawson III (Baton Rouge, Louisiana: Louisiana State University Press, 1990), 241.

445   Bennett H. Wall, ed., *Louisiana: A History, 3rd Edition* (Harlan Davidson, 1997), 269.

446   Henry C. Dethloff, "Huey P. Long," In *The Louisiana Governors: From Iberville to Edwards*, edited by Joseph G. Dawson III (Baton Rouge, Louisiana: Louisiana State University Press, 1990), 228.

447   Betty M. Field, "Oscar K. Allen," In *The Louisiana Governors: From Iberville to Edwards*, edited by Joseph G. Dawson III (Baton Rouge, Louisiana: Louisiana State University Press, 1990), 240.

448   Bennett H. Wall, ed., *Louisiana: A History, 3rd Edition* (Harlan Davidson, 1997), 254

449   Ibid, 258

450   Harnett T. Kane, *Louisiana Hayride: The American Rehearsal for Dictatorship 1928-1940* (Gretna, Louisiana: Pelican Publishing Company, 1971), v.

451   Ibid.

452   Jeff Crouere, "Louisiana Double Standard." (Downloaded from http://www.BayouBuzz.com on 1/ 20/2004)

453   Louisiana Economic Development Council, *Louisiana: Vision 2020-2003 Update: Master Plan for Economic Development, http://Vision2020/louisiana.gov/*, 12.

454   Personal experience of the author. Tour of Louisiana Capitol.

455   John Maginnis, "Blanco built agenda along the way," *New Orleans Times-Picayune*, 23 June 2004, B7.

456   Ibid., 75, 78.

457   Ibid., 83.

458   Ibid., 83.

459   David M. Landry and Joseph B. Parker, "The Louisiana Political Culture," In *Louisiana Politics: Festival in a Labyrinth*, edited by James Bolner, Chapter 1, 1-13 (Baton Rouge, Louisiana: Louisiana State University Press), 10.

460   Ibid., 1.

461   Stuart Grayson Noble, "Governor Claiborne and the Public School System of the Territorial Government of Louisiana," In *The Louisiana Purchase Bicentennial Series in Louisiana History, Volume XVIII, Education in Louisiana*, edited by Michael G. Wade (Lafayette, Louisiana: Center for Louisiana Studies, 1999), 52.

462   Hodding Carter. "Huey Long: American Dictator," *The Louisiana Purchase Bicentennial Series in Louisiana History, Volume VIII, The Age of the Longs: Louisiana 1928-1960,* edited by Edward F. Haas (Lafayette, Louisiana: Center for Louisiana Studies, 2001), 42.

463   Ed Renwick, "The Governor," In *Louisiana Politics: Festival in a Labyrinth*, edited by James Bolner, Chapter 4, 75-88 (Baton Rouge, Louisiana: Louisiana State University Press), 84.

464   Public Affairs Research Council of Louisiana, Inc., *PAR 1998 Guide to the Constitutional Amendments*, August 1998, 1.

465   Mark T. Carleton, "The Louisiana Constitution of 1974," In *Louisiana Politics: Festival in a Labyrinth,* edited by James Bolner (Baton Rouge, Louisiana: Louisiana State University Press, 1982), 15.

466   Public Affairs Research Council of Louisiana, Inc., *PAR 1998 Guide to the Constitutional Amendments,* August 1998, 1.

467   Henry C. Dethloff, "Huey P. Long," In *The Louisiana Governors: From Iberville to Edwards*, edited by Joseph G. Dawson III (Baton Rouge, Louisiana: Louisiana State University Press, 1990).

468   Ibid, 228.

469   Ibid, 229.

470   Ibid, 233.

471   Betty M. Field, "Alvin Olin King," In *The Louisiana Governors: From Iberville to Edwards*, edited by Joseph G. Dawson III (Baton Rouge, Louisiana: Louisiana State University Press, 1990).

472   Betty M. Field, "Oscar K. Allen," In *The Louisiana Governors: From Iberville to Edwards*, edited by Joseph G. Dawson III (Baton Rouge, Louisiana: Louisiana State University Press, 1990), 239.

473   Ibid, 240.

474   Betty M. Field, "James A. Noe," In *The Louisiana Governors: From Iberville to Edwards*, edited by Joseph G. Dawson III (Baton Rouge, Louisiana: Louisiana State University Press, 1990).

475   Mark T. Carleton, "Richard Webster Leche," In *The Louisiana Governors: From Iberville to Edwards*, edited by Joseph G. Dawson III (Baton Rouge, Louisiana: Louisiana State University Press, 1990), 242.

476   Ibid, 247.

477   Ibid, 249.

478   J. Paul Leslie, Jr., "Earl K. Long," In *The Louisiana Governors: From Iberville to Edwards*, edited by Joseph G. Dawson III (Baton Rouge, Louisiana: Louisiana State University Press, 1990), 249-55.

479   Associated Press, "Long Still Seeks New L.S.U. Coach," *New York Times*, 20 December 1934, 32.

480   Russell Owen, "Huey Long Gives His View of Dictators," *New York Times*, 10 February 1935, SM3.

481   Associated Press, "Long Usurps Rule At State Capital," *New York Times*, 20 December 1934, 25.

482   John R. Thelin, *A History of American Higher Education* (Baltimore: Johns Hopkins University Press, 2004), 205.

483   Ibid.

484   Harnett T. Kane, *Louisiana Hayride: The American Rehearsal for Dictatorship 1928-1940*, (Gretna, Louisiana: Pelican Publishing Company, 1971), 211.

485   Ibid.

486   Michael L. Kurtz and Morgan D. Peoples, *Earl K. Long: The Saga of Uncle Earl and Louisiana Politics* (Baton Rouge: Louisiana State University Press, 1990), 93-4.

487   Harnett T. Kane, *Louisiana Hayride: The American Rehearsal for Dictatorship 1928-1940*, (Gretna, Louisiana: Pelican Publishing Company, 1971), 213.

488   Ibid, 216.

489   Ibid, 226.

490 Ibid, 234.

491 Ibid, 235.

492 Ibid, 223.

493 Ibid, 212.

494 Ibid, 225.

495 Michael L. Kurtz and Morgan D. Peoples, *Earl K. Long: The Saga of Uncle Earl and Louisiana Politics* (Baton Rouge: Louisiana State University Press, 1990), 93.

496 Hodding Carter, "Huey Long: American Dictator," In *The Louisiana Purchase Bicentennial Series in Louisiana History, Volume VIII, The Age of the Longs: Louisiana 1928-1960,* edited by Edward F. Haas (Lafayette, Louisiana: Center for Louisiana Studies, 2001), 41.

497 Harnett T. Kane, *Louisiana Hayride: The American Rehearsal for Dictatorship 1928-1940,* (Gretna, Louisiana: Pelican Publishing Company, 1971), 217.

498 Bennett H. Wall, ed., *Louisiana: A History, 3rd Edition* (Harlan Davidson, 1997), 258.

499 Harnett T. Kane, *Louisiana Hayride: The American Rehearsal for Dictatorship 1928-1940,* (Gretna, Louisiana: Pelican Publishing Company, 1971), 219.

500 Glen Jeansonne, "Sam Houston Jones and the Revolution of 1940," In *The Louisiana Purchase Bicentennial Series in Louisiana History, Volume VIII, The Age of the Longs: Louisiana 1928-1960,* edited by Edward F. Haas (Lafayette, Louisiana: Center for Louisiana Studies, 2001), 357-8.

501 Harnett T. Kane, *Louisiana Hayride: The American Rehearsal for Dictatorship 1928-1940,* (Gretna, Louisiana: Pelican Publishing Company, 1971), 224-5.

502 Glen Jeansonne, "Sam Houston Jones and the Revolution of 1940," In *The Louisiana Purchase Bicentennial Series in Louisiana History, Volume VIII, The Age of the Longs: Louisiana 1928-1960,* edited by Edward F. Haas (Lafayette, Louisiana: Center for Louisiana Studies, 2001), 357-8.

503 Hodding Carter, "Huey Long: American Dictator," In *The Louisiana Purchase Bicentennial Series in Louisiana History, Volume VIII, The Age of the Longs: Louisiana 1928-1960,* edited by Edward F. Haas (Lafayette, Louisiana: Center for Louisiana Studies, 2001), 41.

504 Harnett T. Kane, *Louisiana Hayride: The American Rehearsal for Dictatorship 1928-1940,* (Gretna, Louisiana: Pelican Publishing Company, 1971), 227.

505 Michael L. Kurtz and Morgan D. Peoples, *Earl K. Long: The Saga of Uncle Earl and Louisiana Politics* (Baton Rouge: Louisiana State University Press, 1990), 98-9.

506 Harnett T. Kane, *Louisiana Hayride: The American Rehearsal for Dictatorship 1928-1940,* (Gretna, Louisiana: Pelican Publishing Company, 1971), 230.

507 Ibid, 232.

508 Betty M. Field, "The Louisiana Scandals," In *The Louisiana Purchase Bicentennial Series in Louisiana History, Volume VIII, The Age of the Longs: Louisiana 1928-1960,* edited by Edward F. Haas (Lafayette, Louisiana: Center for Louisiana Studies, 2001), 278.

509 Glen Jeansonne, "Sam Houston Jones and the Revolution of 1940," In *The Louisiana Purchase Bicentennial Series in Louisiana History, Volume VIII, The Age of the Longs: Louisiana 1928-1960,* edited by Edward F. Haas (Lafayette, Louisiana: Center for Louisiana Studies, 2001), 357.

[510]   Ibid, 358.

[511]   Marietta M. LeBreton, *Northwestern State University of Louisiana 1884-1984: A History* (Natchitoches, Louisiana: Northwestern State University Press, 1985), 120-1.

[512]   Ibid, 121.

[513]   Ibid, 121f.

[514]   Ibid, 122.

[515]   Ibid, 123.

[516]   Ibid, 153.

[517]   Ibid, 124.

[518]   Ibid, 164.

[519]   University of Louisiana at Lafayette, *100 Years: The University of Louisiana at Lafayette: 1900-2000* (Lafayette, Louisiana: The University of Louisiana at Lafayette Office of Public Relations and News Services, 1999), 43.

[520]   Marietta M. LeBreton, *Northwestern State University of Louisiana 1884-1984: A History* (Natchitoches, Louisiana: Northwestern State University Press, 1985), 154.

[521]   Ibid, 155.

[522]   Ibid, 177.

[523]   Ibid.

[524]   Ibid, 176-7.

[525]   Ibid, 178.

[526]   University of Louisiana at Lafayette, *100 Years: The University of Louisiana at Lafayette: 1900-2000* (Lafayette, Louisiana: The University of Louisiana at Lafayette Office of Public Relations and News Services, 1999), 42.

[527]   Ibid, 49.

[528]   Florent Hardy, Jr., *A Brief History of the University of Southwestern Louisiana: 1900 to 1960* (Baton Rouge: Claitor's Publishing Division, 1973), 43.

[529]   University of Louisiana at Lafayette, *100 Years: The University of Louisiana at Lafayette: 1900-2000* (Lafayette, Louisiana: The University of Louisiana at Lafayette Office of Public Relations and News Services, 1999), 43.

[530]   Florent Hardy, Jr., *A Brief History of the University of Southwestern Louisiana: 1900 to 1960* (Baton Rouge: Claitor's Publishing Division, 1973), 48.

[531]   Ibid, 48.

[532]   Ibid, 49.

[533]   Doris Dorcas Carter, "Charles P. Adams and Grambling State University: The Formative Years (1901-1928)," In *The Louisiana Purchase Bicentennial Series in Louisiana History, Volume XVIII, Education in Louisiana*, edited by Michael G. Wade (Lafayette, Louisiana: Center for Louisiana Studies, 1999), 459-61.

[534]   Mildred B. G. Gallot, A History of Grambling State University (Lanham, MD: University Press of America, Inc., 1985), 35.

[535]   Ibid, 37.

[536]   Ibid, 38.

[537]   Ibid, 40.

538 Ibid, 41.

539 Ibid, 52.

540 Ibid, 53.

541 Ibid, 49-51

542 Ibid, 27.

543 Ibid, 77.

544 Ibid, 83.

545 Ronald Harris, *We Hail Thee Now Southeastern: Remembering the First Seventy-Five Years of Southeastern Louisiana University* (Hammond, Louisiana: Southeastern Development Foundation, 2001), 2.

546 Ibid, 1.

547 Ibid, 11, 14.

548 Ibid, 15.

549 Ibid, 24.

550 Ibid, 21-2.

551 Ibid, 25.

552 Ibid.

553 Ibid, 29.

554 Ibid.

555 Ibid, 33.

556 George Thomas Walker, *The Building of a University* (Dallas, Texas: Taylor Publishing Company, 1991), 72.

557 Ibid, ix.

558 Ibid.

559 Ibid.

560 John A. Knesel and Holly B. Casey, *"I think you can, and I believe you will:" selected writings of C. C. Colvert, 1932-1943* (Monroe, Louisiana: ULM Friends of the Library, 2003), vii.

561 Gregory Lang Goodwin, "The Historical Development of the Community-Junior College Ideology: An Analysis and Interpretation of the Writings of Selected Community-Junior College National Leaders from 1890 to 1970" (Ph.D. diss., University of Illinois at Urbana-Champaign, 1971), 210-1.

562 Ibid, 212.

563 John A. Knesel and Holly B. Casey, *"I think you can, and I believe you will:" selected writings of C. C. Colvert, 1932-1943* (Monroe, Louisiana: ULM Friends of the Library, 2003), x.

564 Ibid, ix.

565 Gregory Lang Goodwin, "The Historical Development of the Community-Junior College Ideology: An Analysis and Interpretation of the Writings of Selected Community-Junior College National Leaders from 1890 to 1970" (Ph.D. diss., University of Illinois at Urbana-Champaign, 1971), 210.

566 John A. Knesel and Holly B. Casey, *"I think you can, and I believe you will:" selected writings of C. C. Colvert, 1932-1943* (Monroe, Louisiana: ULM Friends of the Library, 2003), x.

[567] John P. Dyer, *Tulane: The Biography of a University* (New York: Harper & Row, Publishers, 1966), 216.

[568] Ibid, 218.

[569] Ibid.

[570] Ibid, 219.

[571] John P. Dyer, *Tulane: The Biography of a University* (New York: Harper & Row, Publishers, 1966), 240.

[572] Ibid.

[573] Joe M. Richardson, "Edgar B. Stern: A White New Orleans Philanthropist Helps Build a Black University," *The Journal of Negro History*, Vol. 82, No. 3 (Summer, 1997), 328-342 (Downloaded from *www.jstor.org* on April 10, 2005), 331.

[574] Ibid.

[575] Ibid, 336.

[576] Ibid.

[577] Ibid, 334.

[578] Ibid, 333.

[579] Ibid.

[580] Ibid, 330.

[581] Ibid.

[582] Ibid, 331.

[583] Ibid, 332.

[584] Ibid.

[585] Ibid.

[586] Ibid, 333.

[587] Ibid, 335.

[588] Ibid, 336.

[589] Ibid.

[590] Ibid.

[591] Ibid, 337.

[592] Ibid, 338.

[593] Joe Gray Taylor, *McNeese State University, 1939-1987: A Chronicle* (McNeese State University, 1990), 7.

[594] Ibid, 8.

[595] Ibid.

[596] Ibid, 7.

[597] Ibid, 11.

[598] Ibid, 1-3.

[599] Ibid, 32.

[600] Edward Daniel Schumacher, *The Struggle Against Adult Functional Illiteracy in Louisiana: A Historical Analysis* (Sulphur, Louisiana: Maplewood Books, 1973), 2.

[601] John P. Dyer, *Tulane: The Biography of a University* (New York: Harper & Row, Publishers, 1966), 244.

602 George B. Vaughan, *The Community College Story* (Washington, D. C.: Community College Press, 2000), 24.

603 John R. Thelin, *A History of American Higher Education* (Baltimore: Johns Hopkins University Press, 2004), 262-3.

604 George F. Will, "Echoes of the GI Bill," *Newsweek,* 27 October 1997, 82.

605 John R. Thelin, *A History of American Higher Education* (Baltimore: Johns Hopkins University Press, 2004), 262-3.

606 George F. Will, "Echoes of the GI Bill," *Newsweek,* 27 October 1997, 82.

607 John R. Thelin, *A History of American Higher Education* (Baltimore: Johns Hopkins University Press, 2004), 264.

608 George F. Will, "Echoes of the GI Bill," *Newsweek,* 27 October 1997, 82.

609 Ibid.

610 Ronald Harris, *We Hail Thee Now Southeastern: Remembering the First Seventy-Five Years of Southeastern Louisiana University* (Hammond, Louisiana: Southeastern Development Foundation, 2001), 55.

611 George F. Will, "Echoes of the GI Bill," *Newsweek,* 27 October 1997, 82.

612 J. Paul Leslie, Jr., "Earl K. Long," In *The Louisiana Governors: From Iberville to Edwards,* edited by Joseph G. Dawson III (Baton Rouge, Louisiana: Louisiana State University Press, 1990), 253.

613 Morgan D. Peoples, "Earl Kemp Long: The Man from Pea Patch Farm," In *The Louisiana Purchase Bicentennial Series in Louisiana History, Volume VIII, The Age of the Longs: Louisiana 1928-1960,* edited by Edward F. Haas (Lafayette, Louisiana: Center for Louisiana Studies, 2001), 439-40.

614 J. Paul Leslie, Jr., "Earl K. Long," In *The Louisiana Governors: From Iberville to Edwards,* edited by Joseph G. Dawson III (Baton Rouge, Louisiana: Louisiana State University Press, 1990).

615 Floyd M. Clay, "Jimmie Davis," In *The Louisiana Governors: From Iberville to Edwards,* edited by Joseph G. Dawson III (Baton Rouge, Louisiana: Louisiana State University Press, 1990), 260-1.

616 Michael L. Kurtz, "Robert F. Kennon," In *The Louisiana Governors: From Iberville to Edwards,* edited by Joseph G. Dawson III (Baton Rouge, Louisiana: Louisiana State University Press, 1990), 263.

617 Alfred N. Delahaye, *Nicholls State University: The Elkins-Galliano Years, 1948-1983* (Thibodaux, Louisiana: Nicholls State University Foundation, 1999), 48.

618 Ibid, 3.

619 University of Louisiana at Lafayette, *100 Years: The University of Louisiana at Lafayette: 1900-2000* (Lafayette, Louisiana: The University of Louisiana at Lafayette Office of Public Relations and News Services, 1999), 51.

620 Florent Hardy, Jr., *A Brief History of the University of Southwestern Louisiana: 1900 to 1960* (Baton Rouge: Claitor's Publishing Division, 1973), 51.

621 Ronald Harris, *We Hail Thee Now Southeastern: Remembering the First Seventy-Five Years of Southeastern Louisiana University* (Hammond, Louisiana: Southeastern Development Foundation, 2001), 55-6.

[622] Alfred N. Delahaye, *Nicholls State University: The Elkins-Galliano Years, 1948-1983* (Thibodaux, Louisiana: Nicholls State University Foundation, 1999), 3.

[623] Ibid, 104.

[624] Ibid.

[625] Ibid, 2.

[626] Ibid, 18.

[627] Ibid, 3.

[628] Ibid, 9.

[629] Ibid, 8.

[630] Ibid, 10-11.

[631] Ibid, 11.

[632] Ibid, 1.

[633] Ibid, 21.

[634] Ibid, 23.

[635] Ibid, 36.

[636] Ibid, 197.

[637] Ibid, 51, 70.

[638] Ibid, 19.

[639] Ibid, 20.

[640] Ibid, 25.

[641] Ibid, 53.

[642] Ibid, 31.

[643] Ibid, 160, 167.

[644] Ibid, 78.

[645] Ibid, 161.

[646] Ibid, 81.

[647] Ibid, 79.

[648] Ibid, 82.

[649] Ibid, 202.

[650] John P. Dyer, *Tulane: The Biography of a University* (New York: Harper & Row, Publishers, 1966), 255.

[651] Ibid.

[652] Joe Gray Taylor, *McNeese State University, 1939-1987: A Chronicle* (McNeese State University, 1990), 49.

[653] Ibid, 49.

[654] Ibid, 51.

[655] Ibid, 86.

[656] Adam Fairclough, *Race & Democracy: The Civil Rights Struggle in Louisiana, 1915-1972* (Athens, Georgia: the University of Georgia Press, 1995), 153.

[657] Ibid, 170.

[658] Ibid, 170.

[659] Alfred N. Delahaye, *Nicholls State University: The Elkins-Galliano Years, 1948-1983* (Thibodaux, Louisiana: Nicholls State University Foundation, 1999), 176.

[660] Ibid, 77.

[661] Joe Gray Taylor, *McNeese State University, 1939-1987: A Chronicle* (McNeese State University, 1990), 85.

[662] Ibid.

[663] George Thomas Walker, *The Building of a University* (Dallas, Texas: Taylor Publishing Company, 1991), 234.

[664] Ibid, 233.

[665] Joe Gray Taylor, *McNeese State University, 1939-1987: A Chronicle* (McNeese State University, 1990), 127.

[666] Ibid, 171.

[667] Michael L. Kurtz and Morgan D. Peoples, *Earl K. Long: The Saga of Uncle Earl and Louisiana Politics* (Baton Rouge: Louisiana State University Press, 1990), 200-1.

[668] Ibid, 204.

[669] Ibid, 201-2

[670] Ibid, 202.

[671] J. Paul Leslie, Jr., "Earl K. Long," In *The Louisiana Governors: From Iberville to Edwards*, edited by Joseph G. Dawson III (Baton Rouge, Louisiana: Louisiana State University Press, 1990), 253.

[672] Charles Vincent, *A Centennial History of Southern University and A&M College, 1880-1980* (Charles Vincent, 1981), 165.

[673] Valera Theresa Francis, "Pride and Paradox: The History and Development of Southern University at New Orleans, 1954-1975" (Ph.D. diss., University of New Orleans, 2004), 10.

[674] Ibid, 60.

[675] Ibid, 61.

[676] Ibid, 56.

[677] Ibid, 57.

[678] Ibid, 67.

[679] Mildred B. G. Gallot, A History of Grambling State University (Lanham, MD: University Press of America, Inc., 1985), 100.

[680] Valera Theresa Francis, "Pride and Paradox: The History and Development of Southern University at New Orleans, 1954-1975" (Ph.D. diss., University of New Orleans, 2004), 172.

[681] Ibid, 173.

[682] Ibid, 174.

[683] Mildred B. G. Gallot, A History of Grambling State University (Lanham, MD: University Press of America, Inc., 1985), 91.

[684] Ibid, 94.

[685] Charles Vincent, *A Centennial History of Southern University and A&M College, 1880-1980* (Charles Vincent, 1981), 166.

686   Ibid, 166.

687   Adam Fairclough, *Race & Democracy: The Civil Rights Struggle in Louisiana, 1915-1972* (Athens, Georgia: the University of Georgia Press, 1995), 153.

688   Alfred N. Delahaye, *Nicholls State University: The Elkins-Galliano Years, 1948-1983* (Thibodaux, Louisiana: Nicholls State University Foundation, 1999), 76.

689   Adam Fairclough, *Race & Democracy: The Civil Rights Struggle in Louisiana, 1915-1972* (Athens, Georgia: the University of Georgia Press, 1995), 155.

690   Ibid.

691   Ibid, 219.

692   Florent Hardy, Jr., *A Brief History of the University of Southwestern Louisiana: 1900 to 1960* (Baton Rouge: Claitor's Publishing Division, 1973), 60.

693   Ibid, 61.

694   University of Louisiana at Lafayette, *100 Years: The University of Louisiana at Lafayette: 1900-2000* (Lafayette, Louisiana: The University of Louisiana at Lafayette Office of Public Relations and News Services, 1999), 65.

695   Joe Gray Taylor, *McNeese State University, 1939-1987: A Chronicle* (McNeese State University, 1990), 83.

696   Alfred N. Delahaye, *Nicholls State University: The Elkins-Galliano Years, 1948-1983* (Thibodaux, Louisiana: Nicholls State University Foundation, 1999), 76.

697   Ibid, 77.

698   Ibid, 177.

699   Ibid.

700   Ibid, 176.

701   John P. Dyer, *Tulane: The Biography of a University* (New York: Harper & Row, Publishers, 1966), 287.

702   Ibid.

703   Ibid.

704   Ibid.

705   Ibid, 287-9.

706   Ibid, 289.

707   Adam Fairclough, *Race & Democracy: The Civil Rights Struggle in Louisiana, 1915-1972* (Athens, Georgia: the University of Georgia Press, 1995), 379-80.

708   Arthur W. Bergeron, Jr., "John J. McKeithen," In *The Louisiana Governors: From Iberville to Edwards*, edited by Joseph G. Dawson III (Baton Rouge, Louisiana: Louisiana State University Press, 1990), 269.

709   Ibid.

710   Valera Theresa Francis, "Pride and Paradox: The History and Development of Southern University at New Orleans, 1954-1975" (Ph.D. diss., University of New Orleans, 2004), 150.

711   Arthur W. Bergeron, Jr., "John J. McKeithen," In *The Louisiana Governors: From Iberville to Edwards*, edited by Joseph G. Dawson III (Baton Rouge, Louisiana: Louisiana State University Press, 1990), 269.

[712] William H. Honan, "J. J. McKeithen, 81, Governor of Louisiana, 1964 to 1972," *New York Times*, June 5, 1999.

[713] Bennett H. Wall, ed., *Louisiana: A History, 3rd Edition* (Harlan Davidson, 1997), 337.

[714] Rochelle Nash Alexis, *A Description and Analysis of the Perceived Impact of the Academic Governance Structure of Higher Education in the State of Louisiana After the Adoption of the Constitution of 1974* (Ph.D. Dissertation presented to UNO. Located at UNO Library, Louisiana Collection, 1985), 15.

[715] Alfred N. Delahaye, *Nicholls State University: The Elkins-Galliano Years, 1948-1983* (Thibodaux, Louisiana: Nicholls State University Foundation, 1999), 247.

[716] Ronald Harris, *We Hail Thee Now Southeastern: Remembering the First Seventy-Five Years of Southeastern Louisiana University* (Hammond, Louisiana: Southeastern Development Foundation, 2001), 101.

[717] Ibid, 102.

[718] Alfred N. Delahaye, *Nicholls State University: The Elkins-Galliano Years, 1948-1983* (Thibodaux, Louisiana: Nicholls State University Foundation, 1999), 274.

[719] Ibid, 243.

[720] Marietta M. LeBreton, *Northwestern State University of Louisiana 1884-1984: A History* (Natchitoches, Louisiana: Northwestern State University Press, 1985), 246.

[721] Edward Daniel Schumacher, *The Struggle Against Adult Functional Illiteracy in Louisiana: A Historical Analysis* (Sulphur, Louisiana: Maplewood Books, 1973), 189.

[722] Louisiana State University at Eunice website, "Establishment of LSU at Eunice." Downloaded from *http://www.lsue.edu/about.html* on 11/8/2003.

[723] Southern University at Shreveport website, "Historical Sketch of Southern University at Shreveport." Downloaded from *http://www.susla.edu/html/catalog/general/history.htm* on 11/8/2003.

[724] John J. McKeithen, interview by Mark Carleton, located at LSU Libraries Special Collections (call number L4700.0334), 1993, 42-3.

[725] Ibid, 53.

[726] John J. McKeithen, interview by Jack Fiser, located at LSU Libraries Special Collections (call number L4700.0042), 1982, 9, 14.

[727] Ibid, 17-8.

[728] Ibid, 33.

[729] Ibid, 14.

[730] Ibid, 15.

[731] John J. McKeithen, interview by Mark Carleton, located at LSU Libraries Special Collections (call number L4700.0334), 1993, 9, 11.

[732] Ibid, 11.

[733] Edward Daniel Schumacher, *The Struggle Against Adult Functional Illiteracy in Louisiana: A Historical Analysis* (Sulphur, Louisiana: Maplewood Books, 1973), 220.

[734] Bennett H. Wall, ed., *Louisiana: A History, 3rd Edition* (Harlan Davidson, 1997), 334.

[735] Mildred B. G. Gallot, A History of Grambling State University (Lanham, MD: University Press of America, Inc., 1985), 103.

736   Ibid.

737   Valera Theresa Francis, "Pride and Paradox: The History and Development of Southern University at New Orleans, 1954-1975" (Ph.D. diss., University of New Orleans, 2004), 150-1, 153.

738   Charles Vincent, *A Centennial History of Southern University and A&M College, 1880-1980* (Charles Vincent, 1981), 185.

739   Ibid, 190.

740   Ibid, 191.

741   Ibid, 192.

742   Ibid, 194-5.

743   Ibid, 210.

744   Ibid, 211-2.

745   Ibid, 213.

746   Ibid, 213-4.

747   Ibid, 214-5.

748   Ibid, 215.

749   Ibid, 215-6.

750   Adam Fairclough, *Race & Democracy: The Civil Rights Struggle in Louisiana, 1915-1972* (Athens, Georgia: the University of Georgia Press, 1995), 460.

751   Ibid.

752   Charles Vincent, *A Centennial History of Southern University and A&M College, 1880-1980* (Charles Vincent, 1981), 217.

753   Ibid, 218.

754   Carl H. Degel, *Creation of the Louisiana Coordinating Counicl for Higher Education: Perspectives in Public Organizational Decision-making* (Masters Thesis for Tulane Graduate School, May 28, 1971), 16.

755   Marietta M. LeBreton, *Northwestern State University of Louisiana 1884-1984: A History* (Natchitoches, Louisiana: Northwestern State University Press, 1985), 92.

756   Carl H. Degel, *Creation of the Louisiana Coordinating Counicl for Higher Education: Perspectives in Public Organizational Decision-making* (Masters Thesis for Tulane Graduate School, May 28, 1971), 20.

757   Mildred B. G. Gallot, A History of Grambling State University (Lanham, MD: University Press of America, Inc., 1985), 91.

758   Alfred N. Delahaye, *Nicholls State University: The Elkins-Galliano Years, 1948-1983* (Thibodaux, Louisiana: Nicholls State University Foundation, 1999), 83.

759   Carl H. Degel, *Creation of the Louisiana Coordinating Counicl for Higher Education: Perspectives in Public Organizational Decision-making* (Masters Thesis for Tulane Graduate School, May 28, 1971), 26.

760   Ibid, 27.

761   Ibid, 28.

762   Ibid, 29.

763   Ibid, 71.

[764]   Ibid, 73.

[765]   Ibid, 37.

[766]   Ibid, 52.

[767]   Marietta M. LeBreton, *Northwestern State University of Louisiana 1884-1984: A History* (Natchitoches, Louisiana: Northwestern State University Press, 1985), 249.

[768]   Jerry Pinsel, "A Brief Historic Profile of the Louisiana Higher Education Community: An Unfinished Journey" (Unpublished Draft), 2003.

[769]   Rochelle Nash Alexis, *A Description and Analysis of the Perceived Impact of the Academic Governance Structure of Higher Education in the State of Louisiana After the Adoption of the Constitution of 1974* (Ph.D. Dissertation presented to UNO. Located at UNO Library, Louisiana Collection, 1985), 17.

[770]   Jerry Pinsel, "A Brief Historic Profile of the Louisiana Higher Education Community: An Unfinished Journey" (Unpublished Draft), 2003.

[771]   Walter Crosby Eells, *The Junior College,* (Boston: Houghton Mifflin Company, 1931), 190.

[772]   Ibid., 191.

[773]   Ibid., 192.

[774]   Ibid., 193.

[775]   Ibid., 191.

[776]   Clyde E. Blocker, Robert H. Plummer, and Richard C. Richardson, Jr., *The Two-Year College: A Social Synthesis* (Englewood Cliffs, NJ: Prentice-Hall, Inc., 1965), 31; Judith S. Eaton, *Colleges of Choice: The Enabling Impact of the Community College*, (New York: American Council of Education and Macmillan Publishing Company, 1988), 6.

[777]   Walter Crosby Eells, *The Junior College* (Boston: Houghton Mifflin Company, 1931), 191.

[778]   Walter Crosby Eells, *The Junior College* (Boston: Houghton Mifflin Company, 1931), 191-2.

[779]   David W. Breneman and Susan C. Nelson, *Financing Community Colleges: An Economic Perspective* (Washington, D. C.: Brookings Institution, 1981), 19.

[780]   Clyde E. Blocker, Robert H. Plummer, and Richard C. Richardson, Jr., *The Two-Year College: A Social Synthesis.* (Englewood Cliffs, NJ: Prentice-Hall, Inc., 1965), 35.

[781]   Thomas Diener, *Growth of an American Invention: A Documentary History of the Junior and Community College Movement* (New York: Greenwood Press, 1986), 7.

[782]   Gregory Lang Goodwin, "The Historical Development of the Community-Junior College Ideology: An Analysis and Interpretation of the Writings of Selected Community-Junior College National Leaders from 1890 to 1970" (Ph.D. diss., University of Illinois at Urbana-Champaign, 1971), 7.

[783]   *USA Today,* "Western states yield high graduation rates," 15 December 2003, 6D.

[784]   Louisiana Economic Development Council, *Louisiana: Vision 2020-2003 Update: Master Plan for Economic Development, http://Vision2020/louisiana.gov/*, 11.

[785]   Ibid, 18.

[786]   Ibid, 7.

[787]   Southwest Educational Development Laboratory, Downloaded from www.sedl.org/pubs/pic01/priority.html on 11/13/2003.

[788]   Louisiana Economic Development Council, *Louisiana: Vision 2020-2003 Update: Master Plan for Economic Development*, *http://Vision2020/louisiana.gov/*, 11.

[789]   Ibid, 14.

[790]   Southwest Educational Development Laboratory, Downloaded from www.sedl.org/pubs/pic01/priority.html on 11/13/2003.

[791]   Ibid.

[792]   David M. Landry and Joseph B. Parker, "The Louisiana Political Culture," In *Louisiana Politics: Festival in a Labyrinth*, edited by James Bolner, Chapter 1, 1-13, (Baton Rouge, Louisiana: Louisiana State University Press), 7.

[793]   Ibid., 7.

[794]   Southwest Educational Development Laboratory, Downloaded from www.sedl.org/pubs/pic01/priority.html on 11/13/2003.

[795]   Ibid.

[796]   Bennett H. Wall, ed., *Louisiana: A History, 3rd Edition* (Harlan Davidson, 1997), 346

[797]   Ibid.

[798]   Ibid, 353-4

[799]   Ibid, 354

[800]   Ibid, 385

[801]   Ibid, 354

[802]   Joseph B. Parker, "Edwin Edwards," In *The Louisiana Governors: From Iberville to Edwards*, edited by Joseph G. Dawson III (Baton Rouge, Louisiana: Louisiana State University Press, 1990), 276.

[803]   John Hill, "From powerhouse to prisoner: Former La. governor prepares to serve jail time," *Louisiana Gannett News,* 20 October 2002. Downloaded from *www.shreveporttimes.com* on 3/18/2004.

[804]   Chris Frink, "Gov. Mike Foster's legacy," *The Advocate,* 28 December 2003. Downloaded from 2theadvocate.com on 3/18/2004.

[805]   Joseph B. Parker, "Edwin Edwards," In *The Louisiana Governors: From Iberville to Edwards*, edited by Joseph G. Dawson III (Baton Rouge, Louisiana: Louisiana State University Press, 1990), 272.

[806]   Mary Crystal Cage, "Higher-Education Probes by Crusty Louisiana Watchdog Bring Headlines and Headaches," *The Chronicle of Higher Education*, 18 October 1989. Downloaded from *http://chronicle.com* on 4/9/2004.

[807]   Tonya Whitfield, "Louisiana Official Stopped From Investigating Colleges," *The Chronicle of Higher Education*, 2 September 1992. Downloaded from *http://chronicle.com* on 4/9/2004.

[808]   Mary Crystal Cage, "Reform Plan Stymied: Governor's Effort to Simplify Louisiana's Higher-Education System Deepens the Bitter Divisions Created by Years of Segregation and Political Turf Wars," *The Chronicle of Higher Education*, 18 October 1989, A29-31, 29.

[809]   Ibid.

[810]   Bennett H. Wall, ed., *Louisiana: A History, 3rd Edition* (Harlan Davidson, 1997), 344.

[811] Southwest Educational Development Laboratory, Downloaded from www.sedl.org/pubs/ pic01/priority.html on 11/13/2003.

[812] Public Affairs Research Council of Louisiana, Inc., *PAR Analysis: Meeting Louisiana's Need For Vocational-Technical Education: A Summary,* Number 184?, 1973.

[813] Public Affairs Research Council of Louisiana, Inc., *PAR Analysis: Vo-tech—In Search of A System,* Number 254, December 1981, 33.

[814] Ibid.

[815] Louisiana Board of Regents, *Board of Regents—The 2000 Accountability Report,* ii.

[816] Louisiana Technical College, *History of LTC,* Downloaded from *http://www.theltc.net/ ltc_history.htm* on 6/14/2004.

[817] Ibid.

[818] Public Affairs Research Council of Louisiana, Inc., *PAR Analysis: Vo-tech—In Search of A System,* Number 254, December 1981, 24.

[819] Public Affairs Research Council of Louisiana, Inc., *PAR Analysis: Meeting Louisiana's Need For Vocational-Technical Education: A Summary,* Number 184?, 1973, 38.

[820] Ibid.

[821] Public Affairs Research Council of Louisiana, Inc., *PAR Analysis: Vo-tech—In Search of A System,* Number 254, December 1981, 33.

[822] Ibid, 15.

[823] Ibid.

[824] Ibid, 24.

[825] Valera Theresa Francis, "Pride and Paradox: The History and Development of Southern University at New Orleans, 1954-1975" (Ph.D. diss., University of New Orleans, 2004), 175.

[826] Jerry Pinsel, "A Brief Historic Profile of the Louisiana Higher Education Community: An Unfinished Journey" (Unpublished Draft), 2003.

[827] Ibid.

[828] Ibid.

[829] Sara Hebel, "Desegregation Pacts Set in Maryland, Tennessee, and Louisiana," *The Chronicle of Higher Education,* 5 January 2001. Downloaded from *http://chronicle.com* on 4/9/2004.

[830] Sara Hebel, "Segregation's Legacy Still Troubles Campuses," *The Chronicle of Higher Education.* 14 May 2004. Downloaded from *http://chronicle.com* on 5/10/2004.

[831] Ibid.

[832] Sara Hebel, "Desegregation Pacts Set in Maryland, Tennessee, and Louisiana," *The Chronicle of Higher Education,* 5 January 2001. Downloaded from *http://chronicle.com* on 4/9/2004.

[833] Sara Hebel, "Segregation's Legacy Still Troubles Campuses," *The Chronicle of Higher Education.* 14 May 2004. Downloaded from *http://chronicle.com* on 5/10/2004.

[834] Scott Jaschik, "U. S. Judge Reverses Order to Reorganize Higher Education," *The Chronicle of Higher Education,* 7 November 1990. Downloaded from *http://chronicle.com* on 4/9/2004.

[835] Joye Mercer, "Louisiana Desegregation Trial is Delayed Until March," *The Chronicle of Higher Education,* 3 August 1994. Downloaded from *http://chronicle.com* on 4/9/2004.

836 Jerry Pinsel, "A Brief Historic Profile of the Louisiana Higher Education Community: An Unfinished Journey" (Unpublished Draft), 2003.

837 Ibid

838 Mildred B. G. Gallot, A History of Grambling State University (Lanham, MD: University Press of America, Inc., 1985), 179-180; 182-4.

839 Scott Jaschik, "U. S. Judge Reverses Order to Reorganize Higher Education," *The Chronicle of Higher Education*, 7 November 1990. Downloaded from *http://chronicle.com* on 4/9/2004; Scott Jaschik, "Overhaul to End Segregation Ordered in Louisiana," *The Chronicle of Higher Education*, 6 January 1993. Downloaded from *http://chronicle.com* on 4/9/2004.

840 Mary Crystal Cage, "Supreme Court Says It Lacks Jurisdiction in La. Desegregation Dispute," *The Chronicle of Higher Education*, 17 January 1990. Downloaded from *http://chronicle.com* on 4/9/2004.

841 Scott Jaschik, "Overhaul to End Segregation Ordered in Louisiana," *The Chronicle of Higher Education*, 6 January 1993. Downloaded from *http://chronicle.com* on 4/9/2004.

842 Mary Crystal Cage, "Supreme Court Says It Lacks Jurisdiction in La. Desegregation Dispute," *The Chronicle of Higher Education*, 17 January 1990. Downloaded from *http://chronicle.com* on 4/9/2004.

843 Scott Jaschik, "U. S. Judge Reverses Order to Reorganize Higher Education," *The Chronicle of Higher Education*, 7 November 1990. Downloaded from *http://chronicle.com* on 4/9/2004.

844 Ibid.

845 Ibid.

846 Ibid.

847 Sara Hebel, "Desegregation Pacts Set in Maryland, Tennessee, and Louisiana, *The Chronicle of Higher Education*, 5 January 2001. Downloaded from *http://chronicle.com* on 4/9/2004.

848 Joye Mercer, "La. Board Proposes Higher-Education Desgregation Plan, *The Chronicle of Higher Education*, 16 December 1992. Downloaded from *http://chronicle.com* on 4/9/2004.

849 Ibid.

850 Ibid.

851 Scott Jaschik, "Overhaul to End Segregation Ordered in Louisiana," *The Chronicle of Higher Education*, 6 January 1993. Downloaded from *http://chronicle.com* on 4/9/2004.

852 Joye Mercer, "Judge Refuses to Delay Louisiana Desegregation Order, *The Chronicle of Higher Education*, 3 March 1993. Downloaded from *http://chronicle.com* on 4/9/2004.

853 Joye Mercer, "Order for La. 'Superboard' Blocked by Appeals Court, *The Chronicle of Higher Education*. 17 March 1993. Downloaded from *http://chronicle.com* on 4/9/2004.

854 Scott Jaschik, "Back to the Drawing Board in Louisiana, *The Chronicle of Higher Education*. 5 January 1994. Downloaded from *http://chronicle.com* on 4/9/2004.

855 Joye Mercer, "Louisiana Desegregation Trial is Delayed Until March, *The Chronicle of Higher Education*, 3 August 1994. Downloaded from *http://chronicle.com* on 4/9/2004.

856 Patrick Healy, "Louisiana NAACP May Challenge State's Desegregation Plan," *The Chronicle*

of Higher Education, 23 November 1994. Downloaded from *http://chronicle.com* on 4/9/ 2004.

[857]   Patrick Healy, "Black Educators in Louisiana Unhappy With Pace of Desegregation," *The Chronicle of Higher Education*, 30 June 1995. Downloaded from *http://chronicle.com* on 4/ 9/2004.

[858]   Jerry Pinsel, "A Brief Historic Profile of the Louisiana Higher Education Community: An Unfinished Journey" (Unpublished Draft), 2003.

[859]   No author. "BRCC to offer more aid," *The Advocate Online.* Downloaded from *http:// www.theadvocate.com/stories/121102/new_aid001.shtml* on 12/19/2002.

[860]   Mary Owen, "A Desegregation Success Story in the Making in Louisiana," *The Chronicle of Higher Education,* 14 April 1998. Downloaded from *http://chronicle.com* on 4/9/2004.

[861]   John Laplante, "Higher education integration a costly failure," *The Advocate,* 26 July 2004, Downloaded from *http://www.2theadvocate.com* on 7/26/2004).

[862]   Ibid.

[863]   Joseph B. Parker, "David Treen," In *The Louisiana Governors: From Iberville to Edwards*, edited by Joseph G. Dawson III (Baton Rouge, Louisiana: Louisiana State University Press, 1990), 277.

[864]   Ibid, 279.

[865]   No Author. "State Notes: Louisiana's Gov. Said to Interfere in President Search," *The Chronicle of Higher Education*, 14 November 1990. Downloaded from *http://chronicle.com* on 4/9/ 2004.

[866]   Mary Crystal Cage, "Academics Protest Governor's Choice to head La. University," *The Chronicle of Higher Education*, 16 January 1991. Downloaded from *http://chronicle.com* on 4/9/2004.

[867]   Ibid.

[868]   Mary Crystal Cage, "Southern Voters Defeat 2 Pro-Education Governors," *The Chronicle of Higher Education*. 20 November 1991. Downloaded from *http://chronicle.com* on 4/9/ 2004.

[869]   Spencer J. Maxcy and Doreen O. Maxcy, "Educational Reform in Louisiana," *International Journal of Educational Reform* (Volume 2, No. 3, July 1993, 236-241), 236.

[870]   Mary Crystal Cage, "Southern Voters Defeat 2 Pro-Education Governors," *The Chronicle of Higher Education*. 20 November 1991. Downloaded from *http://chronicle.com* on 4/9/2004.

[871]   Spencer J. Maxcy and Doreen O. Maxcy, "Educational Reform in Louisiana," *International Journal of Educational Reform* (Volume 2, No. 3, July 1993, 236-241), 238.

[872]   Bennett H. Wall, ed., *Louisiana: A History, 3rd Edition* (Harlan Davidson, 1997), 371.

[873]   Spencer J. Maxcy and Doreen O. Maxcy, "Educational Reform in Louisiana," *International Journal of Educational Reform* (Volume 2, No. 3, July 1993, 236-241), 241.

[874]   Ibid, 239-40.

[875]   Mary Crystal Cage, "Reform Plan Stymied: Governor's Effort to Simplify Louisiana's Higher-Education System Deepens the Bitter Divisions Created by Years of Segregation and Political Turf Wars," *The Chronicle of Higher Education*, 18 October 1989, 29.

876   Mary Crystal Cage, "Gubernatorial Contest Poses Distinct Choices for Future of Higher Education in Louisiana," *The Chronicle of Higher Education*, 16 October 1991. Downloaded from *http://chronicle.com* on 4/9/2004.

877   Ibid.

878   Ibid.

879   Ibid.

880   Ibid.

881   Mary Crystal Cage, "Southern Voters Defeat 2 Pro-Education Governors," *The Chronicle of Higher Education*. 20 November 1991. Downloaded from *http://chronicle.com* on 4/9/2004.

882   Mary Crystal Cage, "Reform Plan Stymied: Governor's Effort to Simplify Louisiana's Higher-Education System Deepens the Bitter Divisions Created by Years of Segregation and Political Turf Wars," *The Chronicle of Higher Education*, 18 October 1989, 29.

883   Bennett H. Wall, ed., *Louisiana: A History, 3rd Edition* (Harlan Davidson, 1997), 371.

884   Mary Crystal Cage, "Reform Plan Stymied: Governor's Effort to Simplify Louisiana's Higher-Education System Deepens the Bitter Divisions Created by Years of Segregation and Political Turf Wars," *The Chronicle of Higher Education*, 18 October 1989, 29.

885   Ed Anderson," Foster: Set up 1 board for colleges; Push connected to money plans," *New Orleans Times-Picayune*, 10 February 1996; Patrick Healy, "Louisiana Governor's Chief of Staff . . . ," *The Chronicle of Higher Education*, 1 May 1998.

886   Mary Crystal Cage, "Gubernatorial Contest Poses Distinct Choices for Future of Higher Education in Louisiana," *The Chronicle of Higher Education*, 16 October 1991. Downloaded from *http://chronicle.com* on 4/9/2004.

887   Ibid.

888   Scott Jaschik, "Overhaul to End Segregation Ordered in Louisiana," *The Chronicle of Higher Education*, 6 January 1993. Downloaded from *http://chronicle.com* on 4/9/2004.

889   Ibid

890   Carl H. Degel, *Creation of the Louisiana Coordinating Counicl for Higher Education: Perspectives in Public Organizational Decision-making* (Masters Thesis for Tulane Graduate School, May 28, 1971), 21.

891   Ibid, 39.

892   Mary Crystal Cage, "Gubernatorial Contest Poses Distinct Choices for Future of Higher Education in Louisiana," *The Chronicle of Higher Education*, 16 October 1991. Downloaded from *http://chronicle.com* on 4/9/2004.

893   Mary Crystal Cage, "Southern Voters Defeat 2 Pro-Education Governors," *The Chronicle of Higher Education*. 20 November 1991. Downloaded from *http://chronicle.com* on 4/9/2004.

894   Jerry Pinsel, "A Brief Historic Profile of the Louisiana Higher Education Community: An Unfinished Journey" (Unpublished Draft), 2003.

895   Diane Ravitch, *Left Back: A Century of Battles Over School Reform* (New York: Simon & Schuster, 2000), 429-30.

896   Patrick M. Callan, "Reframing Access and Opportunity: Problematic State and Federal Higher Education Policy in the 1990s," In *The States and Public Higher Education Policy:*

Affordability, Access, and Accountability, edited by Donald Heller, 83-99. (Baltimore, Maryland: The John Hopkins University Press, 2001), 85.

897   Ibid.

898   Ibid.

899   Ibid.

900   Ibid., 430.

901   J. Wade Gilley, "Governors versus College Presidents: Who Leads?" In *ASHE Reader: Public Policy and Higher Education*, edited by Lester F. Goodchild, Cheryl D. Lovell, Edward R. Hines, and Judith I. Gill (Ginn Press, 1997), 160.

902   Ibid., 161.

903   Ibid.

904   Ibid.

905   By the Center for Policy Study in Education at George Mason University

906   Ibid., 162.

907   Mary Crystal Cage, "Gubernatorial Contest Poses Distinct Choices for Future of Higher Education in Louisiana," *The Chronicle of Higher Education*, 16 October 1991. Downloaded from *http://chronicle.com* on 4/9/2004.

908   John Hill, "From powerhouse to prisoner: Former La. governor prepares to serve jail time," *Louisiana Gannett News*, 20 October 2002. Downloaded from *www.shreveporttimes.com* on 3/18/2004.

909   Spencer J. Maxcy and Doreen O. Maxcy, "Educational Reform in Louisiana," *International Journal of Educational Reform* (Volume 2, No. 3, July 1993, 236-241), 236.

910   Mary Crystal Cage, "Supreme Court Says It Lacks Jurisdiction in La. Desegregation Dispute," *The Chronicle of Higher Education*, 17 January 1990. Downloaded from *http://chronicle.com* on 4/9/2004.

911   Mary Crystal Cage, "Gubernatorial Contest Poses Distinct Choices for Future of Higher Education in Louisiana," *The Chronicle of Higher Education*, 16 October 1991. Downloaded from *http://chronicle.com* on 4/9/2004.

912   Mary Crystal Cage, "Louisiana's College Officials Fear the Consequences if Ex-Leader of Ku Klux Klan Becomes Governor," *The Chronicle of Higher Education*, 6 November 1991. Downloaded from *http://chronicle.com* on 4/9/2004.

913   Mary Crystal Cage, "College Leaders Pleased With Outcome of La. Governor's Race," *The Chronicle of Higher Education*, 27 November 1991. Downloaded from *http://chronicle.com* on 4/9/2004.

914   Mary Crystal Cage, "Gubernatorial Contest Poses Distinct Choices for Future of Higher Education in Louisiana," *The Chronicle of Higher Education*, 16 October 1991. Downloaded from *http://chronicle.com* on 4/9/2004.

915   Bennett H. Wall, ed., *Louisiana: A History, 3rd Edition* (Harlan Davidson, 1997), 392.

916   Larry Johnson, "Politics, Markets, and Ideology: The Transformation of a Technical College into a Community College," (Ph.D. diss., University of Utah, May 2000), 20.

917   John Aubrey Douglass, *The California Idea and American Higher Education: 1850 to the 1960 Master Plan* (Stanford, California: Stanford University Press, 2000), 1.

918   Public Affairs Research Council of La., Inc., *The Community College Question: Summary Report*, August 1997, 7.

919   Ibid., 9.

920   Ibid., 309.

921   Ibid., 283.

922   Ibid., 296.

923   Ibid., 314.

924   Ibid., 297.

925   Ibid., 12.

926   Ibid., 316.

927   Ibid., 314.

928   Ibid., 316.

929   Louisiana Economic Development Council, *Louisiana: Vision 2020-2003 Update: Master Plan for Economic Development*, *http://Vision2020/louisiana.gov/*, 8.

930   Ibid, 9.

931   Ibid, 18.

932   Ibid.

933   Louisiana Board of Regents, *Master Plan for Public Postsecondary Education: 2001*, 10.

934   Chris Frink, "Gov. Mike Foster's legacy," *The Advocate*, 28 December 2003. Downloaded from 2theadvocate.com on 3/18/2004.

935   Ibid.

936   Katherine S. Mangan, "La. Governor Threatens to End Tax Breaks for Tulane U. in Dispute Over Law Clinic," *The Chronicle of Higher Education*, 5 September 1997. Downloaded from *http://chronicle.com* on 4/9/2004.

937   No author. "Ways and Means: 27-Year-Old Nominee to Lead U. of Louisiana System Lands on Fast Track," *The Chronicle of Higher Education*, 30 April 1999. Downloaded from *http://chronicle.com* on 4/9/2004.

938   Southwest Educational Development Laboratory, Downloaded from www.sedl.org/pubs/pic01/priority.html on 11/13/2003.

939   Patrick Healy, "Louisiana's Governor-Elect Promises to Support Colleges," *The Chronicle of Higher Education*, 1 December 1995. Downloaded from *http://chronicle.com* on 4/9/2004.

940   Patrick Healy, "Proposal to Merge Louisiana Colleges Worries Black Colleges," *The Chronicle of Higher Education*, 2 February 1996. Downloaded from *http://chronicle.com* on 4/9/2004.

941   Patrick Healy, "Plan for Public-College 'Superboard' Irks Louisiana Educators," *The Chronicle of Higher Education*, 1 March 1996. Downloaded from *http://chronicle.com* on 4/9/2004.

942   Ibid.

943   Jeffrey Selingo, "Louisiana Judge Blocks Law Expanding Authority of Board of Regents," *The Chronicle of Higher Education*, 16 January 1998. Downloaded from *http://chronicle.com* on 4/9/2004.

944   Ibid.

945 Public Affairs Research Council of La., Inc., *The Community College Question: Summary Report*, August 1997, 8.

946 Hayes Ferguson, "First Grads Leave Nunez: College Being Used As Model," *New Orleans Times-Picayune*, 20 May 1993, B1.

947 In 1990, a legislative act dropped the "vocational" from all of the vocational-technical institutes.

948 Louisiana Board of Regents, *Board of Regents' Feasibility Study: Proposed Merging of St. Bernard Parish Community College with the Elaine P. Nunez Vocational-Technical Institute Prepared in Response to Senate Concurrent Resolution Number 50 of the 1992 Regular Session of the Louisiana Legislature—Staff Draft—May 1992*, 6

949 Hayes Ferguson, "First Grads Leave Nunez: College Being Used As Model," *New Orleans Times-Picayune*, 20 May 1993, B1.

950 Karen Turni, "College Merger Plan Studied," *New Orleans Times-Picayune*, 19 November 1994, B1.

951 Public Affairs Research Council of La., Inc., *The Community College Question: Summary Report*, August 1997, 9.

952 Ibid.

953 Scott Dyer, "Community college system creation studied by group," *The Advocate*, 11 March 1996.

954 Ibid.

955 Jerry Pinsel, "A Brief Historic Profile of the Louisiana Higher Education Community: An Unfinished Journey" (Unpublished Draft), 2003.

956 Ed Anderson," Foster quietly signs community college bill," *New Orleans Times-Picayune*, 8 May 1998, A3.

957 Harold Callais, "Regents to Voters: OK Community College Plan," *New Orleans Times-Picayune*, 25 September 1998, B6.

958 No Author. "Ways & Means: Louisiana Voters Approve New 2-Year-College System," *The Chronicle of Higher Education*. 16 October 1998. Downloaded from *http://chronicle.com* on 4/9/2004.

959 Littice Bacon-Blood, "Community College System to Debut; Single Board Touted As Way To Improve La. Job Training," *New Orleans Times-Picayune*, 1 July 1999, A1.

960 Ibid.

961 Jerry Pinsel, "A Brief Historic Profile of the Louisiana Higher Education Community: An Unfinished Journey" (Unpublished Draft), 2003.

962 Public Affairs Research Council of La., Inc., *The Community College Question: Summary Report*, August 1997, 5.

963 Jerry Pinsel, "A Brief Historic Profile of the Louisiana Higher Education Community: An Unfinished Journey" (Unpublished Draft), 2003.

964 Public Affairs Research Council of La., Inc., *The Community College Question: Summary Report*, August 1997, 5.

965 Ibid, 6.

[966] Patrick Healy, "Louisiana Plans to Meld 50 Campuses Into a Coherent 2-Year College System," *The Chronicle of Higher Education*, 1 May 1998, A41.

[967] Patrick Healy, "Louisiana Governor's Chief of Staff …," *The Chronicle of Higher Education*, 1 May 1998.

[968] Littice Bacon-Blood, "Community College System to Debut; Single Board Touted As Way To Improve La. Job Training," *New Orleans Times-Picayune*, 1 July 1999, A1.

[969] Public Affairs Research Council of La., Inc., *The Community College Question: Summary Report*, August 1997, 12.

[970] Thomas R. Bailey and Irina E. Averianova, *Multiple Missions of Community Colleges: Conflicting or Complementary?* (New York: Community College Research Center, 1998), 12.

[971] Ibid.

[972] Ibid, 10.

[973] Patrick Healy, "Louisiana Plans to Meld 50 Campuses Into a Coherent 2-Year College System," *The Chronicle of Higher Education*, 1 May 1998, A40.

[974] Ibid, A41.

[975] Ibid.

[976] Harold Callais, "Regents to Voters: OK Community College Plan," *New Orleans Times-Picayune*, 25 September 1998, B6.

[977] Patrick Healy, "Louisiana Plans to Meld 50 Campuses Into a Coherent 2-Year College System," *The Chronicle of Higher Education*, 1 May 1998, A40.

[978] Ibid.

[979] Louisiana Community and Technical College System, *LCTCS Mission*. Downloaded from www.lctcs.net/about/mission.htm.

[980] Louisiana Community and Technical College System, *LCTCS Policy #I.1.003—Title: Elements of Two-Year Institutional Mission*. Downloaded from www.lctcs.net.

[981] Public Affairs Research Council of La., Inc., *The Community College Question: Summary Report*, August 1997, 4.

[982] Peter Schmidt, "A Small Team of Consultants With Large Sway in Higher Education," *The Chronicle of Higher Education*, 29 September 2000. Downloaded from *http://chronicle.com* on 4/9/2004.

[983] Ibid.

[984] Ibid.

[985] Jerry Pinsel, Vice President for Academic and Student Affairs of the Louisiana Community and Technical College System, informal correspondence.

[986] Edward Daniel Schumacher, *The Struggle Against Adult Functional Illiteracy in Louisiana: A Historical Analysis* (Sulphur, Louisiana: Maplewood Books, 1973), 6.

[987] Joanna Weiss, "Nunez Kicks Off Campaign For Re-Election At College," *New Orleans Times-Picayune,* 2 August 1995, B3.

[988] St. Bernard Parish Community College, *Catalog for St. Bernard Parish Community College, 1970-71 School Session*, 2.

[989] St. Bernard Parish Community College, *Catalog for St. Bernard Parish Thirteenth and Fourteenth Grades, 1968-69 School Session.*

[990] St. Bernard Parish Community College, *Catalog for St. Bernard Parish Community College, 1970-71 School Session,* 2.

[991] Louisiana Board of Regents, *Board of Regents' Feasibility Study: Proposed Merging of St. Bernard Parish Community College with the Elaine P. Nunez Vocational-Technical Institute Prepared in Response to Senate Concurrent Resolution Number 50 of the 1992 Regular Session of the Louisiana Legislature—Staff Draft—May 1992,* 2.

[992] Louisiana State Legislature, *State of Louisiana Acts of the Legislature Volume I—Regular Session 1992,* 955-8.

[993] Ibid., 26-8.

[994] Ibid., 13.

[995] Ibid., 15.

[996] Ibid., 26.

[997] Ibid., 16.

[998] Public Affairs Research Council of La., Inc., *White Paper on Higher Education* (Issue 1, April 2003), 1.

[999] Ibid.

[1000] Ibid.

[1001] John Maginnis, Business Report.com, 17 March 2003.

[1002] No author. "Louisiana lost way in policy," *2theadvocate.com.* Downloaded from *http://www.2theadvocate.com/stories/120403/opi_edi001.shtml* on 12/4/2003.

[1003] Ibid.

[1004] Ibid.

[1005] Council for a Better Louisiana, *Community and Technical Colleges,* Downloaded from *http://cabl.org* - Education Issues -> Community and Technical Colleges on 9/14/2003.

[1006] Dennis Stine, *A Vision of Louisiana's Community and Technical College System,* March 1999. Downloaded from *http://cabl.org* - Briefings -> Community and Technical College System on 9/14/2003.

[1007] Coleman Warner, "TOPS ups retention, test scores: But lawmakers say many miss benefits," *New Orleans Times-Picayune,* 17 November 2004, A1.

[1008] U. S. Census Bureau, *Educational Attainment of the Population 25 Years and Over for the United States, Regions, and States, and for Puerto Rico: 1990 and 2000.* Downloaded from *www.census.gov/prod/cen2000/doc/st3.pdf.*

[1009] Ibid., 7.

[1010] Ibid., 7.

[1011] Ibid., 18.

[1012] Patrick M. Callan, "Measuring Up 2002: Introduction," *National Center for Public Policy and Higher Education.* Downloaded from *http://measuringup.highereducation.org/2002/articles/introduction.htm* on 11/15/2003.

[1013] Ibid.

1014 The standard measure used by the federal government for graduation rates is to track full-time, first-time freshmen that graduate in six years. This is a suitable measure for "traditional" students at four-year colleges and universities. For two-year colleges, where many students are "non-traditional" and part-time, the measure often is not an accurate representation of whether the college is fulfilling its mission.

1015 Steven Brint and Jerome Karabel, *The Diverted Dream: Community Colleges and the Promise of Educational Opportunity in America, 1900-1985* (New York: Oxford University Press, 1989), 129.

1016 Donna Clark, Vice Chancellor for Student Affairs at Nunez Community College, Interview on June 27, 2002.

1017 Ibid.

1018 Public Affairs Research Council of La., Inc., *The Community College Question: Summary Report*, August 1997, 2.

1019 Patrick Healy, "Louisiana Plans to Meld 50 Campuses Into a Coherent 2-Year College System," *The Chronicle of Higher Education*, 1 May 1998, A40.

1020 Associated Press, "Nola.com Newsflash—Louisiana Editorial Roundup" 14 May 2003.

1021 Patrick Healy, "Louisiana Plans to Meld 50 Campuses Into a Coherent 2-Year College System," *The Chronicle of Higher Education*, 1 May 1998, A40.

1022 Ibid, A41.

1023 Ibid.

1024 Ibid.

1025 Shannon Reilly and Robert W. Ahrens, "USA Today Snapshots: Paychecks increase with education," *USA Today*, 22 April 2005, 1A.

1026 David Glenn, "Education Researchers Use Survey Data to Discern Trends and Differences Among Community-College Students," *The Chronicle of Higher Education*, 12 April 2005. Downloaded from http://chronicle.com/free/2005/04/2005041202n.htm on 4/20/2005.

INDEX